To

(I... a good choice, but
you can always swap
it with Anthony)

bb
Mildred + Pat

Merry Xmas Dad 2022
I suppose Mildred (?)
was wrong and Pat
was right....
But I know this is a
good choice for you!
lots o loves
Katie xxx

P.S. I wonder why they
inscribed a book they
thought was a bad choice...

COURT AND BOWLED

Tales of Cricket and the Law

COURT AND BOWLED

Tales of Cricket and the Law

JAMES WILSON

Wildy, Simmonds & Hill Publishing

© James Wilson 2014

ISBN 9780854901401

British Library Cataloguing in Publication Data
A catalogue record for this book is available from the British Library

Wilson, J

Court and Bowled: Tales of Cricket and the Law

First published in 2014 by
Wildy, Simmonds & Hill Publishing
58 Carey Street
London WC2A 2JF
England
www.wildy.com

Printed in Great Britain by CPI Antony Rowe, Chippenham, Wiltshire

MIX
Paper from
responsible sources
FSC
www.fsc.org   FSC® C013604

For Aran and Sam

The laws of cricket tell of the English love of compromise between a particular freedom and a general orderliness, or legality.

— Sir Neville Cardus

Serious sport has nothing to do with fair play. It is bound up with hatred, jealousy, boastfulness, disregard of all rules and sadistic pleasure in witnessing violence: in other words it is war without the shooting.

— George Orwell

Cricket is not illegal, for it is a manly game.

— Queen Anne

I don't wonder at the courage of you English, when you teach your children to play with cannon balls.

— Czar Nicholas I

'The facts as found in the present case show that, for some people, the reach of cricket has extended far beyond any boundary imaginable when CLR James wrote his celebrated book some fifty years ago.'

— Mr Justice Hamblen,
Kaneria v The England & Wales Cricket Board Limited
[2014] EWHC 1348 (Comm).

ACKNOWLEDGEMENTS

The idea for this book arose in conversation with Andrew Riddoch of Wildy, Simmonds & Hill about a possible follow-up to my 2012 book *Cases, Causes and Controversies*.[1] Andrew and the team at Wildy have given their customary professional support to the project throughout.

I am most grateful to Lintz Cricket Club for supplying the cover image, and to Bob Jackson for supplying first-hand recollections of *Miller v Jackson*, which will forever remain the first case that comes to mind when anyone thinks of cricket and the law.

My brother John Wilson occupied first slip in the proofreading cordon, reading several drafts of the entire book. He also reminded me of a number of the better cricket stories and anecdotes, and offered numerous suggestions about the more philosophical arguments. The rest of my immediate family were roped in towards the end, and so thanks are due as well to Annette and Neil Harris and my parents Bob and Penny Wilson.

Andrew Johnson and Vanessa Cortis generously provided the benefit of Andrew's cricket knowledge and Vanessa's legal knowledge, and the wine expertise of both. Helen Sheridan, Sally Thomas and Aaron Turpin kindly read several draft chapters. Needless to say, any remaining editorial misfields are solely my responsibility.

As ever, the greatest support came from home. My biggest debt therefore is to Mona, Sam and Aran for their love and support, as well as their tolerance for the demands the book inevitably placed on time, money and space on the bookshelf.

James Wilson
Dulwich
April 2014

---

[1] *Cases, Causes and Controversies: Fifty Tales from the Law* (Wildy, Simmonds & Hill, 2012). To save space I will refer to the book hereafter simply as *Cases, Causes and Controversies*.

CONTENTS

INTRODUCTION

CRICKET, JUSTICE AND NOT-CRICKET

Having written stories about law for some years now, and having read stories about cricket for much longer, it occurred to me that cricket and the law share a few things in common.

First, over the years both have stood for something more than merely a game on the one hand or a set of rules on the other. Lionel, Lord Tennyson (grandson of the poet) wrote: 'Cricket, however, has more in it than mere efficiency. There is something called the spirit of cricket, which cannot be defined.' And the former British Prime Minister Stanley Baldwin said: 'One could not define what cricket was, as one could not define a gentleman, but one knew it, as one knew a gentleman when one met a gentleman.' Such sentiments reflected the cliché about anything unsporting or unfair being 'not cricket'. The first recorded use of the phrase 'not cricket' was probably by one of the earliest cricket historians, Reverend Pycroft, in 1851[1] – when he used it to denounce overarm bowling. Before the end of the nineteenth century, the phrase had entered the vernacular with its more general meaning. In 1896, for example, *The Times* thundered: 'Cricket is a kind of synonym for generous behaviour, nor can we condemn any conduct more severely and succinctly than by saying that "it is not cricket".'[2]

For the law, any number of great quotes about justice might be cited from across the ages. Here is one not so well known, from the unlikely source of what used to be called 'horse operas':[3]

> A man just naturally can't take the law into his own hands and hang people without hurtin' everybody in the world, 'cause then he's just

---

[1] Rev. James Pycroft's *The Cricket-Field* was one of the very earliest cricket books. At the time of writing, the second edition (A & G A Spottiswoode, 1854), was available free online on Google Books.

[2] Quoted in Andy Bull, 'What's Not Cricket', *Wisden Cricketer's Almanack 2012*.

[3] By 'horse operas' I mean of course Westerns, once the dominant genre in Hollywood in both film and television. The quote is from *The Ox-Bow Incident* (1943), a film where a lynch mob is formed and hangs the wrong people for a crime while (unbeknownst to them) the sheriff is away catching the right villains.

not breaking one law but all laws. Law is a lot more than words you put in a book, or judges or lawyers or sheriffs you hire to carry it out. It's everything people ever have found out about justice and what's right and wrong. It's the very conscience of humanity. There can't be any such thing as civilization unless people have a conscience, because if people touch God anywhere, where is it except through their conscience? And what is anybody's conscience except a little piece of the conscience of all men that ever lived?

In turn such ideas have given rise to the concept of the rule of law, the central idea of which is that lawmakers are required to exercise their power in accordance with fixed rules and principles set out in advance, and may be brought to account in an independent tribunal if they fail to do so. Needless to say, both cricketers and lawyers have often fallen short of those lofty standards, and in doing so have provided much material for this book.

Secondly, without sounding too much like the pontiff's scriptwriter, one can draw inferences about any particular society both from the cricket it plays and from the legal system which governs it. Any society's criminal justice system, for example, provides a telling commentary on that society's values and an historical guide to how they have developed. Nelson Mandela once said: 'No-one truly knows a nation until one has been inside its jails. A nation should not be judged by how it treats its highest citizens, but its lowest ones.'

Equally, a number of authors have looked to cricket to tell larger stories about the countries and communities in which it has been played. One of cricket's most revered writers, Neville Cardus, wrote that if everything about England was destroyed except the laws of cricket, 'then life in this country could be recreated', [4] while G M Trevelyan suggested that 'if the French noblesse had been capable of playing cricket with their peasants, their chateaux would never have been burnt'.[5] In a more serious vein, C L R James wrote a classic account of colonization and cricket in his *Beyond a Boundary* (1963).

---

[4] Neville Cardus, *Cardus on Cricket: A selection from the cricket writings of Sir Neville Cardus, chosen and introduced by Sir Rupert Hart-Davis* (Souvenir Press, 1949, reprint 1976).
[5] Quoted in Lawrence Booth, *Arm-ball to Zooter: A Sideways Look at the Language of Cricket* (Penguin, 2007).

Ramachandra Guha's *A Corner of a Foreign Field: The Indian History of a British Sport* (2002) provided an intelligent commentary on Indian history and particularly the caste system, while the Bollywood film *Lagaan* (2001) aimed a bouncer at the British occupation of India, by way of a fictional story about a cricket match.[6]

Of course, one should not get too carried away with cricket's importance. 'What really shines through', wrote Sir Michael Parkinson about Jack Fingleton's *Brightly Fades the Don* (1949), 'is one man's belief that cricket is about fellowship and humour and that in the real scale of human values it matters little except as a game.' Of a similar generation to Fingleton was Keith Miller, the great Australian all-rounder, who was once asked about the pressure of playing test cricket. 'Pressure', the former wartime Mosquito pilot corrected his interlocutor, 'is a Messerschmitt up the arse.'

Having said that, the fact that Muttiah Muralitharan was a Tamil surely added a touch of poignancy to his status as Sri Lanka's greatest cricketer and a national hero, given that civil war raged in his home country between the minority Tamils and the majority Singhalese throughout most of his career. Or one could look to the saga of Basil D'Oliveira, which caused ructions going well beyond the selectors' smoke-filled rooms and into the highest echelons of power in both South Africa and the United Kingdom. Before both of them was Sir Donald Bradman, whose status as an Australian icon went far beyond mere cricketing circles. The author Thomas Keneally once wrote: 'The only history we were taught was European. Poetry cut out after Tennyson. If we spoke of literary figures, we spoke of Englishmen. Cricket was the great way out of Australian cultural ignominy for, while no Australian had written *Paradise Lost*, we knew Don Bradman had made 100 before lunch at Lord's.'[7] Bradman became an

---

[6] Two books published in 2013 on similar themes were Shaharyar M Khan and Ali Khan's *Cricket Cauldron: The Turbulent Politics of Sport in Pakistan* (I B Tauris), a book which sets out in meticulous detail the maelstrom that is Pakistani cricket and how it has been continually bedevilled by politics, and James Astill's *The Great Tamasha: Cricket, Corruption and the Turbulent Rise of Modern India* (Wisden Sports Writing), which charts the emergence of India as a superpower by telling the story of how cricket became transformed from entertainment to a vehicle for resisting colonialism and finally an economic and cultural phenomenon.

[7] Here it seems to me Keneally is being a bit harsh on Dorothea Mackellar and

icon beyond Australian shores too: it is said that Nelson Mandela's first question to an international delegation that came to visit him while he was in jail in 1986 was whether Bradman was still alive.

Thirdly, both law and cricket give a stage to participants great and small. Both seem to attract the eccentrics, the characters and generally what Dennis Potter once deliberately misquoted as the 'warp and woof of life in all its rich texture'. Lawyers all know of distinctive characters who have held forth in the courtroom over the years. There are the great advocates such as Edward Carson or Sir Edward Marshall Hall. There are the famous judges such as the cerebral Lord Atkin, the popular (if controversial) Lord Denning and the infamous Hanging Judge Jeffreys. But there are also the ordinary citizens whose everyday doings led by chance and happenstance to great legal landmarks, such as Mrs Donoghue of the snail and the ginger beer, or Mrs Carlill of the smoke ball and the influenza epidemic.

Cricket fans for their part all know of the likes of Bradman, Sobers and Tendulkar, but some of the best cricketing stories also concern the 'one-test wonders' – the walk-on parts involving players whose lives were otherwise led in cricketing obscurity. Jack MacBryan's name regularly turns up in pub quizzes, because in his sole test in 1924 he did not bat, bowl or field before the match was rained off.[8] Footage of Andy Lloyd's half-hour-long test career – ending when he was felled by a bouncer from Malcolm Marshall – has received more hits on YouTube than many clips of players who had veteran careers. Gary Pratt spent only a handful of sessions on a test ground in his life, but managed in that time to run out the Australian captain, Ricky Ponting, in the 2005 Ashes. More than any other incident in the series to that point, Ponting's expletive-ridden tirade that followed his dismissal showed the pressure the Australians found themselves under for the first time against the Old Enemy in nearly twenty years. Pratt earned himself a place on the victory bus tour across London accordingly.

Banjo Paterson, but I should probably defer to him on the matter of Australian poetry.
[8] Frederick Hyland suffered a similar fate in his only first-class match, though he did become the subject of a superb profile by Ronald Mason in his book *Sing All a Green Willow* (Epworth, 1967). At p 129 Mason wrote: 'No sooner did Mr Hyland come than he went, not only by that same door but almost in that same breath. *Le silence éternel de ces espaces infinis m'effraie*, said Pascal; the monumental brevity of this cricketer's career does the same to me.'

Fourthly, the law in one form or another can be found in virtually every aspect of human activity and cricket is no exception. Almost uniquely among major sports, cricket does not have rules, but rather the appropriately more august 'Laws of Cricket'. And inevitably officious lawyers have not always left cricketers alone. Hence the idea arose for a compilation of stories of the law and cricket, and the laws of cricket.

The most obvious stories of law and cricket involve cricketers breaking the law. These can range in seriousness from the unfortunate Pakistani cricketer S S Naik, convicted of stealing four pairs of socks with a combined value of £1.20 from Marks & Spencer in Oxford Street in 1974, to the former West Indian test cricketer Leslie Hylton, who was hanged in 1955 for the murder of his wife. At other times cricketers are the victims of crime. Two serious examples are the horrendous assault meted out to the New Zealander Jesse Ryder in 2013 and the tragic death of the Australian David Hookes in 2011, both the result of nights out gone wrong. Unquestionably the worst criminal incident in cricket history, however, was the terrorist attack on the Sri Lankan team in Pakistan in 2009. Astonishingly, none of the players was seriously hurt, even though hundreds of rounds were fired by automatic weapons and six police and two civilians died.

Next there are cricketers suing or being sued, in what lawyers refer to as civil (that is to say, non-criminal) law. The more notable cases include *Bolton v Stone*, an important precedent in the English law of negligence, and the Packer litigation of *Greig and others v Insole and others*. The ruling in *Bolton v Stone* affected village and impromptu cricketers everywhere, while if Mr Justice Slade in *Greig and others v Insole and others* had not decided the case in the players' favour, the Packer Revolution of the late 1970s would have been over before it started. *Bolton v Stone* had a successor in the form of *Miller v Jackson*, a case where Lord Denning obtained cricketing as well as legal immortality with his legendary paean to the delights of village cricket. There are also a number of libel actions which, as ever, involve some of the more scandalous background facts.

On other occasions, disputes involving cricketers might raise legal issues but manage to be resolved outside the courtroom. An obvious example is where a player is banned or otherwise threatened with a sanction for misbehaviour. Ultimately, what is being decided is a special contractual dispute, in the form of the legal rights and duties between players and administrators. Normally these are resolved by the club or organization responsible, though the courts might retain a supervisory jurisdiction, if a manifestly unfair procedure has been followed.

Contractual disputes can raise major issues: Darrell Hair's umpiring career and perhaps even the future of sporting relations between two countries were placed on the line after Hair ruled that Pakistan had forfeited a test in England. They can also be rather less significant in the grand scheme of things, such as the tale of the mischievous Australian county cricketer whose first-class career was threatened after he had in cricketing parlance 'exposed his middle stump' in the team photograph for the 2000 edition of *Wisden*.[9] S F Barnes – statistically one of the greatest bowlers in history – refused to play the final test on his final tour because of a dispute over his wife's expenses. His petulance probably affected nothing more than his opportunity to finish with 200 test wickets. On the other hand, the contractual wrangling of the West Indian side on the eve of its first official tour to South Africa was an altogether more depressing affair, given that the intended fixture had been laden with significance going well beyond a few extra pages in *Wisden*.

In years past, playing sport was considered an almost exclusively private activity, not the business of the general law. Thus, a player could not sue over a career-ending wrong decision by an umpire, or sue the selectors for leaving him out. Also, governments did not feel they had the right to ban private individuals from maintaining sporting contacts with rogue regimes. In recent times, a number of those formerly sacrosanct principles have come under attack – with varying degrees of success – as will be seen throughout the book.

---

[9] After realizing his place in the side was under threat thanks to the indiscretion, the player concerned complained that it was 'all a misunderstanding'. He also said that the picture was ambiguous, and it could have been a little finger on display. The editor of *Wisden* at the time, Matthew Engel, responded by asking what was the misunderstanding, and observing that if the offending member could be confused with a little finger, perhaps the player should not quite have been so ready to show himself off.

Elsewhere, cricket and the law find strange and somewhat random connections. On the wall of the United Kingdom Supreme Court there is a tribute to the honorary Lieutenant-Colonel Bernard Bosanquet, who wrote a book 120 years ago advising fellow bankers on the importance of cash reserves, but who is more famous because his son invented the googly.[10]

Finally, in my opinion anyway, cricket has a richer literature than any other sport and law has a richer literature than any other profession. There has accordingly been no shortage of inspiration or material on which to draw for this book.

The book

The book begins with a short survey of cricket's origins, how its laws developed, and some instances where it intersected with the law up until the late nineteenth century. Thereafter it follows a thematic approach, covering a number of stories from W G Grace to the twenty-first century concerns such as the 20/20 revolution and recent match-fixing disasters. It considers whether there might ever be a chance of the law interfering with play itself, in the form of a negligence action or a criminal prosecution for something happening on the field. The final chapters then seek to draw upon all the legal themes discussed and apply them to both the spirit and the laws of cricket themselves, with a few thoughts on some controversial subjects including 'Mankading', walking and the role of umpires in a technological age.

I have not attempted to be comprehensive and cover every possible interaction between cricket and the law. Aside from rendering the book of inordinate length, such an objective would have risked the book becoming out of date even before going to print. After I had started writing, Mickey Arthur resigned as Australian coach and threatened to sue (he settled out of court); a spat began over nationality in the Australian team; Kevin Pietersen settled a libel claim in his favour and then became embroiled in an online quarrel about his own nationality, before being removed in a *coup de théâtre* that was bizarre even by the standards of English cricket; Lalit Modi's contractual disputes reached the Indian Supreme Court; very serious

---

[10] See 'Did You Know?', Supreme Court website, www.supremecourt.uk/about/did-you-know.html (retrieved 14 April 2014).

match-fixing allegations continued to be made (and in some cases confidential testimony leaked to the press).

As for old cases that have been left out, it would have been nice to include something about Arthur Coningham (1863–1939), who played a solitary test for Australia (in which he dismissed Archie MacLaren with his first ball), but who also had several less than happy encounters with the divorce courts in later life. Then there was Montague John Druitt, a journeyman Victorian cricketer and a journeyman Victorian barrister, who might also have been the most famous criminal in history: for years he was one of the leading Jack the Ripper suspects. Modern historians usually discount him because, thanks to his cricket career, his movements can be traced with some accuracy, and they make his involvement in some of the Whitechapel murders unlikely.

From more recent times, I would have liked to say something about the investigation into Bob Woolmer's death, and the Allen Stanford 20/20 fiasco, the latter making for an interesting contrast in how fraud is dealt with in the United States and the United Kingdom. But there had to be some limits. Ultimately, I employed the simple criterion of writing about the stories I had enjoyed researching the most. In *Wisden* 1910 Sydney Pardon said of the English selectors that their choices were 'touch[ing] the confines of lunacy' and that 'the despised man in the street could not have been guilty of such folly'. I can only hope my own selections are let off a bit more lightly.

For many of the background cricket facts before the 1980s I have been reliant on secondary sources, albeit *Wisden* just about qualifies as a primary source, and I have been careful to check original scorecards and video footage where available (YouTube has been a revolutionary historian's tool in this respect). For most of the law, on the other hand, I have used only primary sources (original judgments and legislation), and what appears are therefore solely my own arguments and interpretation. That compels me to add the rider that nothing herein constitutes legal advice, and should not be relied upon as such.

Pedant's corner

Wisden Cricketers' Almanack is referred to throughout simply as *Wisden*, save where it is necessary to distinguish it from *Wisden*

Cricketers' Monthly. I have assumed that readers will be familiar with ESPN Cricinfo and other major websites such as YouTube. I have used common abbreviations such as TCCB for the Test and County Cricket Board and ECB for its successor, the England and Wales Cricket Board; ICC for both the International Cricket Council and its archaic-sounding predecessor, the Imperial Cricket Conference; IPL for the Indian Premier League; and MCC for Marylebone Cricket Club.

On the legal side of things, I have used the terminology appropriate to the time and place. Thus, English judges are referred to as Mr Justice Smith (thereafter Smith J), Lord Justice Smith (thereafter Smith LJ) and Lord Smith, depending on whether they are in the High Court, Court of Appeal or House of Lords/Supreme Court respectively. Australia calls appellate judges Smith JA, while New Zealand has long dispensed with 'Mr' before High Court judges. I have used 'plaintiff' and 'claimant' interchangeably, depending on which terminology was current in the case.[11] I hope no confusion results.

The goal

The most talented individual ever to have picked up a stick of willow and taken a swish at a spherical object once said: 'Reading poetry and watching cricket were the sum of my world, and the two are not so far apart as many aesthetes might believe.'[12] Reading law and watching cricket amounts to a substantial chunk of my world, and it is the object of this book to show that those two are not so far apart either.

---

[11] The use of the latter term was introduced in England by the Civil Procedure Rules 1998, for no particularly good reason. In fact it only served to muddy the waters, since the word 'claimant' is used in a variety of other contexts in England (someone applying for a social welfare benefit, for example), whereas 'plaintiff' was never used outside the legal world and was reasonably well known in common parlance anyway. More pointless changes included replacing the foreboding 'writ' with the lame 'claim form' and the easily understood 'third party' with the obscure 'Pt 20 defendant'. Most other jurisdictions did not follow suit.

[12] Sir Donald Bradman, as if it needed to be said.

Chapter 1
THE BEGINNINGS

THE ORIGINS

Where did cricket come from? Sir Neville Cardus made an accurate analogy with the legal system when he observed that 'like the British constitution, cricket was not made: it has "grown"'. Just as with the common law, the emergence of cricket was a process of slow evolution. The common law was developed by judges trying to recognize and give effect to the dealings of the ordinary citizens who appeared before them, unlike some other legal systems where the rulers devised their own standards and then expected the citizenry to comply. Similarly, cricket was played in one form or another for centuries before the first written laws of the game appeared – there was no cricketing equivalent of Dr James Naismith[1] – and most probably the original drafters tried to reflect their own experiences of playing the game.

That informal process means that the origins of cricket, including the word itself, have now been lost with time. There is, however, a consensus, supported by the *Oxford English Dictionary*, that the first recorded use of the word 'cricket' is actually found in the law books. In 1597,[2] one John Derrick gave evidence to a court in Guildford which was hearing a dispute over a plot of land. The dispute had arisen because the land in question had been appropriated by one John Parvish. He had enclosed the plot and intended to use it as a timber yard. The Royal Grammar School in Guildford (established 1509) claimed to be the true owner. The record of Derrick's deposition stated (spelling modernized):[3] 'Being a scholar in the free school of Guildford he and divers of his fellows did run and play there at cricket and other plays.'

---

[1]   The inventor of basketball, who wrote down a set of rules after observing other games and trying to eliminate what he saw as the flaws in each. If there was any cricket equivalent, he or she has long been lost to history.
[2]   By the Julian calendar; it would be 1598 by the Gregorian.
[3]   The record appears in *The Constitution Book of Guildford*. Note that 'divers' is an archaic word meaning 'several', not an early spelling of 'diverse'.

There is good reason to accept the veracity of Derrick's account. He was Queen's Coroner for Surrey and would have been giving evidence under oath. Also, whether he played cricket as opposed to any other pastime was irrelevant in the context of the case – it could not have affected the outcome – and therefore he had no incentive to offer false testimony on the point. Nor is there any reason to suspect that the word 'cricket' referred to a game other than hitting a ball with a bat, as there is no other recorded contemporary use of the word suggesting an alternative meaning.

Since Derrick used the word without explanation, it had to have already been in general use, at least in the community in which he lived. So where did the word come from? Henry Blofeld, in an irreverent account of cricket's history,[4] begins by suggesting that 'any fool can see' that the early Anglo-Saxon word *creag* meant 'cricket'. The word *creag* appeared in the wardrobe accounts of Edward I in the context of a game being played by his teenage son, the future Edward II. A similarly irreverent book by Simon Hughes restates the same theory.[5] Both to some extent echo Rev. Pycroft,[6] who observed that *creag* was close to *cricce*, the Anglo-Saxon for a crooked stick, which early cricket bats resembled.

It is a plausible enough inference, but the former Prime Minister Sir John Major, author of an impressive study of cricket's origins,[7] suggests that it takes a 'mighty leap of faith' to infer that *creag* equals cricket. Indeed, 'creag' might not even have been a game: a case might equally be made that it was an earlier form of the Irish *craic*, which translates roughly as 'pleasure derived from friendship'.

The late Sir Derek Birley, in another important historical survey, exercised similar caution to Major. He stated that cricket's putative

---

[4]   Henry Blofeld, *Cricket and All That* (Coronet, 2001), p 1.
[5]   Simon Hughes, *And God Created Cricket* (Black Swan, 2010, p 11).
[6]   At p 8 of *The Cricket-Field*, Pycroft stated that he applied a sort of lawyer's forensic approach to the evidence as to cricket's origins, reasoning that just because the name is hard to find before the eighteenth century did not mean that the game itself did not exist before then, since the game might have been older than its name, or records might simply have been lost. Pycroft was proved correct in his caution when Derrick's testimony was discovered later.
[7]   John Major, *More than a Game: The Story of Cricket's Early Years* (Harper Perennial, 2007), p 18.

ancestor was '*pila baculorea* (usually translated as "club-ball"), which Edward III banned in 1369 as detrimental to his war effort. The usefulness of this impressive-sounding theory is somewhat limited by our ignorance of what "club-ball" was. We do not even know whether it was a specific game, or whether, as seems more likely, it was a catch-all term to cover any form of ball-bashing the citizenry were apt to waste their time on.'[8]

More martial interference is found in another legal context, a statute of King Edward IV in 1477/8 (17 Edw IV c3) which made the playing of 'handyn' and 'handoute' illegal because they 'interfered with the compulsory practice of archery'. One has to have priorities. As with 'club-ball', both 'handyn' and 'handoute' might also be ancestors of cricket, at least somewhere in the game's family tree if not its direct progenitors.

Wisden contends that cricket evolved in the Dark Ages, between the Romans and the Normans.[9] If so, that makes it rather older than Edward I's wardrobe. But let us return to John Derrick and the first incontrovertible reference to the game. Derrick testified that he had had knowledge of the disputed land for fifty years (he was aged 59 at the time of the case), which means his 'cricket and other plays' would have taken place around the middle of the 1500s. It can therefore be said with reasonable certainty that something close to the modern game – close enough that it used the same name – existed by the mid-sixteenth century. Major imagines an unknown hero unwittingly leaving an immortal bequest: 'In the midst of this tumultuous century [the 1500s] an unknown rural genius, somewhere in the Weald of south-east England, tweaked some ancient game and cricket was born. As anonymous as his ancient forebear, the inventor of the wheel, he would have gained immortality had his name become known. Alas, it did not, though his shade can rest content that he built a game for all time.'[10]

It might render the imagery somewhat less poetic, but, as Major would likely concede, it was probably a collection of geniuses rather than an individual. Perhaps there was a group of shepherds who

[8] Derek Birley, *A Social History of English Cricket* (Aurum, 1999), p 2.
[9] *Wisden* 2009, p 1638.
[10] Major, op cit, p 21.

derived so much enjoyment from knocking something small and roundish around with a crook that they started to refine the rules. They decided that the striker had to defend a fence post or a tree or – dare one say it – the stump of a tree (later replaced by the wicket-gate through which sheep would pass). They determined that the value of each hit would be measured by the number of times that the striker could run between two markers before the ball was returned. Then their neighbours noticed the enjoyment (craic?) so much that they asked to join in, or started their own variation. Then parents in the area might have discovered that sending children to join in the increasingly popular game was a good way of keeping them out of trouble. Formalizing and refining the rules might have become a common talking point at the local ale house. And so it would have proceeded.

Another reason to assume that shepherds were involved in fashioning cricket's antecedents into something like its modern form is that the sheep would have kept the grass short – something necessary for a game in which the ball was rolled along the ground, as most conclude it was by early bowlers. Then again, perhaps the shepherds simply varied an earlier game in which balls were lobbed or otherwise delivered as a full toss – though long grass would have made finding the ball maddeningly frustrating, as all who have played the game in improvised circumstances can confirm. All of the above chimes with *Wisden*'s conclusion: 'All research concedes that the game derived from a very old, widespread and uncomplicated pastime by which one player served up an object, be it a small piece of wood or a ball, and another hit it with a suitably fashioned club.'[11]

Perhaps the shepherds now lost in time provided the etymological origin too: as we have seen, early cricket bats were crooked, like a shepherd's crook, and so one might infer 'crooked' became 'cracce' and then 'cricket'. As against that, different scholars have offered alternative explanations based on Celtic, Scandinavian, Anglo-Saxon, Dutch and Norman French sources. In 1935 the poet Thomas Moult delivered some robust common sense on their combined speculation:

---

[11] *Wisden* 2009, p 1638.

Time and time again, indeed, have we been told that the origins of the game are lost in rounders, cat and dog, stob-ball, or the stool ball which Nausicaa and her girls – see Chapman's Homer – played in old Greece, playing it, we are informed, 'with wrists of ivory', a term which will doubtless be used by some cricket writer when the modern Nausicaas come again into their own …

It has been claimed that allusions to cricket are to be found in documents of the Plantagenet period, but even if the claim is a true one, it does not matter, because there may be all the difference in the world between an organised pastime and its throwbacks. Adam, no doubt, whiled away some of his golden hours in the Garden of Eden by using a pebble as a ball and smiting it hard with a stick. But that does not make Adam a cricketer.[12]

Moult's warning remains just as valid today.

SLIM PICKINGS

So much for the very beginnings. Unfortunately, further written evidence of cricket is hard to come by for several centuries after John Derrick's fragment. This is not surprising, because few written records of anything from that time exist outside the government, the church and the law. As John Major says, 'what scraps we know of it come from court hearings, inquests, church records and the pitiful number of letters and diaries that have survived the years'.[13]

Of the official records only the law was ever likely to be much concerned with cricket. Prior to the nineteenth and especially the twentieth century, the state existed on a far smaller and generally less intrusive scale than at present. Also, until at least the seventeenth century, when literacy levels increased significantly, most of those who were able to write things down were not the same class of people likely to be concerned with playing cricket. Rev Pycroft was appalled to find a record from 1700 which listed cricket as one of the pastimes of the 'lower classes,'[14] though he might have been mollified by the

---

[12] Thomas Moult, 'The Story of the Game', in Thomas Moult (ed), *Bat and Ball: A New Book of Cricket* (Magna, [1935] 1994), pp 18–20.

[13] Major, op cit, p 23.

[14] Pycroft rants: 'Nevertheless we have a catalogue of games about 1700 in Stow's "Survey of London," and there Cricket is mentioned; but, remarkably

fact that the Earl of Sussex in 1677 was recorded drawing £3 from his treasurer to attend a local cricket match, which was listed among other presumably non-lower-class pursuits such as hunting, hawking and ninepins.[15]

LEGAL PROBLEMS

Then there are problems with legal records themselves. Records of litigation prior to the nineteenth century are extensive, but not always in a satisfactory state. It comes as a surprise for most laypeople to learn that, with some highly specialized exceptions,[16] the state in England and Wales has never taken responsibility for publishing judgments of the courts. Thus, although the law of the land has been developed in large part by the common law, through the system of precedent, and it is a basic legal maxim that ignorance of the law is no excuse, there has never been a formal, state-funded repository of decisions of binding precedent handed down by the courts.

The earliest records of the common law start in the thirteenth century, with the first of the year books. These were published annually until the mid-sixteenth century. The books were written in Norman French (sometimes pejoratively called 'Dog French', it was the official language of the common law courts until 1730, though it had a long and slow decline in actual usage before the official abolition.[17]) and recorded argument and judicial rulings during

---

enough, it is particularised as one of the amusements of "the lower classes." The whole passage is curious:- "The modern sports of the citizens *besides drinking (!)* are cock fighting, bowling upon greens, backgammon, cards, dice, billiards, also musical entertainments, dancing, masks, balls, stage plays, and club meetings in the evening; they sometimes ride out on horseback, and hunt with the lord mayor's pack of dogs, when the common hunt goes on. The *lower classes* divert themselves at foot-ball, wrestling, cudgels, ninepins, shovel board, cricket stow-ball, ringing bells, quoits, pitching the bar, bull and bear baitings, throwing at cocks, and lying at ale houses."(!)' (Pycroft, op cit, p 7; the emphasis is Pycroft's.)

[15]   Birley, op cit, p 12.

[16]   These include Reports of Patent Cases, which are published under the authority of the Intellectual Property Office (formerly the Patent Office), and Reports of Tax Cases, reported under the direction of HM Revenue and Customs. Increasingly, tribunals (such as the Employment Appeal Tribunal) also publish judgments on their website, though not as traditional law reports, but rather raw transcripts, occasionally with a rudimentary summary and catchwords at the start.

[17]   Also, many legal terms survive from those times. Interestingly, the development

sittings of the courts in a particular legal term. The successors to the year books were the 'nominate reports', so called because the name of the reporter appeared on each series.[18] Some of the reporters gained great respect and authority:[19] the one-time Chief Justice Sir Edward Coke was arguably respected in legal circles as much for his reports as for his career as a barrister and judge.

Other series of reports developed a less impressive reputation: 'Particularly notorious were those produced at the turn of the 18th and 19th centuries by Isaac Espinasse, of whom it was said that he heard only half of what went on in court and reported the other half. One exasperated judge, faced with counsel seeking to cite one of Espinasse's reports, was said to have exclaimed that he would not hear anything from Espinasse or any other ass.'[20] Worst of all, sometimes different reports of the same case reported entirely different outcomes.[21]

Chief Justice Holt once said despairingly:[22]

---

of 'standard English' is usually attributed to the Chancery. English replaced Norman French in administrative documents from about 1430 and the version of written English used in the Court of Chancery became the standard in respect of grammar, spelling and handwriting. See for example Malcolm Richardson, 'Henry V, the English Chancery, and Chancery English', [1980] *Speculum* 55(4), pp 726–50.

[18] Opinion has it that the year books, which were mostly written by anonymous authors, were originally compiled not for barristers to use in court, but rather for students of the law. See J H Baker, *An Introduction to English Legal History* (Butterworths, 4th edn, 2002), pp 178–83; S F C Milsom, *Historical Foundations of the Common Law* (Oxford University Press, 2nd edn, 1981); W T S Daniel QC, *The History and Origin of the Law Reports* (William Clowes, 1884). A copy of the last of those mentioned has been digitized and is freely available online at the time of writing. Those sources reveal some differences over precisely when the year books began. As early as the 1220s, lawyers were extracting cases from the formal plea rolls as illustrations of the law, though the first year book as such came later in the same century.

[19] Starting with Edmund Plowden, whose reports were published from the 1550s until the 1570s.

[20] Craig Rose, *From the Year Books to the Internet: Seven Centuries of Law Reporting in England* (LexisNexis, 2008). Rose also points out that, despite Espinasse's asinine reputation, his reports were still being cited by the House of Lords as recently as 2006, in *Bradford & Bingley plc v Rashid* [2006] 4 All ER 705.

[21] See *A-G v Reynolds* [1911] 2 KB 888, where the court had to resolve the competing reports of *Costard and Wingfield*'s case.

[22] *Slater v May* (1704) 2 Ld Raym 1071 at 1072.

'these scrambling reports . . . will make us [judges] appear to posterity
for a parcel of blockheads.'

In the mid-nineteenth century, a concerted attempt was made
by barristers to improve matters, culminating in the formation of
the Incorporated Council of Law Reporting (ICLR) in 1865.[23] The
ICLR's objects were stated as being the 'preparation and publication,
in a convenient form, at a moderate price, and under gratuitous
professional control, of Reports of Judicial Decisions of the Superior
and Appellate Courts in England and Wales'. In time, the reports
produced by the ICLR were required by the judiciary to be cited
in preference to any other series, and hence became known as the
'official law reports'.[24] In the early to mid-twentieth century, they were
joined by commercial ventures such as the All England Law Reports,
which also gained judicial approbation, as did a variety of specialist
reports.[25] Then, in the 1990s, judgments started to be recorded online,
with important implications for the functioning of the common law.[26]

[23]   One other important tidying-up exercise was the creation of the English Reports
in the early twentieth century, which consolidated more than 100,000 pre-1865 cases
into 178 weighty volumes.
[24]   All of that was achieved without any state intervention: the ICLR to this day
remains a private charity, not a government department, and the status of its reports
is established not by legislation but by practice notes issued by the judiciary. There
is also the Bailii service, which publishes judgments on a free website, but it too
is a charity, not an arm of the state. At the time of writing it was also not fully
comprehensive, with regard to either present-day cases or historical ones.
[25]   Under the current practice direction ([2012] 2 All ER 255), the official reports of
the AC, QB, ChD and Fam have the first priority, the All England Reports (All ER)
and the Weekly Law Reports (WLR) are equal second, then the various specialist
reports, and finally official transcripts. Reports of extempore judgments may be
admissible if signed by a barrister or a solicitor.
[26]   Judgments have grown exponentially in length in the past twenty years or so. In
the 1980s there was the 'photocopying disease', which gave way in turn to the cut-
and-paste of the 1990s and unreported judgments becoming easily available for the
first time, thanks to the internet. As a result counsel were able –and some felt obliged
– to cite many cases where in the past one or two would have sufficed, and the judges
in turn felt obliged to deal with all of them. Previously, unreported judgments would
effectively vanish (which meant also that legal editors wielded great unspoken power
in the development of the law…), unless someone involved in a later case happened
to have personal knowledge of an earlier unreported decision.
    It has not helped either that the law in recent decades has become much more
complex thanks to the plethora of statute and statutory regulation, much of which

It remains the case, though, even today, that most cases are reported only by non-state entities.

Moreover, the creation of the ICLR and subsequent commercial equivalents only solved the problem for judgments of the superior courts (the High Court and above). The decisions of the lower courts – the magistrates' court, county court, crown court and all of their antecedents (in which most of the fragments about cricket appear) – were never collected in a central state repository and are still not in a satisfactory state today. Hence, pre-nineteenth-century cricket fragments are often found in church records or publications such as *Fog's Weekly Journal*, none of which could be called an approximation of a modern law report. Even though lower court decisions do not have precedent value, the principle of open justice ought to require more consolidated and publicly accessible records than has ever been the case.

FRAGMENTS

For cases prior to 1865, therefore, historians are left sifting through legal records of distinctly uneven quality when trying to find mentions of cricket. One would expect references to cricket in those early centuries to be infrequent, since the law would usually encounter it only if someone was seriously hurt while playing, justifying litigation of some sort, or if an incident occurred along the lines of smashed windows or boundary disputes (of the land, rather than of the six and four, variety).

That was the case at least until the seventeenth century, when the rising Puritan tide washed over cricket, and compulsory church attendance on Sundays conflicted with the only chance most people had to play the game. In 1611, for example, two youths from the village of Sidlesham in the Chichester district of West Sussex were 'fined for playing cricket' instead of going to church. Two years later, in Wanborough, near Guildford, an assault with a 'cricket staffe' was recorded.[27] In 1622 in Boxgrove, also in the Chichester district, six

---

derives from the European Union and the very different form of statute law that exists in most of its member states, but that is for another day.

[27] Geoff Tibballs, *No-Balls and Googlies: A Cricket Companion* (Michael O'Mara, new edn, 2013), p 10.

men were impugned by the churchwardens not simply for playing on the Sabbath but also because 'they use to breake the church windows with the ball' and, more gruesomely, 'a little childe had like to have her braynes beaten out with a crickett batt'.[28] Then, in 1624, one unfortunate Jasper Vinnall is said to have been killed playing the game: he was hit by a bat while trying to catch the ball at Horsted Green, also in Sussex. In 1629, more ecclesiastical issues appeared when Henry Cuffin, curate of Ruckinge, Kent, was hauled before the archdeacon's court because he had been playing cricket immediately following a service.

It is usually assumed the game did not prosper under the Protector, but the evidence is fairly light on the point and the subject of some dispute. There are claims that Cromwell himself played the game in his youth,[29] but even if true that does not provide compelling evidence as to what his government did with the game years later. It is also said that he or his commissioners banned the playing of 'krickett' in Ireland in the 1650s and, by way of enforcement, ordered that all sticks and balls used in the game be 'burnt by the common hangman'; if so, whether the measure was intended to be more anti-cricket or anti-Irish is another question.

Other seventeenth-century repression included banning of theatres by the Long Parliament. Also, in 1643, before the Commonwealth itself, Parliament had ordered the Book of Sports to be publicly burned.[30] In terms of cricket specifically, three players in Eltham, Kent, were fined for breaching the Sabbath at the beginning of the interregnum.[31]

---

[28]   Birley, op cit, p 7.
[29]   Harry Altham, *A History of Cricket, vol 1: From the Beginnings to the First World War* (George Allen & Unwin, 1962), ch 1. One has to be careful about contemporary references to Cromwell having misspent his youth playing cricket, as some of the authors were hostile to Cromwell, and may have wanted to paint him as a hypocrite in the light of his later Puritanism.
[30]   James I's Declaration of Sports of 1617, also known as the Book of Sports, listed the sports and recreations that were permitted on Sundays and other holy days. It did not refer to cricket. James wavered in the application of the declaration, sensitive to Puritan opposition, though Charles I in 1633 reissued it and ordered it to be read.
[31]   One might note at this point that if they had banned or otherwise harassed cricket the seventeenth-century Puritans would have been going further than even the reasonably notorious Japanese prison guards of the Second World War. The famous

Nevertheless, it is certain that cricket was played during Cromwell's rule in public schools such as Winchester. It has been claimed that wealthy royalists retreated to their country estates during the period and, observing (and clearly enjoying) the game played by estate staff, hit upon the idea of gambling on the result, which they were able to do after the Restoration. Sir Derek Birley concluded that whatever restrictions were placed on adults, school cricket was alive and well during the interregnum,[32] and those who left school and found occupations that allowed for a bit of leisure time were able to continue playing cricket as adults in post-Restoration England.

AFTER THE RESTORATION: TAXES AND GAMBLING

Shortly after the Restoration, another all-pervasive branch of the law provided a reference to cricket: 'In 1668 the landlord of the Ram at Smithfield, London's medieval sports ground, paid rates for a cricket field, and in the same year the Maidstone justices benevolently waived excise duties on the sale of beer at a "kricketing".'[33]

Further evidence of the discarding of Puritanical repression comes from the references to 'wagers' on cricket which appear from 1694. Gambling was central to the formal development of the game (an historical fact which adds more than a touch of irony to the present-day match-fixing affairs, which by necessity occupy a depressing number of pages later in the book). Almost all cricket historians from Pycroft onwards have stressed the importance of this malevolent

---

cricket writer E W 'Jim' Swanton was interned for a number of years after the fall of Singapore, but was allowed to keep a 1939 edition of *Wisden* he happened to have upon him when captured. It soon became a most sought-after item among the prisoners, and had to be rationed accordingly. It survived the war and to this day, preserved in the Lord's museum, one can see the stamp on the inside cover from some officious Japanese censor which translates as 'Not Subversive'.

One can but wonder about what the censor and his translator would have made of the exploits of Bradman, Hammond and Hutton. Perhaps if the edition had been from the early 1930s they might have hit upon the idea of causing dissention among the British and Australian prisoners with a bit of sledging about Mr Jardine and his infamous strategies. Or perhaps they simply thought that the game was so impossible to understand that it would keep the prisoners' minds off escaping.

[32] Birley, op cit, p 10.

[33] Ibid, p 12. Note that income tax did not exist at the time, hence excise duties, licences and the like were of the first importance to the nation's accounts.

component of cricket's past. Simon Rae put it succinctly: 'No phrase could better describe pre-Victorian cricket than "a gigantic gambling transaction".'[34] One exemplar of that tawdry cricketing age was the second-ever president of MCC, the Reverend Lord Frederick Beauclerk (1773–1850). He delivered sermons about the spirit of cricket being 'unalloyed by love of lucre and mean jealousies', but elsewhere boasted of how he made 600 guineas a year gambling on it – not a bad return for a man who had represented the amateurs in the inaugural Gentleman versus Players fixture.

The focus of vice was a London pub known as the Green Man and Still, in Oxford Street, where players and bookmakers used to meet to carve out their squalid deals. But deals were also made at ostensibly more salubrious establishments: Frederick, Prince of Wales (1707–51), for example, developed a keen interest in cricket, partly as an attempt to assimilate into English society (he was German) and partly because he enjoyed betting on the outcome. But his interest in the game appears to have been genuine, and cricket suffered noticeably from the loss of his patronage upon his death.[35] Cricket's loss was magnified considerably by the fact that its greatest patron of the age, the second Duke of Richmond, had died the previous year.

Naturally gamblers, legal or otherwise, are never all that far from lawyers. In 1719 the press reported what was probably a representative or at least not unknown event: 'Last week a Tryal was brought at Guildhall before Lord Chief Justice Pratt, between two Companies of Cricket Players, the Men of Kent Plaintiffs and the Men of London Defendants, for Sixty Pounds played for at cricket, and after a long hearing and near 200*l.* expended in the cause, my Lord not understanding the Game, ordered them to play it over again.'[36] But there was not much the authorities could do on a practical level.

---

[34] Simon Rae, *It's Not Cricket: Skullduggery, Sharp Practice and Downright Cheating in the Noble Game* (Faber & Faber, 2001), p 55.

[35] Frederick also gave cricket's first trophy (as opposed to hard cash) to the winners of a match in 1733. It is sometimes said, though without much evidence, that his death was caused by a blow from a cricket ball.

[36] Quoted in Rob Light, 'Cricket in the Eighteenth Century', in Anthony Bateman and Jeffrey Hill (eds), *The Cambridge Companion to Cricket* (Cambridge University Press, 2011), p 31.

Bookmakers could be barred from entry to grounds, but no-one would have been under any illusion that that would put them out of business.

Obviously, cricket was not the only concern of the authorities; gambling and fixing results were rife throughout other sports and pastimes such as bare-knuckle boxing and horse racing. In 1740, Parliament passed an Act 'to restrain and to prevent the excessive increase in horse racing'. It banned stakes of less than £50, a substantial sum at the time, the intention being to make racing the preserve of the wealthy. The Act was probably honoured more in the breach than the observance, and even those who did respect the restriction on gambling on horses could simply have switched their activities to other sports. The wealthier among them were known to bet on one result while rigging the match to produce another. They would then collect on a separate, undisclosed bet for a net profit on the combined transactions.[37] All in all, it seems that the pre-Victorian writer Mary Russell Mitford (1787–1855) was a shade detached from reality when she wrote: 'To think of playing cricket for hard cash! Money and gentility would ruin any pastime under the sun.'

THE LAWS TAKE SHAPE

In 1727 came one of the most important early cricket documents, when the Duke of Richmond marshalled a team to play one Mr Broderick in yet another Home Counties fixture (the disparity in rank between the two team captains suggests a portent of the Gentlemen versus Players matches that were to become a feature of English cricket from Victorian times until the early 1960s). The 1727 match was at Peperharow in Surrey. In the spirit of the Court of Chancery, hopefully advised by members thereof, the Duke and Broderick drafted some rather formal-sounding 'Articles of Association' to govern the conduct of the match – the first-ever written record of cricketing rules. Though the articles pertained only to that particular match, it is generally assumed that they were representative of how organized cricket was played at the time.

In August 1731, the Duke's men became embroiled in something more usually found in the magistrates' courts, rather than the

---

[37]   David Frith, 'Corruption in Cricket', in Bateman and Hill, op cit, p 42.

cloistered environs of the Chancery Division: 'The same night the Duke of Richmond and his cricket players were greatly insulted by the mob at Richmond, some of them having their shirts torn off their backs; and it was said a lawsuit would commence about the play.'[38]

The earliest scorecards date from 1743 and 1744. They were compiled in the London Club at the Artillery Ground, Finsbury. A landmark of equal significance occurred at the same venue in 1744, when the first known version of the laws of cricket was published. It has to be said that the first laws were written by draftsmen with no mean legal talent. For example, the first clause reads: 'Ye pitching of ye first Wicket is to be determined by ye cast of a piece of Money', which requires no modern translation and admits of no ambiguity.

The second clause formalized the length of the pitch at 22 yards. It has remained precisely that ever since, in what has to be one of the most remarkable pieces of continuity in all sports. The substantial advances in living conditions and sports science that have occurred over the years – particularly since the Second World War – have not rendered most athletic or ball games obsolete. They have just meant that objects are thrown further and competitors run faster and jump higher and further in track and field sports. In games such as rugby and football they mean that players cover more ground during the course of a game. In cricket, however, greatly increased athleticism has to mean that balls are delivered over the same distance much more quickly in the present day than in 1744 (when they were only bowled underarm, for a start). The game has to have altered significantly as a result, assuming that batsmen's reactions have not sped up in proportion. Yet no-one has ever seriously suggested extending the length of the pitch to compensate.

The section in the 1744 laws headed 'Laws for ye Umpires' was rather telling. It provided among other things that 'each Umpire is sole judge of all Nips and Catches, Ins and Outs, good or bad Runs, at his own Wicket, and his determination shall be absolute, and he shall not be changed for another Umpire without ye consent of both Sides'.[39] Cricket's most important directive was thus laid down from

---

[38]   Extract of a report from *Fog's Weekly Journal*, quoted in Birley, op cit, p 21.

[39]   Quoted in Moult, op cit, pp 271–2. The letter Y in 'ye' would have been a thorn (þ), the predecessor to the modern digraph 'th', which was something beyond early

the start of the modern game. It differed somewhat from the Duke and Broderick's Articles of Association, which left the umpires superior to the players but subordinate to the sponsors.

In 1745 the first recorded ladies' match took place on Gosden Common, Bramley, Surrey. Both teams dressed in white. The Maids of Bramley wore blue ribbons in their hair and scored 119 notches. They were defeated by the Maids of Hambledon, wearing red ribbons in their hair, who scored 127 notches.[40] Had any of the participants lived to what would have been a great age, they might have enjoyed the description of Catherine Morland in Jane Austen's *Northanger Abbey*: 'She was fond of all boy's plays, and greatly preferred cricket not merely to dolls, but to the more heroic enjoyments of infancy, nursing a dormouse, feeding a canary-bird, or watering a rose-bush.'[41]

In 1771 the width of the bat was limited to 4½ inches, another prescription that has not been changed since. The law was introduced after 'Shock' White had used a bat that was wider than the wicket in a match against the famous Hambledon club.[42] Assuming that bats of that width were not common, White might be seen as a forerunner to

printing presses, but like Moult I have not modernized the spelling.

[40] See David Frith, *Guildford's Cricket Story* (Guildford Cricket Club, 2013).

[41] It is also said at the beginning of the book that Catherine enjoyed baseball, which shows that that sport evolved in England as well and was sufficiently well established by 1800 for Austen to refer to it without explanation. Baseball either shared some of cricket's forebears and developed at the same time, or it evolved directly from cricket itself. Its origins were obscured by the nineteenth-century American patriot Albert Spalding, who was so determined to prove that baseball was exclusively American that he set up a commission of inquiry, ignored it when it returned the wrong answer, and set about spreading the myth of General Abner Graves inventing the game in America instead (a sort of parallel with the myth of William Webb Ellis and rugby union). See generally Julian Norridge, *Can We Have Our Balls Back, Please? How the British Invented Sport* (Allen Lane, 2008).

[42] Hambledon's status as the most famous club in England and the presumed cradle of the modern game was established primarily because of a book published in 1833, *The Cricketers of My Time* by John Nyren, which recounted the club's halcyon days in the eighteenth century (it had spluttered on in greatly reduced form into the nineteenth century, but was finished for all intents and purposes before the publication of Nyren's monograph). Other clubs had some significant claims for equal importance in the eighteenth century, but it was Nyren's work and the preservation of records which elevated Hambledon above them – at least until Frith's *Guildford's Cricket Story* (op cit), which set out a case for Guildford, building on the famous testimony of John Derrick all those centuries earlier.

Greg Chappell, who spotted a different loophole two centuries later concerning the permissible methods of bowling, as will be seen later in the book. Three years later the first version of the lbw law was introduced,[43] but surprisingly the earliest scorecard recording anyone falling foul of it dates from 1795 (though that may be nothing more than a reflection of how few scorecards have survived).

Hambledon almost immediately introduced the new width rule, precluding any repeat of White's shock tactic. They also fashioned a metal gauge for enforcement purposes, a sort of cricketing precursor to the platinum metre bar which was stored in the Archives de la République in Paris from 1799.[44]

Another development from the late eighteenth century was the introduction of the middle stump. It came about thanks to the greatest bowler of the age, Edward 'Lumpy' Stevens. During a single-wicket match between Five of Hambledon and Five of England in May 1775, Stevens bowled through the last Hambledon batsman's two-stump wicket no fewer than three times without dislodging the bails.[45]

Round-arm bowling (hand level with the elbow) was illegal before 1828, although it had been experimented with the previous season. The method had been introduced by John Willes when playing for Kent against MCC at Lord's on 15 July 1822. It resulted in him becoming the first bowler to be no-balled for throwing. In 1835 changes to the

---

[43] *Wisden* 1975 stated that 'It seems fairly certain that it was in 1774 that a set of laws was produced which was widely accepted, and which has stood the test of time remarkably well. A Committee of Noblemen and Gentlemen met at The Star and Garter, Pall Mall, on February 25, 1774 and produced New Articles of the Game of Cricket.'

[44] Wikipedia helpfully records that the metre bar remained standard until 1960, when the metre was redefined as '1650763.73 times the wavelength of radiation emitted by the krypton-86 isotope'. It was redefined again in 1983 as 'the length of the path travelled by light in vacuum during a time interval of 1/299,792,458th of a second'. Cricket seems to have managed with slightly less complex definitions.

[45] Stevens's match was played at the Artillery Ground in London, one of the most important early venues. Not long afterwards, in 1787, Thomas Lord, a successful wine merchant as well as a bowler and coach with the White Conduit Club, opened his first ground at what is now Dorset Square in London. That same year the White Conduit Club became the Marylebone Cricket Club. In 1811 Lord moved the ground to Regents Park and in 1814 he did so again, this time to St John's Wood, where it has remained ever since.

laws allowed bowlers to raise their delivery hand to shoulder height. 'Overhand bowling' was authorized by MCC in 1864.

PAGE V WISDEN

Coincidentally, 1864 was the year of the first edition of John Wisden's *The Cricketer's Almanack*.[46] Wisden had a substantial background in cricket not only as a well-known player of his day but also on the business side of things, being the owner of a sports goods store in London. From 1855 until 1858, Wisden worked in partnership with Fred Lillywhite, a member of a famous cricketing family responsible for some of cricket's key moments, including the first-ever overseas tour (to North America, in 1859) and first-ever test match (against Australia in 1877, to which I will return more than once). Wisden went on the 1859 tour as a player, but became Lillywhite's rival in the commercial sphere. His almanack followed Lillywhite's earlier annual, *The Guide to Cricketers*.[47]

Lillywhite used to sell scoring sheets headed 'Lillywhite and Sons' Registered Cricket Scoring-paper'. In 1851, he registered them under the Copyright Act 1842, and re-registered them in 1862 after dissolving another partnership with two of his relatives. The sheets sold well, and hence the copyright became of some value. One Mr Page started selling virtually identical sheets, leading Lillywhite to threaten him with a breach of copyright. Page ignored the threat. Lillywhite's fortunes declined before he could bring proceedings. He became bankrupt in 1866 and died shortly thereafter. Page and Wisden both bid for the copyright in the scoring sheets; Page was the winner. Page then discovered that Wisden was nevertheless

---

[46] The *Almanack* got off to a fairly unpromising start. From the title one infers that Wisden intended the work to be solely about cricket, but he obviously could not find enough material in the first year to fill the desired number of pages, since he padded it out with such random ephemera as the dates of various battles and the length of canals. See Robert Winder, *The Little Wonder: The Remarkable History of Wisden* (Wisden, 2013).

[47] Fred Lillywhite's publication ran from 1849 until his death in 1866; thereafter it was incorporated into John Lillywhite's *Cricketer's Companion*, which had begun in 1865. To add to the confusion, James Lillywhite started his own cricketer's annual in 1872 and incorporated John's from 1885. The combined companions were all out after 1900.

still selling his own scoring sheets. He brought proceedings against Wisden for breach of copyright.

Page faced two obstacles before he started. First, cricket scorecards predated those sold by Lillywhite, as Wisden was able to show by the evidence of three 'experienced cricketers' and by books and other written material. That seems an obvious point: scorecards of one form or another must have been used for as long as cricket has been played – even before John Derrick's time shepherds must have had a method of putting notches (as runs used to be called) on wood. Page was therefore compelled to confine his claim to the one aspect which had been invented by Lillywhite: a section providing for the runs scored at the fall of each wicket, referred to as a 'tablet'. Secondly, there was the fact that Page himself had been selling scorecards before Lillywhite's death, and had been prepared to defend any copyright claim from Lillywhite, giving a hypocritical twist to his own suit against Wisden.

The judge was not much engaged by the affair.[48] He began with the damning words 'This is a litigation with respect to a very small matter' – which indeed it was once Page was compelled to restrict his claim to the tablet. Page admitted that he had earlier defied Lillywhite's threat of copyright litigation, and was commended by the judge for his honesty. But the claim failed anyway, even before the issue of copyright was reached. Page had stated in his pleadings that the copyright was registered in 1863, when, as we have seen, it had been registered in 1851. By putting in a later date he was setting himself up for 12 years more payment than he would otherwise have received, since the copyright would have longer to run (in those days copyright ran for 42 years from the date of publication, or until seven years after the death of the author, whichever was longer). 'The principle', explained the judge, 'is that a person claiming a copyright must state the day when first published.'

The case was therefore dismissed. The judge nevertheless went on to give his opinion of the copyright claim itself. 'I suppose there is a

---

[48] The citation for the report is (1869) 20 LTNS 435. It was heard in the Court of Chancery. In those days, before the Judicature Acts of the 1870s, all puisne Chancery judges had the title 'Vice-Chancellor'. It was later conferred on the head of the division, who since 2005 has simply been known as 'Chancellor'.

copyright,' he said grudgingly, but added: 'On the question whether this is a fit subject for a copyright I have no doubt whatever that it is not.' In a slightly wounding snub to later professionals such as Bill Frindall (who was rather protective of his 'linear scoring method'), he stated: 'To say that a particular mode of ruling a book constituted an object for a copyright is absurd. A solicitor's bill is made out in that way by casting up the totals, and what more is this? It is below all protection, being a mere arithmetical operation, which must have been done over and over again.' Despite the judge's disparagement, the case was later cited in an American judgment and, somewhat surprisingly, in a New Zealand Supreme Court judgment as recently as 2006.[49]

THE MODERN FIXTURES BEGIN

Returning to the governance of cricket, the County Championship regulations were introduced in 1873. The first test match was played in 1877, although it was not called a 'test match' as such; the term gained currency from about 1885. In 1881 the laws underwent a substantial redraft. Needless to say, shortening and simplifying were not among the objectives, though in fairness the game was growing in complexity and the laws had to correspond. At the turn of the century, another major law change came into place with the six-ball over becoming the norm, albeit with a few notable exceptions that lingered for decades.[50]

---

[49] *Henkel KgAA v Holdfast New Zealand Limited* [2006] NZSC 102 at [30]. The case was cited in support of the principle that accurate particulars are required in a copyright case, otherwise the plaintiff will be liable for the costs – reflecting the fact that Page was sunk by putting the wrong dates in his pleadings. Technically the decision on copyright could be said to be *obiter* – not binding on later courts because the issue did not need to be decided in the case – but as far as I am aware no-one has taken the point.

[50] England started a trial of eight-ball overs in 1939. It was supposed to run for two years but was curtailed by the outbreak of the Second World War and not revived thereafter. Eight-ball overs were also used in South Africa from 1938/9 to 1957/8, New Zealand from 1968/9 to 1978/9 and Pakistan from 1974/5 to 1977/8. The Australians continued to use them until the end of the 1970s, before they became another victim of Kerry Packer's revolution: six-ball overs allowed for more ad breaks on television.

At this point, however, the historical sketching can be brought to a close, because we have arrived at the time of W G Grace, who is the subject of the first two individual stories in the book. As will be seen, Grace's career spanned, and was at least partially responsible for, the transition from cricket's patchy early origins to the modern game.

SOME OBSERVATIONS

What observations might be made about the origins of cricket, its early intersections with the law, and the development of its own laws? First, claims for foreign origins can effectively be discarded; it is virtually certain that, even if some of its antecedents were imported, any game recognizable as cricket evolved in England,[51] as for that matter did many other sports which are now played globally including football, rugby and baseball.

Exactly why the English thought up so many great games is a matter of conjecture. After all, other cultures in pre-industrial times were surely just as given to picking up objects, hitting them and chasing them around for their own amusement. I rather like the inference by the anthropologist Kate Fox that the English created organized sport as a means to circumvent traditional social reticence:

> The English are capable of engaging socially with each other, but we need clear and precise guidelines on what to do, what to say, and exactly when and how to do and say it. Games ritualize our social interactions, giving them a reassuring structure and sense of order. By focusing on the detail of the game's rules and rituals, we can pretend that the game itself is really the point, and the social contact a mere incidental side effect.

> In fact it is the other way around: games are a means to an end, the end being the kind of sociable interaction and social bonding that other cultures seem to achieve without all this fuss, subterfuge and self-delusion. The English are human; we are social animals just like

---

[51]   Thomas Moult puts it this way, invoking the sort of patriotism that is a rare find these days: 'All we can be sure about is that as an organized pastime cricket belongs to England, the various learned attempts to prove its foreign ownership by a great flourish of such weird appellations as "cricket-a-wicket" (used in Florio's Italian Dictionary) being merely comic' (Moult, op cit, p 20). For those interested, the text of Florio's non-cricketing flannel is easily found via Google.

all other humans, but we have to trick ourselves into social interaction and bonding by disguising it as something else, such as a game of football, cricket, tennis, rugby, darts, pool, dominoes, cards, scrabble charges, wellie-throwing or toe-wrestling.[52]

That would certainly go some way towards explaining the complexity of the laws of cricket as they have developed, although American football and Australian Rules football suggest the English do not have a monopoly on byzantine rules and peculiar rituals in matters of sport (unless one takes the view that the tendency to create complex sports was part of America and Australia's cultural inheritance from England).

Julian Norridge offers a less genteel explanation: the English formalized physical pastimes into games with fixed rules in order to facilitate gambling.[53] There is certainly much to support that thesis in relation to cricket, considering the actions of the patrons of the Green Man and Still. Either way, the reason for sports invented in Britain later becoming so popular across the globe was undoubtedly the extraordinary breadth and longevity of the British Empire, and, relatedly, the desire of other nations to emulate the success of Britain and the rest of the West. In time, former colonies started to see winning at cricket a means of asserting their independence and getting their own back on their former masters. The influence of nationalism on cricket is found in a variety of different contexts throughout the book.

The second observation I would make from the historical survey is that no-one has really disputed the verdict of the *Oxford English Dictionary* about the first use of the word. It is therefore the law which provides the earliest definitive reference to the game. Opening

---

[52] Kate Fox, *Watching the English: The Hidden Rules of English Behaviour* (Hodder & Stoughton, 2004), p 241. Sir Derek Birley adds a similar comment (op cit, p 27).

[53] Norridge, op cit. Matthew Engel has also quoted an alternative explanation for the importance placed on sport in nineteenth century public schools, from the historian Katherine Mullin: 'The masturbation panic was so ubiquitous that there was a strong emphasis against solitude, against privacy, and against individualism. All sorts of team sports, football in particular, were brought in as an antidote.' As Engel notes, it might be an extreme interpretation. See Matthew Engel, 'It's the Cat's Whisker', Second Oxford Lecture, 1 February 2011, www.matthewengel.co.uk/lectures/oxford/lecture2.html (retrieved 22 April 2014).

myself up to a justifiable charge of sentimentality, I might record that coming across that fact formed part of the inspiration for this book.

Thirdly, state meddling in sports generally can be found from the earliest records of sport being played. The state became very much more prone to involving itself in all forms of human activities from the twentieth century onwards, and cricket was no exception.

Fourthly, several incidents were seen in which village cricketers in the seventeenth century crossed the lawyers of the day. Later in the book it will be shown how in the twentieth century the law (especially in the form of Lord Denning) changed to a more robust defender of the village game and took what I think has generally been a common-sense approach to the risks involved.

Fifthly, it is worth reiterating how the principle of the umpire always being right has stood from the very beginning of the laws of cricket, and how resoundingly it has been stated in every subsequent version. In the penultimate chapter of the book I will look more closely at the past, present and future of umpiring, something which remains at the heart of the spirit of cricket as much as its laws.

Sixthly, inglorious moments were noted in the form of brawling and gambling, and the odd bit of gamesmanship such as Shock White's. Cricket's writers and ex-players have been rather notorious over the years for boring followers into submission with claims that things were superior in some mythical golden age (which usually translates as about a decade before the speaker was born). That sort of cynical faux-nostalgia can usually be dispelled with some historical inquiry. Again, this is something that I will return to more than once.

For the meantime, I shall turn without further ado to Dr Grace.

Chapter 2

THE VICTORIANS

INDIGNATION AND INJUNCTIONS

Great indignation

On 2 April 1874, the Tasmanian paper the *Launceston Examiner* ran its regular column of news from South Australia. The column, which does not appear to have had much prominence in the paper, began:

> March 20. Arrangements having been made with Mr W G Grace to play a match against a twenty-two on the Adelaide Oval, the game was commenced to-day. The Wallaroo Association expressed great indignation owing to the contract, and Mr Panqualin came with the Eleven from the Peninsula to obtain, on behalf of the Yorke's Peninsula Cricketing Association, an injunction to stop them from playing. The game was only commenced at a quarter to 4, Langley (captain of the twenty-two) sending his men first to the wickets.[1]

It gave the score of the twenty-two[2] and went on to give the balance of the match report in among various other news items of the day, including the deaths of a man from thirst in the Gawler Ranges and a woman killed by a train at Port Adelaide while crossing the line in a wagonette driven by her husband.

Anyone in Launceston who took the time to read the column would have spotted the name of the most famous of all nineteenth-century cricketers – indeed, someone who has been called the most famous Victorian behind Gladstone and the Monarch herself. W G Grace had played at Launceston earlier, and that leg of his Australian tour had generally been considered a success on and off the field. Launceston readers might therefore have wondered what on earth he was doing

---

[1]   Retrieved from trove.nla.gov.au/ndp/del/article/52892271 on 15 April 2014.

[2]   The 'twenty-two' refers to the fact that the team playing the English XI had 22 players. Known as 'odds matches', games between teams of different numbers were a common occurrence in Victorian times when two sides were thought to be mismatched.

in a match on the mainland which someone had tried to stop by the drastic measure of a court injunction because of 'great indignation'.

The truth is that Grace deserved the indignation, and the denizens of Wallaroo were not the only mainland Australians he had infuriated. The incident in Adelaide was the final act in a tour in which many Australians had welcomed Grace with fanfare, only to greet his departure with relief coupled with the express hope that they had seen the last of him.

The root of all evil

The basic problem was money: Grace was a great box office attraction, and he knew it. He seems to have decided early on in his career that because he was responsible for bringing in most of the cash, he should get to keep most of it as well. The problem was then compounded by his supposedly amateur status, which forced him to channel his demands in the form of 'expenses' rather than professional fees. At one point even *Wisden* felt compelled to make lame excuses on Grace's behalf for his creative accounting.[3]

On the Australian tour, the locals, being the victims of his sharp practices, were less forgiving. It did not help matters that Grace lived by the rigid class system of the day, represented in cricket by the distinction between amateurs and professionals, and throughout the tour added insult to irony by paying himself a lot more than he paid the professionals. He also relegated them to second-class accommodation while enjoying first-class himself. The more egalitarian Australians would have been about as amused by that state of affairs as the hard-done-by English professionals.

The ill-fated South Australian contest was the last destination for Grace's team on the 1874 tour. Although the tour took place three years before the first official test, and none of the matches were considered first class, the tourists were still seen as representing England at the height of its imperial power and expected to set a standard in gentlemanly conduct accordingly. They were referred to as the 'All England Eleven', and Grace himself had said just before the start of the 52-day voyage that his team 'had a duty to perform

---

[3]   See the notes by Sydney Parton to the 1897 edition.

to maintain the honour of English cricket, and to uphold the high character of English cricketers'.[4]

Because it was assumed that Grace's side would only play one match in South Australia before heading home, a bidding war ensued between prospective promoters in the region. Eventually it was won, not by the official-sounding South Australian Cricket Association (SACA), but by the more remote Yorke's Peninsula Association (YPA). Grace had extracted a heavy price for the YPA's victory – some £800, more than twice his fee for any other match on the tour and a tidy sum in those days.

The scheduled venue for the match was Kadina, one of three small towns surrounding the Wallaroo copper mine. At great expense, the racecourse was converted into what was hoped would be a suitable venue for the fixture (subsequent accounts show a difference of opinion as to how suitable it actually was), and Grace and his team were welcomed with proportionate ceremony. The match was scheduled for three days, but Grace's team easily defeated the locals in only two. His agreement with the organizers provided that in those circumstances an exhibition match would be held on the third day, at not much extra cost. Yet Grace shamelessly asked for more money, despite his prior agreement and despite the fact that the YPA match had already netted him a large sum.

Then came the final straw. At the dinner which followed the conclusion of the cricket, Grace rose and made a short apology, before withdrawing with his team and surreptitiously heading back to Adelaide by coach. The reason soon became apparent: he had double-crossed his hosts. He had negotiated behind the backs of the YPA and agreed on another match in Adelaide with the SACA. Once again he had secured a handsome reward: another not insubstantial appearance fee and half the gate money as well.

The attempted injunction

Not surprisingly, the YPA had had enough. They brought proceedings in the South Australian Supreme Court seeking an injunction holding Grace to the terms of his agreement with them, which had demanded

---

[4]   Simon Rae, *W G Grace: A Life* (Faber & Faber, 1998), p 149.

exclusivity. Unfortunately, it seems that Grace had already received advice that the agreement would be spent after the Kadina match had been played, and so it proved. The application for an injunction was refused and Grace went on to enjoy his extra payday.

Court records of the injunction are sketchy but Australian law (like every other legal system for that matter) was less sophisticated then than now and it can be assumed that the courts would have been more reluctant to intervene in private bargains (no bad thing as an overarching principle). Much would therefore turn on the wording of Grace's contract with the YPA. One frankly brazen excuse offered by Grace was that the Adelaide fixture was not a cricket match but merely 'an exhibition of skill', though even he did not press that one. Instead, he managed to find a loophole in that the tour promoters had contracted for him to play fourteen matches, and once he had completed them (with the Kadina match) he was freed from his obligations and could do as he pleased.[5]

The aftermath

Although the Adelaide match seems to have been more of a success overall than the Kadina affair, which they had so callously undermined, Grace and his team were probably relieved for a variety of reasons when they stepped on board the ship to return to England. In their wake the *Wallaroo Times* and other local newspaper editorials stuck the knife into Grace for supposedly taking legal advice about penalties for breach of contract before he had even arrived at Kadina, and in general for falling well short of the sort of Victorian gentleman he was supposed to personify.

For his own part, Grace blithely recorded that the tour had been a success, and predictably acted in accordance with the advice of another great Victorian, Oscar Wilde, by not apologizing for anything. Back in England he continued annoying Australians almost as much as he had when a guest of their country. Famously he wound up the touring Australians in the test match in 1882, which led to the Ashes mock obituary after England were destroyed by Fred Spofforth in the fourth innings. Indeed, it has been suggested that 'there is a strong case for

---

5   See Robert Low, *WG: A Life of W G Grace* (Richard Cohen, 1997), p 127.

saying that Grace was inadvertently responsible for the creation of the whole Ashes saga'.[6] Yet he was also instrumental in setting up fixtures between Australia and England in the first place, and his competitive nature – of which his gamesmanship was only a part – set the tone for the rivalry that continues to the present day.

Grace returned to Australia nearly twenty years after his first tour, this time with his family in tow. He came with even greater fame than on his previous visit and with a suitably expanded appearance fee to match. Another piece of cricketing immortality was created as a result, because it so happened that the steep financial burden imposed by the grand old man was carried by one Lord Sheffield, who at the conclusion of the tour donated £150 to fund a domestic Australian first-class competition. The Sheffield Shield was thereby born, which went on to become arguably the most hard-fought and respected first-class competition of all. There is, accordingly, good reason for Australians to be grateful to William Gilbert Grace.

AN UNGRACIOUS AFFAIR

The man

It seems appropriate to start the individual tales in the book with Grace, given his unparalleled status in the history of cricket. His career forms the bridge from what might be described as the cricketing Middle Ages to the modern era. He started playing before test matches or the County Championship existed, and at a time when underarm bowling was the norm. He is often said to have invented most of the modern batting shots and techniques, though one detects some exaggeration in such claims given the other great batsmen of the late nineteenth and early twentieth century such as Ranjitsinhji, Trumper and MacLaren. His statistics are impressive by any era (particularly the longevity of his career, which it is safe to assume will never be approached by anyone in modern times), but most of all when compared with those of his contemporaries – none of whom was in any doubt about how good he was.[7] It is said that he rewrote the record books, though as

---

[6]   Rae, op cit, p xiii. I will set out the detail of Grace's offending in the match when discussing the spirit of cricket later in the book.

[7]   See for example the tributes by Lord Harris in *Wisden* 1895 and A G Steel just

others have observed it would be more accurate to say that he was the one who wrote them in the first place, cricket statistics being another facet of the game which developed significantly during the time, and at least partly because, of Grace's career. But there was also the shamateurism, which caused so much trouble throughout his playing days, not simply during the sojourn to that nascent Australian settlement in the early stages of his fame. A circus poster from Grace's era announced 'Being for the benefit of Mr Kite', which a century later would inspire John Lennon to write a song; 'Being for the benefit of Dr Grace' would have accurately summed up most of the cricket matches in which WG was scheduled to play.

In mitigation of Grace's apparent greed, it should be noted that he was not a member of the landed gentry but a middle-class professional (in the non-cricketing sense) who was obliged to maintain a doctor's practice throughout most of his career. He had to pay for a locum when engaged on cricketing matters, and was reputed routinely not to charge indigent patients a fee. He also had financial responsibilities towards his family. Nevertheless, he stretched the concept of amateur expenses well beyond the most generous interpretation, even if he was rarely called to account for his actions. There seems to have been an acceptance that since Grace swelled the gate takings wherever he played, it was fair enough for him to ask for a substantial cut. In that respect, as with so many others, Grace set a trend.[8]

Then there was the gamesmanship. A favourite story from the latter part of his career had Grace supposedly being bowled, then casually replacing the bails and taking guard again. In response to the umpire's umbrage, he offered: 'They've come to see me bat, not you umpire.'

before Grace turned 50. Both are reproduced in Benny Green (ed), *Wisden Anthology 1864–1900* (Queen Anne Press, 1979), pp 959–64.

[8] Grace would not be the last great cricketer to use his name for financial gain in occasionally cynical turns. The two greatest batsmen of all time also trod a questionable path on occasion. Sir Donald Bradman made a comfortable living out of the game before the Second World War, while ostensibly maintaining an amateur status: see Don Heenan and David Dunstan, 'Don Bradman: Just a Boy from Bowral', in Anthony Bateman and Jeffrey Hill (eds), *The Cambridge Companion to Cricket* (Cambridge University Press, 2011), pp 94–5; Brett Hutchins, *Don Bradman: Challenging the Myth* (Cambridge University Press, 2003). Later in the book it will be seen how Sachin Tendulkar managed to be classified for tax purposes as something other than a cricketer..

Elsewhere, one of Grace's great opponents once remarked while he was walking off after being bowled: 'Surely you're not going, Doctor? There's still one stump standing...'[9] Another tale involved him allowing the opposition captain to toss the coin, whereupon Grace would call 'The Lady' while the coin was in the air and, on spotting the coin on the ground, would exclaim 'And the Lady it is'. Given that Queen Victoria was on one side of the coin and Britannia on the other, Grace had secured the Victorian equivalent of 'heads I win, tails you lose'.[10]

Something of Grace's legacy can be gauged from the number of books dedicated to him – about 25 at the time of writing.[11] Two of the more recent and authoritative biographies are *WG* by Robert Low and Simon Rae's *W G Grace*. Both books, particularly Rae's, not only set out in painful detail Grace's cynical and avaricious behaviour on the first Australian tour, but also show how he nearly fell foul of the criminal law later in life (the authors each discovered the event independently).

The assault

Grace, it seems, had remonstrated with some youths who had ignored his sign prohibiting practice on his beloved county ground at Bristol.[12]

---

[9] Simon Rae, *It's Not Cricket: Skullduggery, Sharp Practice and Downright Cheating in the Noble Game* (Faber & Faber, 2001), p 97.

[10] The coin-tossing story is told by Jack Fingleton in *Cricket Crisis: Bodyline and Other Lines* (Pavilion Library, [1946] 1984), p 291.

[11] His autobiography was entitled *WG: Cricketing Reminiscences and Personal Recollections* (James Bowden, 1899). Not long after his death an impressive encomium, *The Memorial Biography of W G Grace*, was published by Lord Hawke, Lord Harris and Sir Home Gordon, which gives a good indication of how much a legend WG had been in his lifetime. Of some of the more modern works Donald Trelford's pocket biography, *W G Grace* (Sutton, 1998), is a good introduction. Bernard Whimpress has written a short and entertaining account of the Kadina debacle (*W G Grace at Kadina: Champion Cricketer or Scoundrel?* (Amazon Media, 2011)), though he does not shed any more light on the injunctive proceedings.

[12] Grace had purchased the land, in the Ashley Down region, in 1889. It remains the home of Gloucester County Cricket Club in the present day.

He later wrote a letter to the club's president,[13] asking for assistance in smoothing things over:[14]

Dear Arrowsmith,

Many thanks for saying you would see White's father about the assault if I wished it. As I did not see him last evening when I saw the son, perhaps it would be as well, if not troubling you too much. The lad I know bears me no ill will, but I fancy, he was kept in bed to make it look worse, you will find this out, if you call. I told the boy's father and mother that I was sorry I had struck the boy, but that 9 out of every 10 persons would have done the same, under the provocation. I could do no more than apologize etc, which I did, and of course would pay the lad for loss of time, etc, but I shall certainly not stand Black Mail being levied on me, which I fancy the father has been put up to, by some of his friends...

Robert Low's verdict is that 'It would appear that Arrowsmith's mediation was successful, and the boy accepted an apology from WG. It would certainly have been highly embarrassing for him if the affair had become public. A charge of assault could have been very awkward for a well-known city doctor, though it would have been a brave magistrate or jury who convicted WG of anything other than constantly wanting his own way on the cricket field.'[15] Sadly Low is probably correct that not all would have been equal – at least, not all would have been equal to W G Grace – before the law, at least in the more minor matters such as the summary offence with which he would most likely have been charged if the incident had gone any further. Such low-level breaches of the rule of law have occurred throughout legal history: many a jury has returned a verdict influenced by a defendant's celebrity status.

A modern equivalent

The incident calls to mind the occasion on which Shane Warne, one of the few cricketers in history to approach Grace's status on and off

---

[13]   The president, one Arrowsmith, was friends with Grace and they planned a book together (Arrowsmith was in the printing and publishing business), leading entirely predictably to a dispute about money: see Low, op cit, pp 213–14.

[14]   Rae, op cit, p 327.

[15]   Low, op cit, p 209.

the field, lost his temper while on tour in New Zealand in 2000. Warne had recently been sponsored $A200,000 by a nicotine patch company to give up smoking, but was caught in the act by a schoolboy, who tried to take a photograph of him. Warne angrily snatched the camera away and returned it only after police intervention.

Warne found making money a lot easier in the much more professional atmosphere which prevailed a century after Grace. But he also had to endure far closer and more relentless media scrutiny during his playing career. One suspects Grace would have been no freer from scandal than Warne had he lived in the modern age, but he might have been just as successful too. After all, neither Warne's 'sexting' humiliations, nor the general media harassment nor the distraction of off-field riches prevented him from enjoying an incredible playing career.[16]

Whatever the truth behind the Bristol incident, it is yet further evidence that WG, as with all cricketers, was not a saint, nor a machine. Nor were any of his various reputations entirely true. He was, after all, merely human, with all the frailties, vices, inconsistencies and passions that come with the territory. And that, perhaps, is the moral of all the stories in this book.

The Man Who Missed the Match

He should have held a unique place in cricketing history. As the foremost wicket keeper of his day, he would have been a certainty for the English side in what has since been deemed the first ever test match. Instead of being behind the stumps at the Melbourne Cricket Ground as Alfred Shaw came in to bowl to Charles Bannerman, however, Edward William 'Ted' Pooley was languishing in jail over a thousand miles away in New Zealand. Pooley's misadventure has become one of the classic cricketing stories, and ironically may have

---

[16] Warne's career still had seven years to run when he was voted one of the top five cricketers of the twentieth century by a panel assembled by *Wisden* in 2000. Other than Bradman, it is hard to think of anyone with a comparable playing record in the Ashes to Warne, who remains easily the highest wicket taker in the history of the contest. Aside from bare numbers Warne's psychological hold over England and his ability to turn a match on its head (such as Adelaide during the 2006/7 Ashes) were the stuff of legend. There is accordingly no hyperbole in mentioning him in the same breath as Grace.

secured him greater fame, albeit of a less desirable kind, than if he had played in that historic match in Melbourne in 1877.

A courageous man

Pooley did not start out as a wicket keeper, but rather batted and bowled without conspicuous success. He was reputed to be a decent batsman, though a first-class average of 15 with a solitary hundred suggests no more than a doughty tail-ender. His own account of how he became a keeper was that he had sauntered up to his captain in a match in 1863 and offered to try his hand because the incumbent was struggling. His captain demurred, but then agreed after another player egged him on. Pooley quickly dismissed several batsmen and never looked back, becoming Surrey's mainstay behind the stumps for much of the 1860s and 1870s.

The pluck with which he secured the keeper's role seems to have been one of the milder manifestations of a tenacious and confrontational character. In 1869, for example, Pooley engaged in some fisticuffs with a journalist who had filed an unflattering match report, and was arrested and bound over to keep the peace.

Certainly his physical courage was never in issue. In those days, it was customary for the keeper to stand up, even against the fastest bowlers and on the worst of what must have been fairly rudimentary pitches (by today's standards) at the best of times. On one occasion at Lord's Pooley was hit flush in the face and lost three teeth. The force of the blow and Pooley's subsequent fortitude prompted one spectator, the well-known bare-knuckle boxer Jem Mace,[17] to remark to Pooley afterwards: 'I would rather stand up against any man in England for an hour than take your place behind the wicket for five minutes. I heard that ball strike you as if it had hit a brick wall.'[18]

---

[17] An interesting sort himself, Mace also toured New Zealand in his sporting capacity, where he discovered the future world champion Bob Fitzsimmons. Mace later supplemented his income by touring with circuses, including that of Pablo Fanque, who was immortalized by the Beatles in 'Being for the Benefit of Mr Kite', the song cited in relation to Grace above.

[18] David Frith, *The Fast Men: A 200-Year Cavalcade of Speed Bowlers* (Corgi, 1975), p 99.

In 1873, the first evidence of Pooley's gambling predilections emerged when he was suspended by Surrey due to an allegation that he had sold a match to Yorkshire for £50. It may be assumed therefore that James Lillywhite and the other organizers of the historic 1877 tour had some idea of what they were letting themselves in for when they selected Pooley as the first-choice keeper. The tour included a few weeks in New Zealand, where Pooley's misadventure occurred.

An elephant trap

While in Christchurch, the English were due to play an odds match, involving eleven visitors against eighteen locals. Pooley made a bet with a local, Ralph Donkin, in which Pooley wagered shillings to pounds – odds of 20 to one – that he could predict the individual scores of the local team.

Donkin had walked into an elephant trap. After securing the odds, Pooley bet that each player would score zero. Obviously, at 20 to one he only had to be successful with one prediction in order to make a profit. Moreover, zero is the most likely score for any batsman in any match. This is partly because players are more vulnerable at the start of their innings, before they have their eye in. But it is also due to the laws of probability, since zero is the only score which every player necessarily spends time on in every innings. For those reasons alone, zero would have been Pooley's best bet. But two other factors weighed more heavily still in his favour. First, the locals were bound to be outclassed by their opponents and one would have expected some of the tail-enders to have had no realistic chance of scoring anything off the English bowlers. Secondly, and somewhat absurdly, Pooley was standing as the umpire in the match. Betting on cricket was legal at the time, but unsurprisingly betting by umpires was not.

In the event, four players were out without scoring, netting Pooley a handsome return. He had not even had to give any controversial decisions as umpire. He went to Donkin and demanded his £4 in exchange for 13 shillings. At that point Donkin might have disputed the enforceability of the contract, since Pooley had stood as an umpire. Instead, he refused to pay on the ground that he was the victim of a 'catch bet'. Pooley in response dispensed with legal niceties and punched Donkin in the face, before going on to smash up his hotel room with the assistance of the team baggage handler, one Alfred Bramhall.

The arrest

Both Pooley and Bramhall were arrested after a later match in Dunedin and returned to Christchurch. Pooley was convicted of assault, the magistrate concluding that he had thrown the first punch. He was fined £5. He and Bramhall were then committed to trial on the charge of destroying property above the value of £5, arising out of the trashing of Donkin's hotel room. Both Englishmen missed the boat to Australia and thus the historic fixture in Melbourne. In the event, they were acquitted, no doubt helped by a lack of sympathy towards Donkin for making a bet and trying to weasel out of it.

For some bizarre reason, possibly an early reflection of the affection in which New Zealand held the 'Mother Country' for many years (and therefore perhaps awarded him a celebrity status he seems not to have earned), Pooley became a rather popular figure while detained in Christchurch. Not only was he acquitted, but a collection held afterwards netted him the not inconsiderable amount of £50 along with a gold watch.

Sadly, Pooley never did play a test match. Worse, it seems he did not invest the £50 or any other money he obtained very wisely, because after his cricket career had finished he fell on hard times and ended up in and out of the notorious workhouses of the day ('It was that or the river,' he told an interviewer who had sought him out). By that stage, the physical demands of wicket-keeping without modern gloves had taken its toll on his hands, which were said to have been reduced to 'mere lumps of deformity'.[19] He died in poverty in 1907.[20] Given the lot of the Victorian and Edwardian poor, missing out on the first ever test was probably the least of his worries in his later years.

[19]   Ibid.
[20]   For further reading on Pooley, see Keith Booth, *His Own Enemy: The Rise and Fall of Edward Pooley* (Belmont, 2000).

Chapter 3
THE DEMON DRINK

In more innocent times, alcohol was usually mentioned in connection with cricketers in an entertaining sense. Ian Botham's rest-day shindigs with the opposition, for example, were the stuff of legend. He has claimed that his 149 not out at Headingley in 1981 was played after just such an occasion, and hence his most feared opponent that day was not Dennis Lillee but his own hangover. Botham's contemporary David Gower exemplified the *bon viveur* both in his effortless batting style and in his highly knowledgeable wine-tasting off the pitch – knowledge he was prepared to pass on (occasionally along with the bar tab) to younger players later in his career.[1]

More recently, the disciplining of the Australian opener David Warner for a lame incident following a lame start to Australia's 2013 trip to England provoked ridicule and reprimand in equal measure. Warner apparently threw a punch at the English player Joe Root in a bar after a match. Various wags on Twitter got to work fairly promptly and suggested that it was about the only time Warner had connected with anything all tour. When the Cricket Australia chief, James Sutherland, wondered what Warner had been doing in a bar in the first place, the Twitterati invoked some Australian backpacker stereotypes by suggesting he had probably been looking for a job. Times had clearly changed since Rod Marsh and Doug Walters competed for the most cans of beer downed on a flight.[2] Warner was suspended, but

---

[1] The story can be inferred from an anecdote in Mike Atherton, *Opening Up: My Autobiography* (Hodder & Stoughton, 2002), p 25.

[2] One of their records may have been broken by David Boon on the 1989 Ashes Tour, when he allegedly drank 52 cans on the flight, though he has always refused to confirm or deny this. To provide some balance regarding the 2013 Ashes series, some English players were alleged to have urinated on the pitch during their drunken celebrations at the Oval after the series finished. Had it been proven, they might have attracted a public order offence. Most likely, though, the authorities would have thought the dent in the individual players' reputations sufficient punishment. And, despite the scoreline showing a heavy defeat, the Australians earned greater respect on and off the pitch as the series went on. I for one was not surprised to see Australia turn the tables at home later in the year, although the margin of victory was certainly

did not have to wait long before exacting revenge on England in the return series later the same year and then going on to play a leading role in Australia's series win in South Africa in early 2014.

For three other cricketers in modern times, however, a night out ended not in tales of revelry but with each of them unconscious. Ricky Ponting was able to make a full recovery and go on to cricketing greatness, Jesse Ryder recovered but faced a long road back to top-level cricket, while tragically David Hookes never woke at all.

Ricky Ponting

Fame arrived early for the young Ricky Ponting. He showed glimpses of his promise in the World Series Cricket tournament of 1994, in which, somewhat farcically, Australia were allowed to field two teams, Australia and 'Australia A'.[3] He scored a breezy 96 on test debut in December 1995, brushing off the missing four runs by saying he would 'gladly cop 96 each hit'. In those days, his hedonistic and apparently addictive personality mixed alcohol and gambling. The latter gave rise to his nickname of 'Punter' and a slightly unusual adjunct to his day job, when in June 1995 he was appointed 'part-time ambassador' for the TAB[4] in his native Tasmania.

If the gambling was potentially bad for his finances, the alcohol was very much worse for his health and his career. In and out of the team in his early days – a startling illustration of the depth of Australian resources at the time – Ponting's alcohol-related problems first came to light on tour in India in 1998. He was evicted from the Equinox nightclub in Kolkata and fined A$1,000. Later that year, he offered the following account, which, it has to be said, is both disarming in its honesty and amusing in its naïveté:

unexpected.
[3]   The reason for the inclusion of 'Australia A' was to try and generate some public interest in the tournament, because the other teams were England and Zimbabwe, and the authorities correctly predicted that Zimbabwe would not be competitive. The A side matches were not full internationals, and the experiment, to the relief of more or less everyone, was not repeated.
[4]   TAB stands for 'Totalisator Agency Board', the monopoly totalisator organisations which were set up in Australia and New Zealand to run sports betting.

What we didn't know was that it was a couples' night which meant the only way men could get in was in the company of a female. We were quite happy just hanging out together and having a few drinks, and for me it was a chance to celebrate North Melbourne's win in the AFL Ansett Cup final in Melbourne. Everyone was having a good time and knocking down a few beers and the next thing I knew I was asked to leave by one of the security guys. I am usually the last one to leave a nightclub and I wanted to stay, and there was a scuffle but that is all there was to it. I didn't realise we were the only single guys there. To be honest I couldn't remember half of what went on during the night because I'd had a skinful but I definitely did not assault women in the nightclub. Thankfully I had enough witnesses to prove it.[5]

Things became worse for Ponting in the following domestic season. In the early hours of 18 January 1999, he found himself in the Bourbon and Beefsteak bar in King's Cross, Sydney, which, it is fair to say, does not constitute the most salubrious district of Australia's largest city. He then found himself in the team hotel with a black left eye, with apparently no recollection of what had happened in the meantime. Cricket Australia was not in a forgiving mood, having just been faced with the infinitely more damaging Shane Warne/Mark Waugh gambling and bookmaking embarrassment. Ponting was suspended pending an investigation. He made a public apology in which he admitted having a drink problem. He was fined A$2,000 and banned for three matches, the fine being suspended on the condition that he undergo treatment for his alcoholism.[6] No criminal proceedings were forthcoming. Perhaps that was because Ponting did not wish to press charges against anyone, as well as (i) a lack of witness evidence (especially with Ponting having no memory of events himself) and (ii) the fact that he was intoxicated and therefore quite possibly not entirely free from blame.[7]

---

[5] Ricky Ponting and Peter Staples, *Punter: First Tests of a Champion* (Ironbark Press, 1998), pp 122–3.

[6] See 'Ponting banned by board', Cricinfo, www.espncricinfo.com/ci/content/story/80202.html (retrieved 15 April 2014).

[7] In his recent autobiography, *At the Close of Play* (HarperSports, 2013), Ponting writes that he was not knocked out as such, just sent flying after a 'king hit' from a formidably sized bouncer (pp 180–81).

His career was in the balance, but Ponting rose to the challenge. He managed to give up drinking altogether, and went on to become one of Australia's greatest post-war batsmen. He equalled Steve Waugh's record for the most test matches played for Australia and, at the time of writing, was the leading test run scorer in Australian history and had played in more winning test matches than anyone from any country. It is true that he suffered three disappointing Ashes defeats (two as captain and one as player) but they were disappointing only because of the standard of Australian cricket that had been set as much by himself as by anyone else. Statistics aside, the rifling pull shot which Ponting played in quite a distinctive style to midwicket deserves the same sort of aesthetic reverence as cover drives by Cowdrey or Hammond, and, taking into account the circumstances of the match, Ponting's hundred against India in the 2003 World Cup final has to be one of the greatest ever captain's knocks in that form of the game. He had many masterful innings in test cricket as well, obviously, one of the best being his 156 to save the third test in England in 2005.

Ponting subsequently denied it,[8] but I cannot help wondering if it was with a nod to his own youthful indiscretions that he came down hard on Andrew Symonds in England early in the 2005 tour, when Symonds had been hitting the town the night before a match and was less than honest with Ponting the next morning about his actions.

David Hookes

The young David Hookes caught the public eye in much the same fashion as the young Ricky Ponting was to do years later. Hookes might have scored fewer runs on his test debut, but if anything he was even more spectacular: in the 1977 Centenary Test, before a full house at the MCG, he hit what was then a record five consecutive boundaries in one over. The unfortunate bowler, Tony Greig, never quite lived that experience down, being ribbed about it for his entire subsequent career as a commentator. Hookes himself used to joke that he was the one who made Greig famous. (That said, Greig may have had other things on his mind during the match, as seen elsewhere in the book.)

[8]   Ricky Ponting and Brian Murgatroyd, *Ashes Diary 2005* (Harper Sports, 2005), pp 151–6.

Hookes became the third highest-scoring Australian batsman in World Series Cricket. He went some way to giving the contest credibility in the public eye by having his jaw shattered by Andy Roberts, thus confirming that the contests were genuinely competitive as opposed to exhibition matches (maybe he was offered up as a cricketing equivalent to Peter Cook's skit about a futile gesture in wartime?). Sadly, though, Hookes's career never went very far from there, mainly, it seems, because his fearlessness against pace was matched only by his haplessness against spin. He finished with a solitary test hundred, made against Sri Lanka, comfortably the weakest side of his era, and generally accepted with humility that he had never had the career once promised.

In retirement Hookes stayed in the game in a variety of coaching and administrative roles. At the beginning of 2004, he was working as coach of the Victoria state cricket team, a position he had held for two years with measurable success. On 18 January, following a win by Victoria over South Australia in a limited-overs match, Hookes and members of both teams went to the bar at the Beaconsfield Hotel in Melbourne to unwind over a few drinks.

It has to be stressed that the accounts of the events which unfolded were and remain conflicting. What undoubtedly did occur was that Hookes became involved in an altercation with one of the bouncers, a professional boxer named Zdravko Mićević. In the course of the struggle Hookes was knocked over by a punch and struck his head on the ground as he landed. He went into a coma and suffered cardiac arrest. He was placed on life support and did not regain consciousness. The next evening, with the consent of his family and the medical professionals responsible for his care, the life support was switched off.

There was no suggestion that Mićević had intended to kill Hookes. Importantly, it was not the punch itself that was fatal, but rather the catastrophic manner in which Hookes's head hit the ground. Thus, Mićević was charged with manslaughter rather than murder.

The charge required the prosecution to prove that Mićević had attacked Hookes with intent to injure him (an accidental shove or an intended 'shadow punch' would not suffice). It also had to show a direct causal link from Mićević's actions to Hookes's death. The case it advanced was that Hookes, intoxicated at the time, was targeted for 'being a smart alec'. In other words, Mićević had singled Hookes out and hit him without any real provocation and without Hookes posing any threat.

The case for Mićević was based on self-defence. It was asserted that he had twice asked Hookes to leave because closing time was imminent, and had twice been told to 'fuck off'. Mićević himself stated: 'When I approached him again, told him to settle down, like I said, he hit me in the guts. He grabbed me by my shirt, he pulled me down, he hit me again, that's where I took a swing back at him.'[9] That 'swing' – a haymaker in boxing terminology – turned out to be the blow with fatal consequences.

No other witness saw Hookes hit Mićević, but his account gained some support from the evidence of Wayne Phillips, a former player whose career had partially overlapped with that of Hookes. Phillips testified that (i) Hookes had been aggressive and (ii) at the time of the fatal blow, Hookes was part of a group who were all pushing and shoving. It seems that the weight of the evidence was that there was a general tussle going on, rather than Mićević singling out Hookes for no reason. That made it harder for the prosecution to prove that Mićević had delivered a blow without provocation or any threat to himself.

The trial lasted two weeks. The jury then deliberated for five days, before returning a verdict of not guilty. The result would have been devastating for Hookes's family, but it is important to reiterate some fundamental legal principles. The most important is that Mićević was innocent until proven guilty beyond reasonable doubt in a court of law, by a jury of his peers. The burden of proof rested on the prosecution throughout.

If Mićević, who had the physique and strength of the professional boxer that he was, had simply walked up to Hookes and hit him with a full-force punch, that would have been one thing. If, however, he had delivered the blow in the course of a general struggle among a group, in which he held reasonable fears for his own safety, then

---

[9] *The 7:30 Report*, ABC, 12 September 2005. Transcript available at www.abc.net. au/7.30/content/2005/s1458713.htm (retrieved 15 April 2014).

one can understand the jury deciding that the charge had not been proved beyond all reasonable doubt. Hookes himself might have not been a match for Mićević on even terms, but he was still a physically strong individual and, if aggressive and intoxicated, would have been a handful for the door staff – particularly if backed up by his companions, who as state-level sportsmen would not, one may infer, have been pushovers either.

Clearly the jury wrestled long and hard over the issue. It might be that they were in doubt over the level of fault, or it might be that some members found it very difficult coming to terms with the fact that a not-guilty verdict would leave a lingering sense of frustration: if any person has been killed by a punch, most people's instinctive reaction would be that the assailant should be punished. But unless one of the jurors chooses – wholly exceptionally – to tell his or her story,[10] we shall never know, since it is a watertight rule of criminal law that the jury's deliberations are confidential and cannot be investigated by a court or any other tribunal.

There was no suggestion that the jury had been misdirected or that it acted improperly. Instead, the case stands as an example of how difficult it is for the prosecution to prove a case when there are conflicting witness statements and there is no compelling forensic or other objective evidence favouring one side or the other – all the more so when most of the witnesses have been drinking, and when some may have been involved in the scuffle themselves. In that light, Mićević's acquittal was understandable, though not inevitable – there was certainly enough objective evidence to provide a case to answer. Instead, the acquittal was a reflection of one of the cornerstones of the criminal justice system, namely the presumption of innocence. That principle, it is worth remembering, exists for the benefit of all, and if it occasionally leads to unsatisfying results, the alternative – locking people up for lesser reasons – has the potential to be much worse.

---

[10] For an interesting study of the jury in action (written by a well-known cricket writer, as it happens), see Malcolm Knox, *Secrets of the Jury Room* (Random House, 2006).

Jesse Ryder

There were echoes of both Ponting and Hookes in the New Zealand cricketer Jesse Ryder. A strong all-rounder, his early promise was blighted by a seemingly endless succession of late-night overindulgences. In a different age they might have attracted little more than amusement and mickey-taking. But in an era of macrobiotic performance diets and institutes of sport, Ryder looked something of an anachronism, a throwback to the more relaxed atmosphere of the Botham era. Not all New Zealand fans were amused. In February 2008, the former test player Adam Parore recorded a most uncharitable verdict in a national newspaper, contending that Ryder was 'too fat' and 'in no fit state to play for New Zealand'.[11]

Shortly after Parore's article appeared, Ryder cut his hand trying to break into a toilet in a bar at 5.30 am, the culmination of a night out celebrating a limited-overs series victory against England. That incident led another commentator in the same newspaper as Parore to argue that the problem was not so much Ryder's weight as his stupidity.[12]

The following year Ryder was dropped after missing a training session, again because of a heavy drinking session. His international career resumed nevertheless, and he went on to a number of significant achievements, including a double century against India. But the controversies and injuries did not abate, and in March 2012, Ryder announced an indefinite break from international cricket. He was aged only 27 at the time. He continued to play domestic cricket and otherwise set about reforming his ways. In March 2013, however, just over a year after announcing his self-imposed exile, Ryder endured a fateful night at a Christchurch bar. He was assaulted outside by four individuals, and was left with serious head and other injuries. He was taken to hospital and placed into a coma. Two men were arrested and charged with assault.

[11]	Adam Parore, 'Ryder is too fat to play for New Zealand', *New Zealand Herald*, 2 February 2008.
[12]	Steve Deane, 'Troubled talent or just village idiot?', *New Zealand Herald*, 27 February 2008.

As is becoming commonplace nowadays, the attack was filmed by some passers-by, who would then have been able to upload the footage to YouTube or other sites within minutes. The possibility of instantly available internet films of criminal actions presents a difficulty for any subsequent trial by jury, since the jurors are not supposed to bring any previous knowledge of the alleged crime or its participants into the courtroom. This is not the only problem that technology presents: a number of recent cases in Britain have concerned jurors playing with their smartphones instead of listening to the evidence. Worse, some have been found googling the participants' names, and in one case even contacting a defendant via Facebook. All of those activities undermine the trial process, for fairly obvious reasons.[13]

To try and prevent any such compromise of the trial of the Ryder accused, the judge ordered that their names be suppressed. Even that measure is problematic, because open justice is every bit as fundamental a principle of a fair trial as the jurors' obligations outlined above. Normally speaking it is the right of the public to know who has been charged with what. Among other things, that right ensures that the state cannot lock up its political opponents on trumped-up charges, or otherwise use the criminal justice process to harass anyone it deems not to be on message. In Ryder's case, despite the judge's order, a video of the assault was posted online by one Jordan Mason. Mason was then charged with a breach of the suppression order. He pleaded guilty and was given a sentence of community detention.

I have written before[14] about the scale of the threat that the internet poses to a number of settled legal rules. Mason was caught and sentenced because he lived in New Zealand and was imprudent enough to post the video despite being personally warned by police. But someone living outside the jurisdiction who had obtained the footage could have uploaded it with impunity. No state's criminal law exceeds its own borders (with rare exceptions). Thus, a person overseas would not be subjected to the court restriction issued by the New Zealand courts and could not be extradited to New Zealand to

---

[13] Nor are the difficulties confined to criminal law: see the problems posed for the Family Division of the High Court as set out by Sir James Munby P in *Re J (A Child)* [2013] EWHC 2694 (Fam).
[14] See *Cases, Causes and Controversies*, pp 149–52.

face trial for breaching the restriction either. Whoever took the original footage in New Zealand and sent it to them would be within the court's jurisdiction, but readers will not need an explanation of how difficult it would be in practice to stop them. The fact is that attempts to censor the internet, at least in countries with any aspiration to be free societies (and therefore where search engines are not barred), may simply end up like King Canute trying to hold back the tide – or, for another pre-internet example, like the hapless Attorney-General in the *Spycatcher* litigation trying to stop publication in different countries of something everyone already knew about.[15]

Aside from the diversion caused by Mason's actions, the impact of YouTube was seen in the prosecution of Ryder's alleged assailants themselves. One pleaded guilty, but the other applied to have the case struck out on the ground that media coverage had made a fair trial impossible. The application was not successful, but it is some indication of the problem of fair trials in a new media age. The answer, I suspect, will simply be that juries will be told to put anything they may have seen or heard about the case out of their mind – as is already done with high-profile cases which have been covered in the traditional media – and will be trusted to do so.[16] Meanwhile, at the time of writing, the trial of the second defendant had not taken place. Ryder himself had taken a further knockback when he was banned for six months for taking a proscribed substance (a weight loss drug, which I will consider in the next section). With a stark demonstration of how much natural talent he possessed, however, he scored a century in his first competitive match after the ban, showing that his cricketing days were far from over, and was recalled to the New Zealand squad before the end of 2013 – only to be suspended in early 2014 for another drink-related episode.

---

[15] *A-G v Guardian Newspapers (No 2)* [1988] 3 All ER 545. The case established the sound principle that there is no point granting an injunction suppressing material already in the public domain.

[16] This point arose again in May 2014, just before this book went to press, when a series of confidential testimony from a number of players to the ICC about match fixing was leaked to the press. The extensive resultant media coverage led to speculation that those subject to the leaks might struggle to receive a fair trial should any proceedings result.

The wrong place at the wrong time

It is important not to read too much into the three incidents, either by finding some connection between each or overanalysing what happened on each of the nights individually. Ponting and Ryder both acknowledged issues with alcohol, while it has never been suggested that Hookes, older and wiser than the other two, had a drink problem, even if on the night in question he happened to be somewhat inebriated. In terms of crime and punishment, Ponting probably suffered enough with the embarrassment and career blight caused by his misadventure. Certainly the classic punishment element of rehabilitation succeeded admirably in his case.

It is a sobering thought, though, if one excuses the pun, that the only difference between Ponting and Hookes might have been that Ponting happened not to fall backwards in the catastrophic manner that Hookes did after being struck. Ponting was hit hard enough to get a black eye and for him apparently not to remember anything of the incident, so he could quite easily have lost his footing in the manner in which Hookes did, in which case he might have hit his head on a hard surface with the same tragic result.

Such are the fine and cruel distinctions upon which life and death can turn. There will always be those who consider that Hookes's assailant should have received punishment, but I hope I have shown enough at least to make the outcome of the trial understandable. It is not always logical to try to distinguish actions which appear similar just because the outcomes happen to be different, though that seems to be the natural reaction; hence Andrew Flintoff, the first English all-rounder to approach Botham's status on and off the pitch, was a folk hero for his drinking when England were winning and a figure of ridicule for it when England were losing.[17] Ryder, for his part, seems clearly to have been the victim of a much more sustained attack than Hookes or Ponting, far exceeding any reasonable response to whatever provocation (if there was any at all) prompted his assailants.

---

[17] Flintoff, incidentally, has the questionable distinction of inadvertently creating a new portmanteau word – 'Fredalo' – after a drunken attempt to board a pleasure craft when on tour in the Caribbean in 2007. He was sacked as vice-captain after the incident. See 'England v Canada', BBC Sport Cricket, 18 March 2007, news.bbc.co.uk/sport1/hi/cricket/england/6464251.stm (retrieved 16 April 2014).

Whatever exactly happened during the three incidents in question, perhaps we can draw no stronger conclusion than simply to say that cricketers, like everyone else, can be in the wrong place at the wrong time, and that sometimes things get out of hand, with tragic consequences.[18] I leave the last word to a master cricketer, Sir Garfield Sobers:

> It always surprises me that some people think a world cricketer should give 100 per cent of his effort and concentration every minute he is playing cricket, and then not relax and enjoy himself after. They seem to have strange ideas about how curfews and conferences and controls should fill his time between play. But if a cricketer does not learn early in his life which things do him good and which are bad for his cricket, and for him, then he does not belong in a world-class team.

[18]   Not that alcohol is always a factor: for other examples of cricketers ending up in trouble off the pitch see Martin Williamson, 'Taking a stand', Cricinfo, 1 August 2006, www.espncricinfo.com/magazine/content/story/255212.html (retrieved 16 April 2014).

Chapter 4

THE DRUGS

W e have just seen with respect to alcohol that top-level cricketers can be prone to the same vices as everyone else. It is no surprise therefore to find that there have been more than a few instances of illegal drug use by professional players over the years as well. As with alcohol, we might begin with Ian Botham. As usual, Botham's actual indulgences were rather less serious than certain of the cricketing press would have had readers believe. He was convicted for possession of marijuana in 1985, though the TCCB took no action. After the disastrous tour of West Indies over the following winter, Botham was quoted in the media admitting that he had smoked marijuana.[1] The resultant uproar was anything but proportionate, with the usual calls for Botham to be excommunicated from English cricket permanently. Frank Keating, one of many Botham biographers,[2] argued instead that he should be praised for bringing the game *into* repute.[3] The English authorities disagreed and banned him from 29 May to 31 July – the height of the season. ('Bad time to lose your all-rounder,' England captain Mike Gatting later mused.) In his comeback match, against New Zealand, Botham quickly equalled and then broke Dennis Lillee's world record for test wickets, prompting Graham Gooch to ask: 'Who writes your bloody scripts then?'

A decade later, in 1996, Ed Giddins was banned for 18 months for cocaine use and expelled from his county, Sussex. He managed to pull himself together enough to play four tests for England at the turn of the century, though he faded quickly from international consideration and retired from first-class cricket in 2003.

---

[1] Botham's admission came after he had sued a newspaper for alleging that he had smoked marijuana on tour in New Zealand in 1984 – before an anti-drugs resolution had been passed by the TCCB.

[2] Frank Keating, *High, Wide and Handsome: Ian Botham – The Story of a Very Special Year* (Collins, 1986).

[3] Martin Williamson and Andrew Miller, 'Dabbling with drugs', Cricinfo, 1 November 2006, www.espncricinfo.com/magazine/content/story/263383.html (retrieved 16 April 2014).

Altogether more serious were the problems which emerged in Warwickshire in the mid-1990s. Most publicity surrounded Paul Smith's brazen admissions about the drugs he had taken over the course of his 12-year career, and how widespread they had been. Smith later wrote a book that suggested he would rather have been a roadie for the rock band Led Zeppelin than a cricketer.[4] The blurb, written in a style consistent with the book itself, set out his version of events: 'Cricketer Paul Smith's life fell apart after he received a drugs ban in 1996, which effectively ended his career. He was made a scapegoat and still believes he was singled-out while several other, favoured players were allowed to continue their careers.' Another Warwickshire player, Keith Piper, was also banned for drug use. By that stage, the problem in the club had become sufficiently serious for external consultants to be hired.

At the more frivolous end of the scale, Phil Tufnell, one of Botham's successors as England's bad boy, was accused in 1997 of having smoked marijuana in a New Zealand nightclub. The club gleefully displayed a sign the next day announcing that Tufnell agreed that it was 'Christchurch's best joint', but the management subsequently cleared him of the allegation.

Much worse than all of the above was the fate of one of Tufnell's contemporaries, Chris Lewis. Lewis was an all-rounder with striking natural ability and athleticism, but for various reasons he ended up not having anything like the career he should have done. His drug problems did not involve personal consumption, but rather the much more serious crime of importation. In 2008, not long after his last effort to play professional cricket had ended in failure, he was arrested at Gatwick airport with some 3.37 kilograms of cocaine hidden in fruit tins and traces of cannabis residue in his luggage. Lewis pleaded not guilty to the resultant criminal charges, but was convicted after a jury trial and sentenced to 13 years' imprisonment. With a certain amount of understatement he told the court: 'Generally throughout my life, my cricket career, when things have gone wrong it's gone wrong in a very public way.'

---

[4]   Paul Smith, *Wasted! The Incredible True Story of Cricket's First Rock 'n' Roll Star* (Know the Score, 2007). The cover picture is not inconsistent with a Zeppelin roadie either, incidentally.

Another English player and, like Lewis, an all-rounder saddled with the 'new Botham' tag for a short time, was Dermot Reeve. He was famous for his self-regard (it was once said that if he went to a nudist beach he would end up only admiring himself). In 2004 he was compelled to resign as a commentator for Channel 4 after being high on cocaine while on air.

However, the nadir of drug use by cricketers in England came early in 2013 with the tragic death of the Surrey professional Tom Maynard, son of the former England international Matthew Maynard. Tom Maynard was seen in the early hours of one morning driving erratically. He was chased by police, during the course of which he abandoned his car. He then ran onto a railway line and was killed almost immediately, either by electrocution or by a train which hit him seconds later. A post-mortem examination showed he was nearly four times over the alcohol limit for driving and had taken both ecstasy and cocaine. Hair samples showed he had been a regular cocaine user in the previous three-and-a-half months.[5] Following an inquest at the end of February, the jury returned a verdict of accidental death.

After Maynard's death it emerged that in the previous five years only one county cricketer had tested positive for recreational drug use. One possible reason for the low detection rate was that players were only tested 'in competition'; in other words, when they were about to play. Only substances taken in the 48 hours before a game would be identified, leaving ample opportunity for players to use drugs at other times.[6]

Somewhat belatedly, the Professional Cricketers' Association (PCA) started a pilot drug testing scheme later in 2013, pending a fixed procedure from 2014 to be established by the ECB. The chief executive of the PCA, Angus Porter, conceded: 'I would be surprised if we got a complete clean sheet simply because of the experience of other sports and the statistics of the age group we're talking about.'[7]

---

[5] See 'Train death cricketer Tom Maynard was high on drugs', BBC News London, 26 February 2013, www.bbc.co.uk/news/uk-england-london-21588586 (retrieved 16 April 2014).

[6] Owen Gibson, 'Tom Maynard inquest casts club cricket drug use in new light', *The Guardian*, 1 March 2013.

[7] Steven Brenkley, 'Positive tests expected in cricket drug survey', *The Independent*, 20 August 2013.

OTHER OFFENDERS

Obviously, English players have not been the only offenders. In the mid-1990s, New Zealand undertook an ill-fated tour of South Africa. The tour began well enough for the tourists, with an upset victory in the first test, but they went on to lose the series and become the first team since W G Grace's time to surrender a one-nil lead in a three-test rubber, though it has happened more regularly since. Three of the more junior players on the tour, Stephen Fleming, Dion Nash and Matthew Hart, received sanctions for smoking marijuana. Nash offered a Clintonesque defence of 'only simulating' smoking, while the other two pleaded guilty. Fleming maintained that they had been made scapegoats when more than half the squad had been involved, and not many players or pundits contradicted him. The South Africans themselves a few years later suffered a similar scandal on a tour of West Indies (in 2000/2001), with the faint mitigation that they at least won on the field.

Elsewhere, the West Indian David Murray's life became blighted by drugs. Murray was a wicket keeper in the 1970s and 1980s who also happened to be the son of the great Everton Weekes. At the start of his international career, it was difficult enough for him to find a place in the side ahead of his unrelated namesake, Deryck Murray, but he also had a more significant handicap in the form of his consumption of cocaine and marijuana. In a less tolerant age, his career might have ended when he was caught using marijuana on tour in Australia in the mid-1970s. As it was, the sympathetic intervention of a senior player, Lance Gibbs, granted him a lifeline. Unfortunately he did not manage to rid himself of the habit, even when given an opportunity to play test cricket during the Packer crisis when most of the senior players were unavailable. After the Packer resolution he faced more competition for the wicket-keeping role from Jeff Dujon. Disillusioned with his prospects, he joined the West Indian rebel tours of South Africa. Afterwards his career as a player was finished, since like all the others involved he was made a pariah upon his return, and once again he descended into drug dependency.

Among Murray's teammates on the rebel tours were Richard 'Danny Germs' Austin, who once had the nickname of the 'right-handed Sobers', and Herbert Chang. Both reportedly became drug addicts upon returning from South Africa and ended up in much-reduced circumstances.[8]

CONCLUSION

It is not difficult to see why cricketers become involved in recreational drugs. The main reason seems to be the same as for other sportsmen, or the likes of rock musicians: the only way they can find of recreating the high of competing or performing is through drug use. Also, being frequent travellers and attendees of fairly hedonistic functions, they tend to have easy access to drugs. Due to the illegal nature of the activity, though, exactly how widespread drug use is in cricket or anywhere else will always be a matter of guesswork.

Underlying all of the incidents considered above is the debate as to whether or not drugs should be banned at all. It is worth considering the debate for a moment because many of the same arguments arise in different contexts later in the book (most obviously with regard to performance-enhancing drugs, but also to a certain extent with respect to ball-tampering and match-fixing as well). Some consider that drugs should be a personal choice and not the business of the state, any more than sexual predilections or, for that matter, legal drugs such as tobacco and alcohol. Moreover, those contemplating banning drugs never take into account the enjoyment that users derive from them, even though there are many risky activities – extreme sports for one – where the only positive benefit is the enjoyment of the user, and the activities are legal presumably because user enjoyment is thought sufficient to outweigh the risks. Then there is the point that a ban necessarily creates a market for criminal gangs, whose stock-in-trade includes violence, extortion and tax evasion. There is more or less a consensus that prohibition did not work in the case of alcohol. Partly this was because individual crime rings grew so wealthy they had greater resources than the police, and even if one was busted, another would quickly move to fill the gap. Moreover, the cost of policing (including housing a startling percentage of the prison population

---

[8] See for example Robert Craddock, 'Tragedy of the West Indian rebels', The Advertiser Sport (Adelaide), 13 April 2007, www.adelaidenow.com.au/sport/cricket/tragedy-of-the-west-indian-rebels/story-e6frectl-1111113339094 (retrieved 16 April 2014).

at any given time) might be better spent on drug education and rehabilitation.

As against all that is the damage that illegal drugs undoubtedly cause to the user and innocent third parties, such as children of heavy users, who might be neglected, or road users if someone drives under the influence, and so forth. There is also the (disputed) empirical evidence from various countries which have experimented with degrees of legalization, which does not seem to present an unambiguous case in favour of decriminalization.

Needless to say, no final conclusions can be offered here. But, whatever one thinks of the wisdom of criminalizing drugs, one can still welcome the initiative of the PCA and ECB in its efforts to identify drug use among players. For reasons of the players' welfare and the reputation of the game they ought to be taking measures to address what does seem to be widespread use of drugs by professional players. It is also necessary because of the obligation of the players themselves not to bring the game into disrepute, or for that matter to attract the interest of law enforcement authorities to cricketing fixtures.

PERFORMANCE-ENHANCING DRUGS

The scandals

At the start of the 2003 World Cup, defending champions Australia looked unstoppable. Linchpin of their bowling attack was Shane Warne, one of the most successful cricketers of all time and a central figure in perhaps the greatest fifty-over match in history, the epic semi-final in the 1999 World Cup, when Australia tied with South Africa and thereby scraped through to the final. It therefore came as something of a shock when Warne was removed without ceremony from the 2003 competition the day before it was due to begin.

The reason for Warne's expulsion was that he had tested positive for a banned diuretic. He admitted taking a single tablet of a prescription drug, Moduretic (a similar drug as that for which Jesse Ryder was suspended a decade later). The Australian Cricket Board found him guilty of breaching its drug code, and imposed a one-year ban. In the event, Warne never played limited-overs cricket for Australia again (not that it made any difference to Australia's chances – they won the tournament, and for that matter the subsequent tournament in 2007, just as easily without him).

A few others have also tested positive for various substances in the past two or three decades, but it is fair to say that there have been relatively few drug-related scandals in cricket compared with some other professional sports. A much bigger scandal enveloped cycling, for example, when it turned out that Lance Armstrong had won his substantial haul of Tour de France victories while using banned substances. A wider picture was given in early 2013 by a major report into Australian sport,[9] which found that the use of what it called 'performance and image-enhancing drugs' (PIEDs) was widespread throughout a number of different sports in that country, though cricket was barely mentioned.

Is it a problem?

It cannot be assumed that cricket is free from PIEDs, even if their use might be less common than in other sports. Every time the subject is raised the media reacts almost uniformly in deploring the use of PIEDs. But there is at least a debate to be had about whether they should be banned. If anything, the arguments in favour of legalizing PIEDs for cricketers are stronger than in the case of recreational drugs in general society. In 2012, Bernard Robertson argued in an editorial for the *New Zealand Law Journal*[10] that objections to PIEDs were reminiscent of the backward-looking 'fuddy duddies' in the film *Chariots of Fire* complaining about professional coaches. He also contended that the state should not involve itself in the private activity that is sport and therefore should not concern itself with whether any particular sport allows or bans drugs.[11] It is therefore worth considering whether there is any justification in banning PIEDs.

---

[9] See the report of the Australian Crime Commission, *Organised Crime and Drugs in Sport*, February 2013.
[10] [2012] *New Zealand Law Journal* 321.
[11] For the competing conceptual arguments about freedom and paternalism, see Simon R Clarke, *Foundations of Freedom: Welfare-Based Arguments against Paternalism* (Routledge, 2012).

The definition

The first problem is to define what PIEDs actually are, as distinct from any other substance. Calling them substances that are 'harmful' will not suffice: *any* substance, including oxygen and water, is harmful in the wrong amount. Nor will it suffice to define PIEDs as substances which 'enhance' performance: a better diet, for example, will improve an athlete's performance. 'Synthetic' substances will not do either: any food or drink that has been processed in some fashion or other is synthetic to some extent. There are also recognized marginal cases, such as athletes training at high altitude and then extracting and storing some of their own blood.

Perhaps it might be said that PIEDs are artificial substances which offer some performance benefits to athletes not normally obtainable in the average diet. That is still not a satisfactory definition, however, because it would include basic painkillers, which might enhance the performance of the person whose pain they alleviate. Is there really a case for banning aspirin?

The short answer, therefore, is that PIEDs are whatever the authorities say they are at any given time. Anything banned would have to be announced in advance and in some considerable technical detail.

The ICC policy

The ICC explains its anti-doping policy in these terms: 'The ICC has a zero-tolerance approach to doping in cricket in support of its continued efforts to: (a) maintain the integrity of the sport of cricket; (b) protect the health and rights of all participants in the sport of cricket; and (c) keep the sport of cricket free from doping.' These are really two objections, since (c) is not a reason as such.

Reason (b) is probably the strongest: drugs harm the user and so should be banned for paternalistic reasons, or on the ground that they are what economists call a 'demerit good' – something which causes clear and measurable harm to users if left unregulated. In the sporting context, however, there are two points against regulation on those paternalistic grounds. First, many PIEDs are not otherwise illegal and so the state does not consider that they pose a significant enough health risk to warrant being outlawed. Secondly, talk of the threat to the health of athletes ignores the fact that many sports at the highest level carry severe long-term health risks anyway. Gymnastics, for example, has well-documented risks of serious back problems, as does weightlifting. Then there is boxing, where tangible brain damage is virtually a mathematical certainty for participants who have any sort of career. There are also more extreme forms of unarmed combat such as Thai boxing or cage fighting, the dangers of which are self-evident.

In cricket, facing fast bowling risks the sort of injuries from short-pitched deliveries that Ewen Chatfield, Mike Gatting and Andy Lloyd among others suffered. In Gatting's case the injury ended his tour. In Lloyd's case the injury ended his career. In Chatfield's case the injury almost ended his life – only the quick thinking of England's physio, Bernard Thomas, saved him from choking to death after he had swallowed his tongue. Moreover, both Gatting and Lloyd were wearing helmets (albeit of an inferior design to those of the twenty-first century), which shows that protective gear cannot eliminate all physical risk.[12]

In each of those sports, it is left to the individual athletes to make the choice about how hard to train and what health implications they are willing to risk. What is the difference between the risks of boxing, for example, and the risks of taking PIEDs? Both, it might be said, are for the individual to judge. Ideally, on that basis, athletes and coaches should be well informed, so they can judge the trade-off between success when young and health issues when old.

Moreover, in the cricketing context one has to consider what drugs are likely to be used. Cricket does not require the extreme physiques of bodybuilding, weightlifting or sprinting, and it would therefore be surprising to find the more harmful anabolic steroids being used by aspiring cricketers. Even fast bowling depends on technique far more than brute strength (as demonstrated by the physiques of great fast bowlers such as Richard Hadlee or Michael Holding). Instead, cricket requires fitness, flexibility (for fast bowlers at least), concentration and, in the case of batting especially, reaction times, most of which

---

[12] As all cricket followers will know, there are many more examples of players receiving injuries from fast bowling, something to which I will return later in the book.

might be impaired if anything by drug-taking. The drugs used by Warne and Ryder would hardly have given them any unfair advantage as players, nor posed such a serious risk to their health as other substances.

Nevertheless, it is possible to push the point too far. There are serious health risks in at least some of the weight-loss drugs on the market.[13] Also, the possible harm done by other forms of PIEDs cannot be dismissed, even if one has to admit to hypocrisy given the other dangerous aspects of sport that no-one is seeking to ban. Moreover, risky activities such as facing short-pitched bowling can be said to be part of the game of cricket, and for such things to be banned would seriously (and in just about everyone's view detrimentally) alter the game. By contrast, banning drugs would not alter the game, or certainly not in any detrimental sense.

The other objection offered by the ICC is (a) above – that PIEDs offend the 'integrity' of the sport. It is not wholly clear what this means. I shall assume it means that PIEDs give the athletes who take them an 'unfair advantage'. But that argument is open to the same objection – inconsistency – as the first. At the level of professional sport, many factors offer advantages to some countries and some athletes over others. The obvious examples are the quality of training facilities and coaching. Some entire sports contain barriers to entry which preclude most of the world's population from ever competing internationally. The cost of an Olympic bicycle, never mind the velodrome in which to ride it, is prohibitive for more than 90 per cent of the global population; so too rowing boats, equestrian facilities (the horses, for a start), yachts and frankly most Olympic sports in which Great Britain tends to win medals.

Even in cricket, where games can be improvised with a bit of wood and a ball of any description, there is a world of difference between

---

[13]   In September 2013, it emerged that a teenager in Britain had died after taking a weight-loss pill containing 2,4-Dinitrophenol (DNP). The *Daily Mail* reported that five people had died in one year after using DNP: see Chris Brooke, 'Tragedy of the gifted rugby player, 18, who died after buying deadly "fat-burning" pills online', Mail Online, 15 September 2013, www.dailymail.co.uk/news/article-2421042/Fat-burning-pills-sold-online-kill-promising-young-rugby-ace-Chris-Maplecroft-18.html (retrieved 16 April 2014).

someone training at the best facilities and someone who can only practise in a remote village with rudimentary equipment. Unfairness, therefore, cannot by itself justify the banning of PIEDs, or at least not without looking like another arbitrary decision compared with all the other equally unfair things currently permitted.

Perhaps, though, by 'integrity' the ICC means that PIEDs are 'unsporting' in some more esoteric sense. This sort of objection is a shade redolent of the debates over amateur and professional sport in years past. The authorities also ignored the fact that the very concept of amateur status – the paradigmatic example of which was the distinction between gentlemen and players in cricket – was originally devised as a way of keeping the working class out of sport, because they could not afford the time off to practice, and in some cases (most notably W G Grace) amateurism was honoured more in the breach than the observance.[14]

By popular demand

Having said all that, the most persuasive argument for banning PIEDs may simply be this: all evidence suggests that the paying public expects PIEDs to be banned as 'unsporting' – whether there is a rational reason for it or not. Watching sport does not have to be a matter of hard logic. To the extent that there is a rational explanation, it would be to the effect that the admiration spectators have for players would not exist so far as their achievements are down to PIEDs as opposed to hard training or natural ability. There is also the basic commercial argument that the paying public will choose to pay for sports that do not involve what the majority of the population, logically or not, deems cheating.[15]

---

[14] In the 1980s, for example, a controversy rumbled on for a while when the All Black captain, Andy Dalton, appeared in a series of television advertisements for tractors, which he claimed was on the basis of his status as a farmer, not a rugby player. No-one believed that the reason Dalton was chosen over the thousands of other farmers in the country was unrelated to his status as an All Black, leading to the usual arguments about the spirit and the letter of the law.

[15] One other point Robertson considers is that an individual country would find itself a pariah if it legalised PIEDs. Or, to put it his way, banning drugs is the game that everyone in the playground is playing. Again, the reasoned arguments do not really come into it; if the overwhelming majority of competing countries believe in a ban, any dissenters will have to go along with the ban in order to be allowed to take

The enforcement

If one accepts that PIEDs (defined as whatever the authorities have listed as PIEDs at any given time) should be banned, the question then arises as to how. Either they could be criminalized, and therefore the ban would be enforced by each individual state's criminal justice system, or the ban could be down to individual sporting authorities, national or international (the ICC in the case of cricket). The International Olympic Committee now requires doping to be a criminal offence in any country bidding to host the Olympics. But it is not clear that the state has to be involved in any way with drugs that it does not choose to ban for the general population.

The arguments against the state's involvement include the following. First, going back to the justification for banning PIEDs being effectively a commercial decision, private sporting bodies are better placed than national authorities to judge what the public might or might not accept. They will learn swiftly by means of gate receipts and television viewing figures if they get it wrong. It is already the case that various substances are banned in some sports and not others. Anabolic steroids would not, one imagines, help someone play snooker, but drugs steadying nerves or sharpening senses might; whereas in sports like weightlifting or sprinting anabolic steroids would confer a substantial advantage.

Secondly, although they cannot impose criminal sanctions, sporting bodies can impose life bans, remove prize money and strip titles from competitors, which would usually be a sufficient deterrent. Thirdly, if it is sporting commercial considerations (as opposed to protection of the public or a section thereof) that are the prime justification for the ban, then it is not clear why the state should have to fund the enforcement mechanism. Fourthly, as mentioned, many substances that might confer an 'unfair' advantage are otherwise legal and would be expected to be otherwise legal, since they might be beneficial as part of general medicine in the right context, or perhaps there would be no use for them in a non-sporting context and therefore no need for a general ban. Fifthly, as a sort of slippery-slope argument, once

part in international fixtures; unless the dissenter wields disproportionate power in some way.

the state takes it upon itself to control the (otherwise legal) drugs involved in the private activity that is sport, it might well decide to regulate other aspects of sport, which might not be so welcome.[16]

Just as with illegal recreational drugs, the ban on PIEDs has resulted in an arms race between methods of detection and methods of evasion. The difficulties in enforcement cannot be a decisive argument against banning drugs, however: if it was difficult to stop murder, it would not be a reason to give up trying. Rather, difficulties in enforcement are an argument for better enforcement techniques, not for giving up on enforcement altogether, unless one reaches the point where the cost of banning drugs unarguably exceeds any benefits from doing so. Accordingly, to the extent that PIEDs ought to be banned from cricket, the decision should be that of the ICC, which would have to provide a list of what is banned and, in co-operation with the boards of member states, the mechanism for detection and punishment.

Coda

Away from cricket an amusing legal story can be found in the United States, where Lance Armstrong's autobiography was moved from the non-fiction sections of some bookshops to the fiction sections after his doping revelations. Rumours started that he was to be sued by readers who thought they were buying the former category of book and not the latter. It ought to go without saying that Armstrong, though purporting to offer a true story of his career in his book, was not making some legally binding commitment to that effect. Otherwise, how many memoirs by retired public figures would be vulnerable to the same sort of challenge?

---

[16] Robertson goes perhaps a bit too far in this regard by invoking the spirit of the east European Communist states, who used to commit all sorts of abuses of citizens to produce Olympic champions, but his underlying point is sound (Robertson, op cit). For a contrary view, see Robert Griffiths QC, 'Fair Play, Cricket and the Law', 22 October 2013, www.4-5.co.uk/uploads/docs/section11/Fairplay.pdf (retrieved 16 April 2014).

Chapter 5

THE DEATHS

Cricketers and suicide generally

Some years ago the leading cricket historian David Frith noticed that a disturbing number of reasonably well-known cricketers had committed suicide. His subsequent research confirmed that the percentage of professional cricketers who had prematurely ended their lives themselves exceeded that of the general population by a considerable margin. He wrote a book, entitled *By His Own Hand*,[1] discussing a number of the cases and pondering what, if anything, the link might be between professional cricket and suicide. The book was later updated and republished as *Silence of the Heart*.[2]

Two of the more notable individuals Frith identified were the Australians Albert Trott and Sid Barnes. Trott's primary claim to fame is that he remains the only player in recorded history to have hit the ball over the Lord's pavilion. Sadly the feat seems to have become a curse: his career declined steadily thereafter, before he was moved to take his life at the age of 41, shortly after it would have been apparent that he could no longer play at first-class level. Sid Barnes, on the other hand, who had a short but brilliant test career, clearly had some psychological problems, including bipolar disorder. His misfortune was to live in an age when diagnosis and treatment of mental illness were much less sophisticated and sympathetic than in the present day. It therefore seems unlikely that Barnes would have had a less troubled life had he chosen other paths than cricket.

I will return to Barnes later in the book when discussing his famous libel case. In the meantime, it should be noted that one needs to be especially careful in cases like his not to fall for the *post hoc ergo propter hoc* fallacy – the trap of assuming that because event *B* followed event *A* then *A* must have caused *B*. In other words, just

---

[1] David Frith, *By His Own Hand: A Study of Cricket's Suicides* (Stanley Paul, 1991).
[2] David Frith, *Silence of the Heart: Cricket Suicides* (Mainstream, 2001).

because someone played cricket and later committed suicide does not mean that their cricket career had anything to do with their later troubles.

An easy example is the suicide of Frederick Hardy in March 1916, which in all probability had nothing to do with his modest cricket career. Hardy played county cricket in Edwardian times, and was described by *Wisden* in his obituary rather blandly as 'a left-handed batsman and a useful right-handed medium-pace bowler'. He was one of the 5.7 million British citizens who served in the Great War, in his case with the County of London Yeomanry. For Hardy, as for a number of other well-documented cases,[3] a return to the trenches was too much. Ordered back to France, he chose instead to end his life by cutting his throat at King's Cross station in London.

In other cases, the cause of death might be ambiguous. One example is Stan McCabe, Sid Barnes's first state captain and, like Barnes, one of the leading Australian batsmen of the era. McCabe died after falling from a cliff. There were rumours of suicide, though it was noted at the inquest that McCabe appeared to have grasped at vegetation on his way down, suggesting that his death might have been an accident (unless the grasping was instinctive).

Cricket and humiliation

More than most sports, cricket has a way of humiliating individuals. Much has been written about the way in which it is ostensibly a team sport but at almost all times is played out by individuals: a single bowler versus a single batsman, hitting the ball to a single fielder. John Arlott once wrote of how 'cricket is a game of the most terrifying stresses with more luck about it than any other game I know. They call it a team game, but in fact it is the loneliest game of all.' While a footballer who misses an easy chance at goal or a rugby player who spills an important pass will usually have (or have had) many chances to make amends in the rest of the game, a batsman dismissed first ball or a fielder who drops an easy chance might have to stand around for days afterwards with no chance of redemption.

---

[3] Including, but not limited to, the approximately 3,000 soldiers convicted of cowardice or similar crimes and sentenced to death. About 90 per cent had their sentences commuted to something less. See *Cases, Causes and Controversies*, ch 9.

Some players have their careers ended by making a single mistake at a critical moment: a nervous debutant might be caught first ball, or hit out of the attack in his first couple of overs, and never be selected again. In 2013 a clinical psychologist spoke of the 'relentless uncertainty' and 'general weirdness' of cricket: 'You're almost waiting for the next failure. Mistakes are punished mercilessly. Sometimes not even your own mistake – an umpire or a teammate might have run you out. The nature of the game is very mentally tough. I don't think there's a tougher game out there.'[4] Robert Winder made the point in somewhat saltier terms when describing a player whose countenance during a poor spell in a test match conveyed a sentiment experienced at times by all who have played the game: 'Fuck I hate cricket'.[5]

One other problem unique to professional cricket as distinct from any other top-level sport is the three different formats in which players are now expected to compete – traditional first-class matches, 50-over matches and 20/20. Then there is the travel associated with the game and the consequent strain on players' personal lives. In the twenty-first century even a team as well resourced as England has seen Marcus Trescothick and Jonathan Trott suffer from stress-related illnesses due to the relentless pressure of the international circuit.

And yet, all of those factors concern players during their careers as opposed to those who have retired. So perhaps it not surprising that Frith concluded at the end of his meticulous research that there was not a compelling case to say that suicides of cricketers derived from the unique facets of the game, at least not in contradistinction with other sports.[6]

That prompts the jejune observation that cricketers are probably prone to depression and other personal issues for much the same reasons

---

[4]   Karen Nimmo, quoted by Dylan Cleaver, 'Mental health and elite sport: Cricket captures the highs and lows', *New Zealand Herald*, 31 October 2013.

[5]   Robert Winder, *Hell for Leather: A Modern Cricket Journey* (Phoenix, 1999). Winder was writing of Devon Malcolm, one of English cricket's many unfulfilled talents of the 1990s, and someone who appears later in this book in a very different context. Winder's description of the pressure falling on Brian Lara, then the leading player in the world, is most insightful as well.

[6]   Incidentally, in the general population the suicide rate has risen 60 per cent in 45 years: see Jennifer Michael Hecht, *Stay: A History of Suicide and the Philosophies against It* (Yale, 2014).

as athletes in general, or anyone else whose career has a comparatively short shelf life. Speaking of Chris Lewis's imprisonment for drug importation, his former teammate Angus Fraser summed up the lot of the ex-player:

> I suppose this highlights how difficult it can be for players to cope once they stop playing cricket. They get used to a lifestyle and a certain standard of living, and a lot of cricketers don't plan for what to do when they stop playing. As a person, Chris liked the nice things in life, the clothes and the cars, but once his playing days were over, his means of income was reduced. He needed the money and it appears he got dragged into something like this. It's very sad.[7]

As well as the income enjoyed by players at the height of their careers, there is also the thrill of playing, the sense of purpose induced by the competition and the camaraderie of the dressing room. The latter is perhaps a watered-down version of the ethos which the armed forces inculcates into its members – homelessness and suicide being disproportionately present among ex-service personnel. Professional cricketers begin their careers as up-and-coming members of a tight-knit unit who play, train and celebrate hard together. They might have a few years as leading members of the team. Then they enter a slow decline, in which they do progressively less well on the field and fit in less well with the social activities off it, before leaving it altogether. That sort of decline and fall would be harsh on even the most robust of characters. It is true that a select few players suffer barely any noticeable loss of form before retiring, and others may attain a sort of elder-statesman status within the team which makes their age an asset rather than a liability, but it is not hard to see how the fading of the light for the more ordinary cricketers might induce some negative feelings, particularly when no equally rewarding second career appears to be in the offing.[8]

---

[7] Andrew Miller 'Lewis case sends a warning – Fraser', Cricinfo, 20 May 2009, www.espncricinfo.com/england/content/story/405230.html (retrieved 16 April 2014).

[8] See also Suresh Menon's article 'The loneliness of the long-distance cricketer', in which he wrote: 'Only superficially is cricket a team game. It is an individual game, and a lonely one. The player has to work out his own solutions (he may borrow from history) in his playing days, and after retirement train himself not to dwell on the past too much' (Suresh Menon, 'The loneliness of the long-distance cricketer',

Some former players manage to segue into roles in the media or coaching and thereby maintain their previous standard of living, as well as staying in touch with the game at the highest level. Necessarily, however, they will be in the minority. Their ranks are also drawn mostly from the best players, and therefore those least in need of financial assistance. Not that media or coaching roles guarantee anything: David Bairstow found modest but respectable opportunities in both, yet still took his own life at the age of just 47.[9] Others are fortunate enough to find second careers away from professional cricket that prove to be as fulfilling, or at least as well paid. The foreword to the second edition of Frith's book was written by Mike Brearley, who went from being an outstanding test captain (if a batsman who was not of the highest class) to being a well-respected psychoanalyst. Doubtless some of his captaincy experience amounted to a transferable skill for his new vocation. He observed:

> Jobs which merely make use of a man's name and previous skills may turn him into a kind of object for use, lured into prostituting himself to make money out of fitting in with the star-struck desires of others. Such a man loses his authenticity. And if he fails, the humiliation, which is felt by some to contrast dramatically with the excitement and successes that went before, may be terrible.

The ultimate example of a second career is probably Imran Khan, the former Pakistani captain. Since his playing days he has taken on such a significant role in the turbulent world of Pakistani politics that his former career – as one of the greatest players in history – sometimes seems little more than a footnote. But few cricketers can ever expect to be as influential and successful off the pitch as Imran, any more than they could expect to be as good a player on it.

The law

From a legal point of view, suicide was an offence at common law in England from the Middle Ages until the enactment of the Suicide Act 1961. The same Act made assisted suicide a criminal offence, which in recent years has received much attention in the media due

---

Cricinfo, 24 February 2008, www.espncricinfo.com/magazine/content/story/337858. html (retrieved 16 April 2014)).

[9]   See Michael Parkinson's obituary of Bairstow, *Daily Telegraph*, 19 January 1998.

to a series of tragic cases[10] and campaigns both for and against the existing law.

The ethics of suicide and assisted suicide constitute a debate which will in all probability never be resolved. Either one believes that there are certain circumstances in which a person should be permitted to end his or her life, with assistance if necessary, or one does not. Either way, one will encounter passionate, articulate and determined opposition. There is no fence to sit upon.

There has been little or no call for suicide to be recriminalized, in Britain at least. Instead, most of the debate has concerned whether assisting suicide ought to remain a crime and, if so, in what circumstances a prosecution should be brought. (One fundamental principle in common law countries is that the prosecutorial authorities have a discretion whether or not to bring a prosecution in any individual case, even when it seems clear that an offence has been committed).[11] On two occasions, the issue even made the cricket pages. First, in September 2010, Michelle Broad, wife of the former England cricketer Chris Broad and step-mother to the England cricketer Stuart Broad, took her own life. A successful businesswoman in her own right, she suffered from motor neurone disease, and tragically explained in notes left to her family that she 'didn't want to become

---

[10] Most prominently the tragic stories of Dianne Pretty and Debbie Purdie: see *Cases, Causes and Controversies*, ch 20.

[11] The Crown Prosecution Service for England and Wales has issued guidelines as to when a prosecution for assisted suicide is likely to be brought. Factors in favour of a prosecution include where the victim was under 18, or lacked the capacity to reach an informed decision, and where the suspect was not wholly motivated by compassion. Factors tending against prosecution include where the victim had reached a voluntary, clear, settled and informed decision, and the suspect was motivated wholly by compassion.

The aim of the ban on assisted suicide is obvious. But if a person is adamant about ending their life before the final stages of a terminal illness, then they might choose to do so before they reach the point of needing assistance (so as not to expose anyone assisting them to a criminal prosecution), and thus die considerably earlier than they would have done had assisted suicide been lawful.

Decriminalizing assisted suicide also has formidable problems on the practical level. Does there have to be a 'death tribunal' to determine which cases involve a genuine decision and which ones involve greedy or otherwise malicious relatives bullying a desperately vulnerable elderly relative? Would its decisions involve the right of appeal? And so on.

a burden'. Then, in August 2013, it was reported that Jonathan Agnew had offered to accompany Brian Dodds, the father of his step-children, to an assisted-suicide clinic in Switzerland. Dodds too had been diagnosed with motor neurone disease, and eventually died from it in England in 2005.

That debate involves the weightiest of questions, which for obvious reasons cannot be explored here. So I shall return instead to the individual cases of suicides of former cricketers.

The mystery

Brearley concluded his foreword to Frith's book by admitting that it was impossible to make more than informed guesses as to why some individuals decide to end everything and others do not. 'Ultimately', he wrote, 'human motivation is mysterious.' Never were those words truer than in the case of Peter Roebuck, who in a grim piece of irony had been the author of the foreword to the first edition of Frith's book. To Roebuck's strange and disturbing tale I shall now turn.

BAD LIGHT STOPS PLAY: THE DEATH OF PETER ROEBUCK

The end

On 12 November 2011, in a hotel in Newlands, Cape Town, the well-known cricket writer and commentator Peter Roebuck telephoned his friend and fellow broadcaster Jim Maxwell, who was staying in the same hotel. Maxwell thought Roebuck sounded highly distressed. He went to Roebuck's room on the sixth floor and found him 'in a state of utter despair'. There were two policemen present, who were in the process of arresting Roebuck. Maxwell was allowed to spend a few minutes with Roebuck, who asked him to contact a few people. One of the officers then escorted Maxwell out of the room.

Moments later Roebuck fell from a window in the room to his death. A complex and mysterious man had died in complex and mysterious circumstances.

Roebuck the player

As a player Roebuck deserves to be remembered as more than just another county journeyman who never quite obtained international honours. His average of 37.27 after 335 first-class matches is respectable enough, but conceals the fact that at his peak in the 1980s he averaged over 40 for four successive seasons, even if he never presented an overwhelming case for test selection. He was appointed captain of his county, Somerset, in 1986. He was one of *Wisden*'s five cricketers of the year in 1988, and was recommended by Somerset to England, though the selectors opted for the experienced Chris Tavaré instead. Around the same time it was even mooted that he might be parachuted in as England captain, though in fairness it was harder to find a player who was *not* then being suggested for that role.[12] He did captain a representative England team in a match in the Netherlands, which was not a success, though it was not a full international. Another of his career highlights was scoring a century in 1989 against Allan Border's tourists, who were the first of the Australian sides that were to bring so much calamity to English cricket over the following decade and a half.

Roebuck's technique included a shot which was somewhat optimistically compared to Greg Chappell's,[13] but a more realistic assessment was that of his former captain Brian Rose, who said: 'He could bat for long periods in his own way, and if anyone can do that they are bound to score runs. He was a great asset.'[14]

Roebuck's achievements on the field during his first class career were overshadowed by his part in the controversy over the sacking of Viv Richards and Joel Garner from Somerset at the end of his first season in charge, which was followed by Ian Botham's furious resignation. Roebuck as captain necessarily bore the brunt of much of the ill-feeling that the affair generated at the club, and began a feud with Botham that would last until Roebuck's death. It did not help that the club's fortunes improved only marginally in the following seasons, and that the new overseas player, Martin Crowe, did not

---

[12]   The rumour of the Roebuck captaincy came after England's 'summer of four captains', used in five tests against West Indies in 1988.
[13]   His former colleague Vic Marks said: 'He had an idiosyncratic shot which we called "the old leg clip", which was a flick off middle and leg, a bit like Greg Chappell' (quoted in Obituary, *Wisden* 2012), though in fairness Marks meant the type of shot, not the end result.
[14]   Ibid.

flourish. 'It was not a career move,' Roebuck later sardonically remarked of his part in the affair.

Roebuck off the pitch

Roebuck started writing about cricket from a fairly early stage in his playing career. The critical acclaim he received for his journalism moved him naturally in that direction and away from playing – a doubly sensible move given how in his most well-received book he had revealed how miserable cricket had made him even before the Richards/Garner affair.[15]

Roebuck had obtained a first in law from Cambridge, and his finely wrought prose often brought to mind some of the best legal authors. His writing also gave rise to no small irony: he had ghosted an autobiography of Botham[16] before they became the most implacable of enemies. Then there was the foreword he had written for the first edition of Frith's study of cricket and suicide. After Roebuck's death, Frith picked out two passages from that foreword which had become especially poignant: 'Cricketers are supposed to be simple, even gung-ho, in sexual matters as in everything else. And yet cricket – and most cricketers – has its dark secrets, its skeletons ... Some people have predicted a gloomy end for this writer. It will not be so.'[17]

Away from his journalism, Roebuck devoted considerable time and money to mentoring youngsters. It was in that capacity that his troubles with the law began.

Roebuck and the law

In the late 1990s, Roebuck had invited three young South Africans to his home in England for coaching and mentoring. He was later

---

[15] See Roebuck, *It Never Rains: A Cricketer's Lot* (Allen & Unwin, new edn, 1985). Roebuck's misery seemed to have derived from the fact that he could not be as good a cricketer as he wanted to be, a feeling familiar to anyone who has played the game, even if it caused Roebuck a good deal more internal torment than most.

[16] Roebuck and Botham, *It Sort of Clicks* (Willow, 1986). The book was sympathetic to Botham – then more or less at the height of his powers as a player – without being a hagiography, although a few of Botham's own quotes would have flattered David Brent from the television comedy *The Office*.

[17] David Frith, 'Cricket has its dark secrets, its skeletons', *The Independent*, 15 November 2011.

charged with causing actual bodily harm after striking them across their exposed buttocks with a cricket bat. Roebuck's explanation was that he had been imposing a punishment as part of his strict disciplinary regime. He initially pleaded not guilty, but changed his mind before trial and pleaded guilty. He was given a suspended sentence of four months' imprisonment.

In his autobiography, Roebuck made two statements about the affair that deserve comment, bearing in mind his legal training as well as his age and high intelligence. The first was that he had had to 'pretend' that the three victims had not consented. 'Of course it was nonsense,' he snarled. Roebuck should have known that consent – leaving aside any technical, legal definition of the word – in the circumstances of the relationship between him and the youngsters was anything but straightforward. Anyone could see that three young people brought to a foreign country by a much older man for his tutelage and mentoring would not be in an equal relationship with that man. Therefore, if a complaint was made about inappropriate physical contact between them, it would and should receive much closer attention from the police than anything comparable between adults. Such was made clear after Roebuck's death by his first 'African son', Psychology Maziwisa, who thanks to Roebuck's financial support had qualified as a lawyer. (Roebuck liked to refer to the youngsters in his charge as his 'sons.') Maziwisa was minded to defend much of what Roebuck had achieved in helping people like himself, while at the same time not holding back about Roebuck's moral and legal transgressions.[18]

Roebuck's second statement was more straightforwardly wrong. He claimed that he did not realize when pleading guilty that the witness statements adduced by the Crown would be taken as proven. That was simply not believable. For a start, Roebuck's legal background would have told him otherwise, even though it was some time since his graduation and he had not worked in law since. Secondly, however, he had been represented by a specialist criminal barrister, who would have advised him of the precise implications of his plea. The Crown pressed charges based on evidence which included witness statements. Roebuck pleaded guilty, meaning he accepted the case against him.

---

[18] See 'Sex, beatings, blackmail: the riddle over Roebuck', *Sydney Morning Herald*, 1 January 2012.

He could not seriously have thought that he could plead guilty and then deny having committed the offences in the manner described by the prosecution.

Nevertheless, Roebuck remained wholly unrepentant. He raged: 'I cannot waste time on accusers who have never produced a player or a young man worth tuppence, and who never will,' and added: 'I stand by my overall record with young people.'

Roebuck the expatriate

Disillusioned with England after the controversy, he moved to Australia and became an Australian citizen. There he developed the bile of the embittered expatriate, rarely missing a chance to denigrate his old country. He reached the point where, commentating on the Ashes, he used the word 'we' when referring to Australia – not that that stopped him from being critical of Australia when he considered it appropriate. He was particularly harsh on Ricky Ponting as a captain, and not just in technical cricketing matters. In the midst of India's acrimonious tour of Australia in 2007/8, Roebuck began a newspaper column in the following terms:

> Ricky Ponting must be sacked as captain of the Australian cricket team. If Cricket Australia cares a fig for the tattered reputation of our national team in our national sport, it will not for a moment longer tolerate the sort of arrogant and abrasive conduct seen from the captain and his senior players over the past few days. Beyond comparison it was the ugliest performance put up by an Australian side for 20 years. The only surprising part of it is that the Indians have not packed their bags and gone home. There is no justice for them in this country, nor any manners.[19]

That sort of criticism – typical of Roebuck – gives some clue about the man and at least some of the trouble in which he found himself. Personal standards were clearly something he held very strong views about – ironically, much in the manner of the traditional upper class in England, whom he professed to despise.

---

[19]   Roebuck, 'Arrogant Ponting must be fired', *Sydney Morning Herald*, 8 January 2008. I should note that Ponting rose above that criticism and offered a generous (and unprompted) tribute to Roebuck upon hearing of his death.

He also started spending time in South Africa, and bought a house in Pietermaritzburg. He continued running mentoring schemes in both Australia and South Africa, helping disadvantaged youngsters as he had before.

Roebuck after death

None of Roebuck's activities attracted media attention until his death, and the subsequent revelation of the charges police had intended to make when they arrived at Roebuck's hotel room. The statements of Maziwisa and the others make for disturbing reading. There is no need to labour the details. In essence, the allegations were that Roebuck had engaged in a number of inappropriate sexual acts with his young charges, passing them off either as disciplinary actions or as acts of affection which he assumed they had received willingly. They had put up with it for some time because Roebuck had provided them with opportunities for education and employment that would not have been available to them otherwise. In some instances he had also helped their family members financially and so they were prepared to suffer humiliation for the good of their relatives.

One of the complainants, a Zimbabwean, had contacted Roebuck through Facebook, asking for assistance with university. He alleged that Roebuck had molested him when they met at the Southern Sun hotel in Newlands on 7 November. Enraged by Roebuck's conduct, he sent a message telling him in no uncertain terms not to try and contact him again. He later told a freelance journalist:[20] 'I was so shocked I couldn't fight him off and it makes me feel like a sissy and a pushover. This man took advantage of me … He preyed on the fact that I was reaching out to him and trusted him and he did this to me.' It should be said that not all of the young people whom Roebuck assisted made allegations against him and some spoke positively in his defence.

An unsatisfactory ending

In the numerous obituaries that followed the news of Roebuck's death, a broad consensus quickly emerged that no-one had really known him, even those who had shared a dressing room with him for

[20] Hedley Thomas, 'Your sick acts humiliated me: Roebuck's alleged victim speaks out', *The Australian*, 18 November 2011.

a decade or more, or who had spent time on tour with him in the press box. His teammate for many years at Somerset, Vic Marks, who like Roebuck had a more successful career as a journalist than a player, delivered a representative verdict: 'He could unravel cricket and cricketers with piercing clarity. Yet if anyone tried to do the same with him, the drawbridge was liable to go up with a resounding clunk.'[21]

Inquests were opened in South Africa and elsewhere, yet none of them seems to have resolved anything about who Roebuck really was or what he had done. At the time of writing, his family remained adamant that no proper inquiry had taken place and doubted even that Roebuck had taken his own life.[22]

We therefore arrive at an unsatisfactory state of affairs from a legal perspective. The police had enough evidence to arrest him, and on the basis of the evidence that has been made public there was, in legal terms, a case to answer. But Roebuck is not here to answer that case. That leaves a lingering sense of injustice in two respects. First, Roebuck cannot defend his name. His family and some of his former colleagues have been anxious to do so on his behalf, but they cannot stand in his place for some sort of putative trial. Second, his accusers will never receive justice either, since they can never see him stand trial. In other words, neither Roebuck nor his accusers will have their day in court.

It might be inferred that since Roebuck apparently took his own life when he was about to be arrested, he was guilty of some or all of the charges. It has to be stressed, however, that such an inference would only be speculation, and however strong the case against him appears to be, there might have been other factors involved. Perhaps even the prospect of being remanded in custody was too much for Roebuck, given the notoriety of certain South African jails. Perhaps he had only done a fraction of what was alleged, but fell into despair as he thought no-one would believe him and a conviction for serious crimes was inevitable, with the attendant horrendous consequences of a lengthy jail term and the destruction of his name and career.

---

[21] Vic Marks, 'Peter Roebuck: a gifted writer and a complex man with a brilliant mind', *The Guardian*, 13 November 2011.

[22] See Nick Miller, 'Peter Roebuck's mystery death must be solved, says mother Elizabeth', *Sydney Morning Herald*, 25 January 2014.

Perhaps he thought he would lose his name and career even if he was found not guilty, and would forever have to put up with people assuming there was no smoke without fire. Perhaps he had wholly unrelated troubles of which no-one knew, and having to face a police investigation on top of those was too much for him.[23] We may never know the full story.

'Don't get bogged down in this. The world is bigger than cricket, and you should see more of it,' Roebuck once advised one of his protégés. It seems that he never quite managed to follow his own advice. In retrospect the comment by the judge in the English trial about Roebuck's actions being the result of an urge to 'satisfy some need' about summed it up: no-one – perhaps not even Roebuck himself – quite understood what his needs were. And so we finish with the verdict that someone no-one really knew in life will remain someone no-one really knows in death.

---

[23] There is something of a parallel with the flood of allegations in the United Kingdom that came a few months after the death of the entertainer Jimmy Savile in 2011. There were rumours from time to time about Savile's activities with young girls while he was alive, though he was never prosecuted. Nor were the rumours considered strong enough to get in the way of him receiving a knighthood in the United Kingdom and a Papal knighthood as late as 1990. A strong if not compelling picture of sexual abuse started to emerge after his death, however, and a police enquiry received information from some 200 witnesses, all claiming to have been victims of sexual abuse from Savile.

There was one problem: while on the evidence a *prima facie* case appeared, Savile was not there to defend his name; it seemed he had been wholly exonerated in life and wholly excoriated in death. As with Roebuck, Savile's death meant that justice could neither be done nor be seen to be done.

Chapter 6

THE MONEY

An indispensable member

In his obituary in *Wisden*, James Seymour (1879–1930) was described as

> an indispensable member of the great Kent elevens before the [Great] War ... He never rose to the highest standard of representative cricket for in his day that standard was very high but as a county player he was in the highest class ... He was not a classic batsman – even in those days his stance was too modern – but he possessed many strokes both skilful and attractive. His flash past cover-point was a thing of special delight, and if he did not always appear sure of himself in playing fast bowling, he was a wonderfully watchful player of the ball on a turning wicket. As a slip fieldsman he ranked with the greatest in that position.

His career average of 32 suggests a good player rather than a great one, as confirmed by the fact he never played a test and only managed three appearances in the Gentlemen v Players matches. Nevertheless, away from the field he achieved a victory in the highest court in the land for which many a county worthy has been grateful ever since. The case of *Seymour v Reed*[1] established that money from benefit seasons did not constitute income (provided the right conditions were met), and was therefore not subject to tax. Hence the fortunate player's cut of exhibition match-takings, tombolas, T-shirt sales and money raised at well-hydrated functions has since been spared the attention of Her Majesty's Revenue and Customs.

The case

Seymour played his benefit match against Hampshire at Canterbury in 1920. It raised enough money for him to buy a farm, so it is not surprising that the Revenue's interest was triggered. They considered

---

[1]   [1927] AC 554.

that the money he received from the day should be subject to income tax, which Seymour disputed.

The matter came before the general commissioners, who held that the money was not subject to income tax because it was a gift, not income as such. The Revenue challenged the decision in the High Court. It did not seek to tax that part of the fund which had been subscribed independently by members of the public. Instead, its case was confined to the money (amounting to about half of the total raised) which had been given to Seymour by the club as representing the gate money, because in the ordinary course of events that money would belong to the club and paying it to a player gave it the appearance of income.

The case was heard before an eminent tax judge, Mr Justice Rowlatt. He formulated the issue as whether the money Seymour had received constituted a 'personal gift' and was therefore exempt, or whether it was 'remuneration' and hence taxable, though neither term actually appeared in the relevant legislation.[2] He decided on the former and therefore upheld the decision of the general commissioners. The Revenue went to the Court of Appeal, which reversed the decision, and Seymour appealed in turn to the House of Lords.

By a majority, the House ruled in Seymour's favour. The Lord Chancellor, Viscount Cave, stated:

> I do not doubt that in the present case the net proceeds of the benefit match should be regarded as a personal gift and not as income from the appellant's employment. The terms of his employment did not entitle him to a benefit, though they provided that if a benefit were granted the committee of the club should have a voice in the application of the proceeds. A benefit is not usually given early in a cricketer's career, but rather towards its close, and in order to provide an endowment for him on retirement; and, except in a very special case, it is not granted more than once. Its purpose is not to encourage the cricketer to further exertions, but to express the gratitude of his employers and of the cricket-loving public for what he has already done and their appreciation of his personal qualities. It is usually associated, as in this case, with a public subscription; and, just as those subscriptions, which are the spontaneous gift of members of the

---

2 Income Tax Act 1918, Sch E.

public, are plainly not income or taxable as such, so the gate moneys taken at the benefit match, which may be regarded as the contribution of the club to the subscription list, are (I think) in the same category. If the benefit had taken place after Seymour's retirement, no one would have sought to tax the proceeds as income; and the circumstance that it was given before but in contemplation of retirement does not alter its quality. The whole sum – gate money and subscriptions alike – is a testimonial and not a perquisite. In the end – that is to say, when all the facts have been considered – it is not remuneration for services, but a personal gift.[3]

Viscount Dunedin agreed, and did not disguise his irritation for anyone who thought otherwise:

When I think of this little nest egg – which, of course, paid income tax as an investment and which, now that it has taken the form of a farm, will pay income tax under Sch A – being treated, the whole sum, as income, honestly, had it not been for the fact that honourable judges, whose opinions I respect, have come to another conclusion, I would have thought the contention was quite preposterous. I therefore concur in the motion which has been made.[4]

In context, 'honourable judges, whose opinions I respect' amounted to damning with faint praise.

Lord Atkinson, whose speech was delivered next, was the dissenting judge and hence one of those earning Viscount Dunedin's scorn. He reasoned:

I think that when no reason is shown for the gift to an official such as Seymour of the large and substantial prize given to him through the medium of a benefit match, it must in reason be assumed that it was given to him for the efficient and satisfactory discharge of the duties he was employed to discharge, and, if so, that the reward which accrued to him came to him from his employment.[5]

In other words, Seymour received a benefit only because he was good at his job as a professional cricketer. The benefit money

---

[3]   [1927] AC 554 at 560.
[4]   Ibid at 560–61.
[5]   Ibid at 561.

constituted payment by his employer for doing his job well, and should therefore be regarded as income.

Lord Atkinson was, however, on his own. The other two judges, Lords Phillimore and Carson, agreed that Seymour should be permitted to keep his benefit in full, and therefore the appeal was allowed.

The later cases

Later judges did not always show a great deal of enthusiasm for the decision. After the Second World War came *Moorhouse (Inspector of Taxes) v Dooland.*[6] The case concerned another professional cricketer, one Bruce Dooland, who played for East Lancashire in the Lancashire League. Dooland was employed under a contract which provided for a salary and certain expenses. In addition, it provided for 'talent money' and collections to be made for him in accordance with the rules of the Lancashire Cricket League for any meritorious performance by him in Lancashire League or Worsley Cup matches (we can observe in passing that collections from spectators would have been something of which W G Grace would have approved, as long as the amount raised proved to be of suitable proportions).

In subsequent litigation between Dooland and the Revenue, the Court of Appeal held that the collections were profits arising from the cricketer's employment and not mere personal presents (in which case Grace certainly would not have approved, since not only would the recipient have to pay tax on them, he would necessarily be classed as a professional). The leading judgment was given by Lord Justice Jenkins, who said that the 'test of liability to tax on a voluntary payment made to the holder of an office or employment is whether, from the standpoint of the person who receives it, it accrues to him by virtue of his office or employment, or in other words, by way of remuneration for his services'. The Seymour case was distinguished on the basis that his benefit match was a one-off occasion and not a contractual right.

---

[6]   (1954) 36 TC 1.

Not long afterwards, Jenkins LJ heard the case of *Wright v Boyce*,[7] which concerned Christmas presents given in the form of cash to a professional 'hunt servant' by people who employed his services. Jenkins LJ said:

> It must, I think, be remembered that *Reed v Seymour* was a case turning very much on its particular facts, and it was, as I see it, a vital element in the case that the benefit match was held and the gate money was collected on the eve of the retirement of Seymour after a long and brilliant career as a county cricketer playing cricket for the county of Kent. It was a 'once and for all' payment after very long service and after a long career spent in entertaining the public. It was made at the proper time for making a testimonial, that is to say, on the eve of the retirement of the person to whom it was being given. That was not so in the present case.

'Turning on its own facts' is usually judge-speak for 'a decision with which I completely disagree but which I do not have the authority to overturn or ignore'. As the quoted passage shows, Jenkins LJ was able to slide around *Seymour* in the Wright case because in the latter case the cash gifts to the individual were part of a long-standing tradition as opposed to a gift at the end of the individual's career as in Seymour. Thus, notwithstanding Jenkins LJ's disgruntlement, the decision in Seymour's case remained applicable to the traditional cricketer's benefit takings, provided that they were derived from precisely the same circumstances as *Seymour*.

The following year the issue came before the House of Lords again, in *Hochstrasser v Mayes*.[8] Lord Radcliffe stated that it was

> not easy in any of these cases in which the holder of an office or employment receives a benefit which he would not have received but for his holding of that office or employment to say precisely why one considers that the money paid in one instance is, and in another instance is not, a 'perquisite or profit ... therefrom'. The test to be applied is the same for all. It is contained in the statutory requirement that the payment, if it is to be the subject of assessment, must arise 'from' the office or employment ... While it is not sufficient to render a payment assessable that an employee would not have received it

7 (1958) 38 TC 160.
8 (1959) 38 TC 673.

unless he had been an employee, it is assessable if it has been paid to him in return for acting as or being an employee.

The benefit today

In the *Seymour* case itself, Viscount Dunedin's derision of anyone who disagreed with him (which included the Court of Appeal in the same case) seems somewhat harsh. As Lord Atkinson pointed out, Seymour's job was playing cricket for Kent, he was awarded the benefit in the course, and precisely because, of that job, and the money was paid to him by his employer just as with his normal income. It did not, therefore, strain credulity that some senior judges would have ruled in favour of the Revenue.

Dunedin stated that Seymour's fund 'paid income tax as an investment and ... now that it has taken the form of a farm, will pay income tax'. With all due respect, that is a rather circuitous point: the same could be said for any set of funds, which in one form or another are bound cross the taxman's path at some point. On the other hand, given that there was a specific exemption in the tax code of the day for gifts by employers, it is equally understandable that the majority of the judges classified a one-off payment made to a specific player – not each member of the team as a matter of course – as a gift and not income.

No doubt the grumblings by later judges, together with their refinement of the circumstances in which a benefit will be found not to be subject to income tax, have led many committees in charge of benefit seasons to exercise considerable caution. But the actual result in *Seymour* has never been challenged.

A general problem

One general problem found throughout tax law is that the moment an exemption to a general rule is granted to one set of people, the opportunity springs up for those on the margins to seek legal advice or possibly engage in litigation to determine whether they fall within that set. Lawyers clearly benefit from that opportunity but others seldom do. Wealthy people can afford to seek the advice and find out if they benefit but others cannot, including people who might have won their cases had they been able to afford representation.

Even worse is where the state decides to make a wholly unjustified exemption for purely political purposes. A high profile example in the cricketing world occurred in 2002, when Ferrari decided to give one of their cars to Sachin Tendulkar by way of congratulations for his 30th test century. Unfortunately for the master batsman, at the time India's tax law imposed a 120 per cent duty on the importation of luxury cars, which rendered the gift more in the nature of a burden. India's finance minister of the day, Jaswant Singh, then suggested the government would waive the application of the duty in Tendulkar's case.

It hardly needs pointing out that Singh's proposal was wholly unprincipled and unjustifiable. Aside from the clear breach of the rule of law (which requires laws to be of equal and general application), there were hundreds of millions of Indians substantially more in need of financial assistance than the great cricketer. Effectively, the proposal would have amounted to an act of attainder in reverse,[9] which would have been no more defensible legally because it was bestowing largesse on the recipient rather than a penalty.

In the event, the outcry was such that Fiat decided to pay the import duty itself and spare everyone's embarrassment. Not that that was the end of Tendulkar's revenue-related headlines: a few years later, it was reported that he had managed to have himself categorized for tax purposes as an 'actor' rather than a sportsman, based on his work on television advertisements, and his tax bill had been reduced accordingly.[10] *India Today* stated:

> Tendulkar had claimed deduction of tax under Section 80RR of the Income Tax Act. The section states that a person can claim tax deduction if he is a playwright, artist, musician, actor or sportsman and the income for which deduction is claimed is derived by him in the exercise of his profession.

---

[9]   An act of attainder was a device in medieval times whereby a particular individual could be punished without the bother of a trial based on evidence. The device was regularly employed during the Wars of the Roses by the competing claimants to the crown, to avenge anyone who had backed the wrong horse.

[10]   Marc Dawson, *Outside Edge: An Eclectic Collection of Cricketing Facts, Feats & Figures* (Pitch, 2013), p 56. It wasn't the end of the Ferrari's time in the limelight either: the plot of the 2012 Bollywood film *Ferrari Ki Sawaari* concerned a young man who stole Tendulkar's Ferrari and had a series of japes behind the wheel.

When the assessing officer asked Tendulkar to explain the nature of his profession, the master blaster submitted that 'he is a popular model who acts in various commercials for endorsing products of various companies'. He further stated that the income derived by him from 'acting' had been reflected as income from 'business and profession' whereas income from playing cricket was reflected as 'income from other sources' since he is a non-professional cricketer. Tendulkar explained that the claimed deduction in tax was from the exercise of his profession as an 'actor'.[11]

It is hard to argue that Tendulkar's classification fell within the spirit of the law. As was pointed out by the assessing officer in the case, if Tendulkar was not a cricketer it was difficult to imagine who might be (it is also unclear why actors and cricketers had different tax rates in the first place).

This brings us back to the never-ending debate over the distinction between tax avoidance (legal) and tax evasion (illegal).[12] It is a debate that bears much resemblance to the spirit of cricket versus the laws of the game, as will be seen at various points later in the book.[13] One of the key problems with curbing tax evasion is that, thanks to cheap air travel and the internet, it has become fairly easy for the wealthy to shift themselves and their money from country to country.[14] All top cricketers might come to fall into this category in future. In fact, given the rise of IPL-cloned 20/20 tournaments in different countries, a class of professional cricketers might evolve who have no national allegiance and no country of domicile for tax purposes.

---

[11] Kiran Tare, 'Actor Sachin Tendulkar gets tax break', *India Today*, 27 May 2011.
[12] There is also a prior question of whether tax is even moral to begin with: some people think that levels of taxation are far too high at present, morally entitling or even obliging people to avoid tax as much as possible, while others maintain that levels of taxation are too low.
[13] It might be observed that the architects of complex trusts designed to avoid tax maintain that they have complied with the letter of the law and should therefore escape censure or criticism. The problem is that unless and until any tax avoidance scheme is reviewed by the always under-resourced authorities and, if necessary, tested in court, it is more in the nature of speculation to say whether it is lawful or not.
[14] With this in mind, in September 2013, the G20 summit came up with various ideas about clamping down on tax havens: see Simon Bowers, 'G20 summit: states chase tax evaders with plan to swap data globally', *The Guardian*, 4 September 2013.

Then again, it is possible to be too naïve in these matters. Financial affairs in modern times are complex primarily because human interactions in modern times are complex.[15] Moreover, the actual issue in the *Seymour* case – what constitutes income as opposed to a gift – is not simple to resolve, because there are so many ways in which money passes between individuals. Thus, while reforming the tax system might always seem desirable[16] there will always be ambiguities and marginal cases that will provide fertile ground for litigation.

Pensioning off the seasons

To twenty-first century eyes, the concept of a benefit season in lieu of a more conventional pension arrangement looks antiquated and not a little absurd. It reflects the fact that county professionals have only recently been able to make a living from the game alone without having to seek winter employment selling blankets in a department store (as Colin Cowdrey was compelled to do for a short time in the mid-1950s, despite being an Oxford graduate and one of the most gifted young cricketers in the country at the time[17]) or by such other occupation as they could find.

The system is also manifestly unfair: benefit seasons are most likely to be awarded to the top players, who are the least in need financially. Benefit seasons are also rarely awarded to players who switch counties several times (much more common nowadays than when benefit seasons were first introduced), because they will be held not to have served their time by any of them. A fairer system would be a general pension scheme akin to those provided by ordinary employers. Alternatively, players could be left to make their own arrangements in the general pensions market, perhaps with the clubs helping to fund independent advice, as some counties have done

---

[15] The Office of the Parliamentary Counsel produced a thoughtful paper on complex legislation generally: see *When Laws Become Too Complex: A Review into the Causes of Complex Legislation* (Office of the Parliamentary Counsel, Cabinet Office, March 2013).

[16] On which see *Cases, Causes and Controversies*, ch 28.

[17] There was some extra compensation for Cowdrey, since he married the proprietor's daughter. See Colin Cowdrey, *MCC: The Autobiography of a Cricketer* (Hodder & Stoughton, 1976).

already (I should emphasize I am not *au fait* with the current British pension legislation, simply noting the outdated nature of the benefit season as a matter of principle).

Pending complete abandonment of the benefit season, however, it can be said that James Seymour deserves to be rather more famous on the county circuit than seems presently to be the case.

NOT GOOD ENOUGH FOR CHARITY

Not long after the House of Lords had decided in favour of James Seymour, thereby doing county cricketers a very substantial favour, the Chancery Division in the case of *Re Patten*[18] had to consider another aspect of cricketing finances, that of bequests to cricket clubs. The court was required to decide whether a trust for a cricket club was charitable, and therefore exempt from tax and the arcane rule against perpetuities.[19] On that occasion the cricketers were the losers, albeit not in terms of an absolute defeat, as will be seen.

The will

The case concerned the will of one William Fletcher Moore Patten, made in 1927. Westminster Bank Ltd was appointed executor and trustee. The will directed the trustees of the testator to retain £3,000 and apply the interest annually in payment of Patten's house, which his aunt was allowed to occupy for life. On the termination of the aunt's occupation, the house was to be sold, and from the proceeds, added to the £3,000, three specific legacies were given. Two of those legacies provided £100 each in funding loan in trust to pay the interest yearly to the staff Christmas funds of the Junior Carlton Club in Pall Mall and the Union Club in Brighton respectively (inflation suggests

---

[18] The full title is *Re Patten; Westminster Bank v Carlyon* [1929] All ER Rep 416.
[19] The rule prevented bequests that would involve legal arrangements that lasted for decades or more after the testator's death. See generally *Tristram and Coote's Probate Practice* (LexisNexis, 30th edn, 2008). Here one can throw a non-cricketing spanner in the works: the America's Cup yachting competition is held pursuant to a deed of gift which has always been assumed to be charitable, or it would not have survived to the present, because of the rule against perpetuities. Interested readers are invited to speculate on the reasons why the America's Cup ought to have charitable status, having regard to Hamish Ross, 'The America's Cup and the Courts', [2013] *New Zealand Law Journal* 359.

they were more generous than certain employers in the present day). The third legacy provided 'to the Sussex County Cricket Club: £300 of Funding Loan in trust to pay the interest yearly to the Nursery Fund'.

Patten died in February 1928, and the will was proved not long afterwards. Westminster Bank took out a summons as executor and trustee, seeking the determination of a number of questions, including whether the legacies to the three clubs were charitable.

Ungodliness and worldly lusts

By way of aside, the bequest to the two social clubs gives an interesting insight into a bygone age. Mr Justice Romer explained:

> It was contended that the two trusts in favour of the Staff Christmas Funds ... are good charitable trusts on the ground that they are trusts for the encouragement of good servants, and I was referred to the cases of *Reeve v Attorney-General* 3 Hare 191 and *Loscombe v Wintringham* 13 Beav 87 as authorities for the proposition that such a trust is charitable. In the former of those cases, a testator [exhorted] servants to be obedient unto their own masters, and to please them well in all things, not answering again, and not purloining, but having all good fidelity and denying ungodliness and worldly lusts, and to live soberly, godly and righteously.

After that rather Cromwellian exhortation, he set out the testator's bequest:

> For such servants, and the like limitation to the principality of Wales, which contains 42,274 female servants, I give 1000*l*. ... in trust to pay the yearly dividends, 35*l*., in sums of 1*l*. to each such female servant, once only, on their producing a certificate, to be entered on the books of the society, signed by the minister and churchwardens of their parish, of their regular attendance at church, and by their masters or mistresses of their ten years' quiet and faithful service, at 5*l*. or less per annum, and of their never having been married or pregnant.

Romer J said the Reeve case seemed to assume that the bequest was charitable. He went on: 'The Vice-Chancellor [the judge in the Reeve case] presumably considered that such a trust was beneficial to the inhabitants of Wales, on the ground that it tended to provide those inhabitants with good servants.' Thus, Romer J implicitly considered that the 'inhabitants of Wales' were distinct from the 'servants of Wales', rather in the manner of the archaic phrase 'my neighbour's wife'. (Note also that the testator required any 'such female servant' not to have been married or pregnant, which raises a question as to how he thought there might be servants for future generations.)

Romer J continued:

> In the second of the two cases there was a bequest of a legacy 'to the governors guardians and trustees of a society instituted for the increase and encouragement of good servants to the intent and purpose that' the legacy 'might be paid to the governors guardians and trustees of the said society for the increase and encouragement of good servants'. No such society could be found, but Lord Langdale MR said he thought there was a sufficient charitable gift.

Having mentioned those two previous authorities, Romer J dealt with the issue of the Christmas fund legacies in a summary fashion: 'I cannot think that the public are in any way interested in the question whether the members of the two clubs are well or ill served. In my opinion these two trusts are not charitable.' This was certainly not the world of the country house as imagined by some modern fictional depictions, where the servants are shown interacting with the above-stairs family, at times on reasonably friendly terms. Romer J's judgment suggests that that would have been as likely as present-day families talking to their microwave ovens. Instead, as the bequests made clear, in pre-war days servants were to keep their mouths permanently shut and know their place.

Manifestations of that rigid class structure were also found in cricket of the time, in the separation of amateurs and professionals. They often had separate dressing rooms, were described differently on the scoreboard, and played each other in the Gentleman v Players match every year. That fixture lasted until 1963 (a watershed year in other respects if Philip Larkin is to be believed), and no professional captained England until Len Hutton in 1953.

Then there was the Bodyline affair, to which I shall return more than once, where MCC disgracefully tried to shift the blame for the controversy onto the working-class professional Harold Larwood.

Larwood quite reasonably responded that he had been following the orders of his captain, Douglas Jardine (who had never blamed him for anything; but then again Jardine never admitted there was anything blameworthy in Bodyline anyway).[20] Those struggling to understand Jardine's complex character should remember that he was a product of his era, and would have been raised by people sharing the same views as Romer J and the 1895 judges who thought that inferior social classes (into which category one suspects Jardine placed all Australians) did not even merit the description 'inhabitants.'[21]

The cricket bequest

Romer J turned to the trust for Sussex County Cricket Club. He recorded:

> It was argued that the trust is one for the 'supportation aid and help of young tradesmen handicraftsmen and persons decayed' within the meaning of the statute of Elizabeth. In my opinion a professional cricketer is neither a tradesman, a handicraftsman nor a person decayed, and though undoubtedly, as a result of the administration of the fund, boys all of the working or lower middle classes and not well off financially may be embarked upon life as professional cricketers, it is, I think, reasonably clear that the object of the fund is the encouragement of the game of cricket and nothing else, and it has been held by authorities that are binding upon me that such a bequest is not charitable.

He referred to the earlier case of *In re Nottage*,[22] where the Court of Appeal held that a gift to support and encourage yacht-racing was not charitable, Lord Justice Lopes explaining:

---

[20] Interestingly, the only amateur among the English fast bowlers was Gubby Allen, who was also the only one to refuse to bowl Bodyline. The class structure of the day would have made it impossible for Larwood or Voce to have taken such a stance whatever their wishes.

[21] One of Jardine's biographers wrote that Jardine was 'strictly speaking, a Victorian by only three months, but in almost every respect – intellect, morality, even appearance – he was a nineteenth century man. His childhood was Victorian, his schooling fiercely so' (Christopher Douglas, *Douglas Jardine: Spartan Cricketer* (Methuen, 2nd edn, 2003), p 1).

[22] [1895] 2 Ch 649.

I am of opinion that a gift, the object of which is the encouragement of a mere sport or game primarily calculated to amuse individuals apart from the community at large, cannot upon the authorities be held to be charitable, though such sport or game is to some extent beneficial to the public. If we were to hold the gift before us to be charitable we should open a very wide door, for it would then be difficult to say that gifts promoting bicycling, cricket, football, lawn tennis, or any outdoor game, were not charitable, for they promote the health and bodily well-being of the community.

In other words, as good for the public as sport might be, it would open the floodgates if gifts for promoting outdoor games were automatically considered charitable. The decision in the *Nottage* case was binding on Romer J, and he therefore held that gifts to cricket clubs would not be charitable per se.

At the time of writing, *Re Patten* had only been considered twice in subsequent cases, and even then only with regard to Romer J's treatment of the bequest to the aunt, not the cricket club.[23] That, however, was not quite the end of the matter. Instead of resolving the point with a degree of finality, it served to offer imaginative trusts lawyers a challenge to find some extra aspect to a sporting bequest that would elevate it to the realms of charity. So rather than just donating to a cricket club, for example, a bequest might leave money sponsoring the poor to learn cricket, or something along those lines.[24]

A shifting of the ground

In 1980, the House of Lords took a somewhat more lenient view of sporting trusts in the case of *Inland Revenue Commissioners v McMullen and others*.[25] The trust in issue had been established by the Football Association. Its objects included:

To organise or provide or assist in the organisation and provision of facilities which will enable and encourage pupils of Schools and Universities in any part of the United Kingdom to play Association Football or other games or sports and thereby to assist in ensuring

---

[23]   See *Re Aberconway's Settlement Trusts* [1953] Ch 647, [1953] 2 All ER 350; *Re Burden* [1948] Ch 160, [1948] 1 All ER 31.
[24]   For recreational charities in general, see *5 Halsbury's Laws* (4th edn), paras 544–7.
[25]   [1980] 1 All ER 884.

that due attention is given to the physical education and development of such pupils as well as to the development and occupation of their minds and with a view to furthering this object.

The House of Lords ruled that, when construing a trust deed where the intention was to set up a charitable trust and where there was an ambiguity, a benign construction should be given if possible. They went on to hold that the particular trust was a valid charitable trust, because, having regard to the educational theory that the provision of sporting facilities contributed to providing a balanced education, the trust could be said to be for the advancement of education. Another important point was that the trust was limited to students at universities and schools (bequests often fail because they are too ill defined).

The decision did not specifically overrule *Re Patten* (or even mention it) nor, importantly, *Re Nottage*, upon which the decision in the *Patten* case had been based. The Lord Chancellor, Lord Hailsham, warned: 'The mere playing of games or enjoyment of amusement or competition is not per se charitable, nor necessarily educational, though they may (or may not) have an educational or beneficial effect if diligently practised.' Nevertheless, the ruling in the case would apply to a cricketing trust that mirrored the football trust. It therefore provided scope for similar cricketing bequests to obtain charitable status.

Trusts today

A number of charitable cricket trusts have been successfully established over the years. One is Cricket for Change,[26] whose main aim is stated as assisting disadvantaged young people. Another is Cricket without Boundaries,[27] which aims

- to spread cricket through coaching children and teaching adults how to coach;
- to link the sport to HIV/AIDS awareness and incorporate these messages into coaching sessions;
- to bring together and empower local communities through cricket.

[26]   www.cricketforchange.org.uk
[27]   www.cricketwithoutboundaries.com

Outside the courts, the Charities Act 2006 has made the advancement of amateur sport a charitable purpose, though s 3(3) of the Act retains the public benefit test. Thus the community, or a sufficient section thereof, has to benefit from the physical activity.[28]

Some parting observations

One of the main legal distinctions between charities and other legal entities is that the former obtain tax exemption and donations to them can be tax deductible. That distinction is based on the assumption that charities do good things for the community, which the state might otherwise have to do itself, and so are to be encouraged, but that leaves endless scope for arguing about what actually constitutes good works as opposed to a normal commercial enterprise.

Here the same general problem as discussed in the chapter on Seymour's benefit arises: the distinction between charities and commercial entities provides opportunities for litigation on the margins to determine who fits where.[29] And that in turn brings us back to the problem in the Patten case: although cricket clubs are undeniably a good thing, they are not sufficiently good to warrant being classed as charities. Something else is required – such as an educational element as approved in the *McMullen* case. The duel between the Revenue and those seeking charitable status can therefore resume.

---

[28] Note that I have remained in the United Kingdom; an interesting article on the New Zealand position is Nicholas Bland, 'Tax, Charities and the Charities Act' [2009] *New Zealand Law Journal* 61.

[29] In the United Kingdom in the early twenty-first century, for example, some trusts for which charitable status had been claimed turned out to be means by which wealthy individuals, often oligarchs from the former Soviet Union, were paying for their children's education. Such trusts should not have been charitable since arranging for one's children's education is a duty, not anything exceptional which deserves charitable status. But the complexity of the law (and of the structures which the oligarchs could pay to have constructed) was such that it was difficult for HMRC to sift through them to find out whether they were lawful or not.

Chapter 7

THE DESPOTS

One would like to say that the apartheid regime in South Africa was uniquely evil in the whole of human history. Sadly, the reality is that many other minority regimes have corruptly assigned to themselves the bulk of their respective countries' resources, rendered the majority of their people second-class citizens, and maintained that state of affairs in a ruthless, violent and corrupt fashion, just as the apartheid regime did.

What was unusual, though not unique, about apartheid South Africa was the lengths to which it was prepared to go and how blatant it was in doing so. The modus operandi of most modern tyrants is to inherit a constitution guaranteeing rights and freedoms for all and then ignore it. By contrast, Dr Verwoerd and his *Broederbond* cohorts, the architects of apartheid, drew up separate laws for people based on the colour of their skin and then diligently enforced them. It was that use of the law that was so extraordinary. It was a stark and brutal illustration of how the law can be used for malign as much as benign purposes.

Among the many millions of innocent victims of apartheid was one Basil D'Oliveira, who would go on to play an unwanted centre-stage role in one of the best-known cricketing stories of the twentieth century. His story forms the first article in this chapter. D'Oliveira was a highly gifted batsman and a quiet man of high personal standards. Both qualities were on display throughout the controversy which made him a household name in two countries. Regrettably, as will be seen, not many others involved in the saga emerged with their integrity similarly intact.

The second article considers another interesting moral and ethical question, and one with which the courts have had to deal with on countless occasions over the years, namely the limits to the right to protest. Are there ever circumstances in which one can break the law to try to force what one thinks is the morally correct outcome? The future United Kingdom cabinet minister Peter Hain thought so when trying to prevent South African cricket teams from playing in England; the barrister Francis Bennion certainly did not. The article tells the story of Hain's protest and Bennion's response.

Finally in this chapter is an afterword, forming a sort of 'what happened next' for D'Oliveira, South Africa, cricket and sport.

THE D'OLIVEIRA AFFAIR

A special talent

Basil D'Oliveira was born in Signal Hill, Cape Town, around 1931.[1] He showed considerable sporting prowess from an early age, especially at cricket. As a 'Cape Coloured', his lot under apartheid was to play cricket all the way up to representing South Africa, but only for a contrived 'coloured team' (which he captained), not their full test side. Nor was he allowed to play against white opponents or use whites-only facilities. But he was able to play enough to show the visiting English journalist John Arlott at the end of the 1950s that he had a special talent.[2]

In 1960 Arlott arranged for D'Oliveira to play professional cricket in England, and the rest, if the cliché can be excused, is history: D'Oliveira struggled initially with English conditions, but his skill and ability quickly won through. He qualified for England by residence and was selected for the national side. He built up a test average around the fifty mark, the sign of a player of the highest class, and was still playing towards the end of the decade when a scheduled

---

[1] There has been some confusion about the year in which D'Oliveira was born. According to Cricinfo, 'he was 30 when he debuted for Worcestershire and 34 when he made his first appearance for England. Pat Murphy, the journalist who wrote his autobiography, said Basil was even older than that because he told the author he was born in 1928. It is currently accepted that he was born in 1931 and died at 80, but his real age may never be known' (Firdose Moonda, 'In Dolly's footsteps', Cricinfo, 30 July 2012, www.espncricinfo.com/magazine/content/story/574510.html (retrieved 17 April 2014)). The most comprehensive work on the D'Oliveira affair is Peter Oborne, *Basil D'Oliveira: Cricket and Conspiracy – The Untold Story* (Sphere, 2005).

[2] See David Rayvern Allen, *Arlott: The Authorised Biography* (Aurum, new edn, 2004), pp 243–7.

tour of South Africa by MCC (under whose aegis England's overseas tours were conducted at the time) came into view.

Not just cricket

The tour was to take place over the English winter in 1968/9. Covert horse-trading between representatives of MCC and the South Africans started some time earlier. The issues being negotiated were not wholly about cricket, or even wholly about apartheid. At the time, the president of MCC was Sir Alec Douglas-Home, former British Prime Minister, who held the foreign affairs portfolio in the shadow cabinet. He was therefore not the neutral, patrician figure one might have imagined. Instead, in his day job he was trying to deal with crises including the fallout from the Rhodesian Unilateral Declaration of Independence (UDI) in 1965, a matter on which Britain was hoping for South African support and which had already caused the cancellation of a cricket tour of Rhodesia.[3]

Outward signals from South Africa were somewhat ambiguous, though one suspects that the South African government, headed by B J 'John' Vorster (a former 'general' in the paramilitary wing of the pro-Nazi Ossewabrandwag organization during the Second World War), never had any intention of allowing D'Oliveira to tour. The embarrassment of a 'coloured' person playing against white opponents in whites-only grounds because he had moved to a different country was something the perverted logic of apartheid could not allow. Still less could it do so when D'Oliveira might excel on the field and thus undermine the whole justification for racial separation, though quite how the lords of apartheid thought they could maintain an argument for racial superiority in cricket in the first place given the performance of the West Indian sides of the era is anyone's guess. Presumably they treated it as what Douglas Adams in *Life, the Universe and Everything*

---

[3] Rhodesia, previously a self-governing British territory, had made the declaration in response to the British requirement for majority rule before full independence would be granted. As the first such unilateral declaration since the American Revolution, it was considered a great embarrassment for Britain. It resulted in the first-ever UN sanctions. Obviously for sanctions to be effective South Africa – as a wealthy country sharing a land border with Rhodesia – would have to be on board. This was crucial since Rhodesia was landlocked, and thus reliant on one of her neighbours providing access to a seaport.

called an 'SEP': a 'Somebody Else's Problem' which others are pathologically unable to register because they do not want to face the consequences. The absurdity of the South African government's position was compounded by the fact that it did not object to white South Africans playing against other races in other countries.

Early in 1968, MCC took formal steps to confirm what South Africa's policy would be, but when Douglas-Home visited (ostensibly wearing his hat as shadow Foreign Secretary, rather than MCC president), Vorster vacillated. Douglas-Home continued to try and find any solution that would not cause controversy. He had been parliamentary aide to Neville Chamberlain in the late 1930s: it seems he had experienced much but learned little.

Douglas-Home was not the only member of MCC who had difficulty with the prospect of quarrels with South Africa. Arthur Gilligan, former England captain and Great War veteran, is usually mentioned disparagingly in this regard because in the 1930s he had belonged to one of the numerous short-lived British fascist parties of the day (in P G Wodehouse's *Code of the Woosters* the proliferation of such parties compelled Roderick Spode to form the Black Shorts, since 'all the shirts had been taken'). It has accordingly been suggested that he was sympathetic to the South African regime itself. But most of the others in MCC at the time, who lacked an equivalently dubious political past, seem to have acted no better.

D'Oliveira falters

In cricketing terms, things had started to fluctuate for D'Oliveira. On the 1967 winter tour in West Indies, he lost form and began seriously to doubt himself. By his own admission, about the only impressive statistics he collected on tour related to how much he had managed to put away in the bar after each game. Then, despite a strong performance in the first Ashes test of 1968, he was dropped (farcically being made the scapegoat for the bowling failure, even though he was a part-time bowler at best), and struggled at county level while England mounted a fightback in the series without him. Meanwhile, cynical efforts were made on behalf of the South Africans to tempt him away with lucrative coaching offers, playing on his faltering confidence as a player. D'Oliveira declined their thirty pieces of silver.[4]

Things therefore looked bleak for D'Oliveira's touring chances. A newspaper lined up an alternative by arranging for him to be offered a job as a journalist covering the tour, something not unprecedented at the time for disappointed players, though there were indications that the South Africans would not have allowed him to perform the role.[5] The suggestion was also made by a South African businessman that a private tour by a 'cavaliers' team including D'Oliveira might be arranged if the MCC tour was not possible – ironically foreshadowing the rebel cricket tours that the South African authorities would later organize themselves to try and get around the ban on international cricket.

Then, dramatically, just before the last Ashes test, the opening batsman, Roger Prideaux, withdrew from the side and D'Oliveira was recalled. Famously, he went on to score a magnificent 158 – one of the greatest innings in Ashes history[6] – and his inclusion in the forthcoming tour seemed assured. His captain, Colin Cowdrey, often considered to be the paragon of the English gentleman (and the man after whom the MCC Spirit of Cricket Lecture was later named), privately promised D'Oliveira his backing.

Utter disbelief

And then came the bombshell. To the disbelief of the players and public alike, the selectors left D'Oliveira out.

To maintain any sort of credibility, the selectors had to convince everyone that the exclusion was on cricketing grounds alone,[7] or

[4]   See D'Oliveira, *Time to Declare: An Autobiography* (J M Dent, 1980), ch 6. See also Oborne, op cit.

[5]   D'Oliveira, op cit, p 71.

[6]   In a bizarre coincidence, another contender for the greatest-ever Ashes hundred was another innings of 158 at the Oval in the final test of a series by a controversial South African import playing for England. In 2005, Kevin Pietersen's memorable fifth-day pyrotechnics secured the match and with it the Ashes for England. The question of Pietersen's nationality, also a cause for controversy, will be considered in more detail in the section on nationality below.

[7]   Colin Cowdrey in his autobiography was adamant that that was the case: see Colin Cowdrey, *MCC: The Autobiography of a Cricketer* (Hodder & Stoughton, 1976). The

at least completely unrelated to the South African objections. The argument they came up with was that D'Oliveira would have upset the 'balance of the side'. Some have speculated that the selectors might have been concerned about a repeat of his off-field behaviour in the Caribbean.[8] The chairman of selectors at the time, Doug Insole, never conceded that anything other than cricketing considerations were involved, though it has to be said that Insole did not look tremendously confident in his own opinions when interviewed on television nearly 35 years after the event.[9] One factor also bandied about by MCC apologists was D'Oliveira's age, and even his staunchest supporters knew he was no youngster.

Whatever the explanation, the South Africans could hardly believe their luck, and the announcement of the tour party was greeted with cheers in Pretoria. Then, just as fate would have it, another English player, Tom Cartwright, withdrew from the touring party with injury, and D'Oliveira was chosen, despite not being a like-for-like replacement. The South African regime were able to spin the turn of events in their favour, by pretending that they were only interested in cricket but that MCC had bowed to political pressure with its *ex post facto* selection of D'Oliveira, since D'Oliveira was not an obvious replacement for Cartwright. Had the selectors included D'Oliveira in the first place and maintained at all times that they had never considered anything other than cricket, the South Africans would either have had to accept the situation or admit that they had been hypocritical all along. Instead, MCC had handed them the excuse they wanted.

book makes for an interesting read: Cowdrey portrays himself as something of a political naïf as far as South Africa was concerned, which might have been the case on his first tour but seems harder to maintain in respect of the D'Oliveira affair, given how much press attention it received and the fact that Cowdrey was by then England captain.

[8] See the D'Oliveira obituary, *Wisden* 2012.

[9] See *Not Cricket: The Basil D'Oliveira Conspiracy* (dir Paul Yule, BBC, 2004). It has been suggested that D'Oliveira was actually the third choice for the tour, but even if so, it might have been the case that he was so low down because the selectors knew the controversy he would likely provoke, and so convinced themselves that there were some cricketing grounds for his exclusion.

Finally MCC was forced to do the right thing. With the South Africans objecting to the team it had chosen, MCC had to stand by its guns and cancel the tour. The reason given was not South Africa's odious domestic policies, but rather the fact that the South Africans were purporting to interfere with MCC's right to select the team it wanted.

To play or not to play

The primary submission of those in favour of sporting relations with South Africa at the time was that politics and sport should not mix. Quite how they could run that argument when it was the South Africans themselves who had brought politics into the equation in the first place is not clear. It was also argued that disastrously bad regimes – some even worse than apartheid – existed around the world without attracting any serious call for a sporting boycott. That argument was encapsulated in the following vituperative *démarche* to the *Daily Telegraph* by one Brigadier C E Lucas Phillips, published on 11 September 1968:

> Sir,
>
> I suggest that the Reverend David Sheppard and those who think like him about racial segregation on the South African cricket field would be fulfilling their Christian mission more effectively if they were to direct their zeal to the far more vicious forms of apartheid practised in the Sudan, Zanzibar, India, Abyssinia, Guyana, Nigeria, Kenya, Egypt and other countries.
>
> The pale discrimination of South Africa fades into insignificance when compared with the bloodshed, persecution, callous neglect and frequently wholesale massacres that occur in such territories from racial, religious, caste and tribal discriminations.
>
> Is it nothing to Christian churchmen that the black, brown and yellow people slaughter and persecute one another? ...
>
> If D'Oliveira had not been a coloured person, no one would have seriously criticised the MCC. No one has made a fuss about the equally unfortunate Milburn.[10]

---

[10] Letter reproduced in Martin Smith (ed), *Not in My Day, Sir: Cricket Letters to*

Moreover, no economic sanctions were in place against South Africa at the time. Thus, the argument ran, it was hypocritical to single out sport in general or cricket in particular. The problem with that argument was that it suggested that sport was nothing other than business, not a view to which I would subscribe. There was also the somewhat stronger point that economic sanctions would harm the majority of the citizens much more than the ruling elite – an argument recycled with some justification every time a rogue regime has come to international attention.

All of those arguments were subsequently repeated a number of times during the years in which the sporting boycott of South Africa was in place. But none was particularly relevant to the narrower question of whether D'Oliveira himself should have been excluded from the 1968 winter tour. Even the most ardent believer in the exclusion of politics from sport should have at least conceded that if sporting relations were to be maintained, they should have been on the basis that both sides were selected on sporting merit alone. South African law at the time precluded that from happening.

The legal angle

What was the legal angle to the story? If D'Oliveira had been an employee and MCC had been a limited company or a partnership, and if he had been excluded from a particular role within the company because of his race, he could have had an action for unfair dismissal or racial discrimination under modern law. At the time, however, both concepts were in their infancy.[11] More to the point, MCC was not a limited company but an unincorporated association. Therefore, any legal action would have had to be taken against the secretary and

---

the Daily Telegraph (Aurum, 2011). The author was referring to Colin Milburn, a cricketer whose reputation as a *bon viveur* probably did for his chances of tour selection, since he would have been considered too much of an off-field risk. The brigadier's assumption was that D'Oliveira was left out on cricketing grounds only. At all events, I prefer another letter sent around the same time, from a reader reporting that his wife was unable to understand why the Irish *Taoiseach* of the day (De Valera) wanted to play cricket for England...

[11] There had obviously been employment laws for a very long time, but even as recently as 1968 the options for employees who had been dismissed were very limited by today's standards (see *Cases, Causes and Controversies*, ch 44).

chief executive personally. But none of that was relevant for players, who were not employees and who understood that they were not guaranteed national selection; legally they were wholly at the whim of the selectors.

As a private club, MCC was beholden to its members, who had the option of bringing a vote of no confidence in the leadership or the selectors. Years later, just such a vote was brought after the controversial omission of David Gower from a tour of India, when the manager of the side gave one explanation and virtually every cricket follower in England believed another.[12] By then, MCC no longer controlled English cricket,[13] rendering the action simply a form of protest – albeit a very public and effective one, especially as the club decided to defend in principle the right of the selectors to do their job, if not necessarily the actual decisions they had made.

That state of affairs reflects the fact that sport has usually been considered a private activity not subject to the supervision of the state. That is not necessarily something to be regretted, even if it leaves private sporting clubs free to make dismal decisions of the calibre of the D'Oliveira omission. If it were otherwise, events would be held up pending the resolution of litigation arising out of selection decisions, and the courts would be left trying to figure out whether player X was excluded on genuine sporting grounds or because the selectors had an axe to grind of some legally indefensible sort. Later in the book I consider the case of the Australian Sid Barnes, who by means of a fortuitous (or contrived) libel action was able to find a way of getting the cricketing authorities into court to explain their actions.

---

[12]   The affair is dealt with ruthlessly in the 1993 edition of *Wisden* by Matthew Engel in his editor's notes and in the 1994 edition by Peter Hayter in his tour report. The South African ban was not wholly irrelevant to the Gower affair, since Gooch had captained the first English rebel tour and Gatting the second, while Emburey was the only player to have gone on both tours. Gower had been on neither. At least there was poetic justice, as England lost every test match, their inept planning clearly not being confined to matters of selection. Gower never played for England again, a fact which added what *Wisden* called a bittersweet touch when Gooch passed his record for the most test runs scored for England – Gower might have set an unbeatable record if Gooch, as captain, had let him play.

[13]   England played as MCC on overseas tours up until the 1976/7 tour of Australia, and continued to wear the colours for another twenty years, the last ever outing being the 1996/7 tour of New Zealand.

Even allowing for the shabby treatment meted out to Barnes, one would not wish to see selection decisions subjected to court cases, and it is therefore fortunate that his case was the exception and not the rule.

But the ultimate legal angle to the D'Oliveira story was that mentioned in the introductory paragraphs above. The whole saga took place because – and only because – of the legal system of South Africa. The South African government chose to write into legislation a set of rules which condemned D'Oliveira to second-class citizenship. From that abuse of the law everything else flowed. It is a reminder that a legal system is not just a set of rules but a yardstick by which any society may be judged.

Meanwhile, the rule of law was about to be tested in England, in a private prosecution that gave rise to a moral and legal issue much wider than the debate about sporting links with rogue regimes.

THE TRIAL OF PETER HAIN

Angry young man

By the early 2010s, the former cabinet minister Peter Hain (b. 1950) had become something of an elder statesman of British politics. In 1969, however, Peter Hain was a rather different political animal: aged 19, not long arrived in Britain from South Africa, and, by his own admission, an angry young man. He and his family had been compelled to flee South Africa because of their anti-apartheid activities. They intended to carry on the fight in England. Despite his youth, Hain became chairman of the Stop the Seventy Tour campaign, which aimed to prevent visits by South African sporting teams and individuals. It led to a prosecution of Hain, which gave rise to an important moral and legal issue, namely the limits of permissible protest in a free society.

The Hain campaign

Hain's campaign aimed to stop fixtures by means of direct action; that is, not with letter-writing campaigns, demonstrations and other forms of lawful protest, but by physically preventing matches taking place. One of the campaign's early targets was a private cricket tour organized by one Wilf Isaacs, a former Second World War fighter pilot who was still playing first-class cricket at the age of 52. With Basil D'Oliveira having been so prominently in the news the year before, cricket was high on the list of South African sporting activities Hain and his associates wished to interrupt.

As to the campaign's methods, Hain explained many years later:

> I was always committed to non-violent direct action. For example, running on tennis courts, as we did in 1969 in Bristol, or running on cricket pitches, sitting down and then being carried off, or we did some imaginative things like people ran on to Twickenham and chained themselves to the goal posts, the rugby posts, and had to be cut free, or an activist booked herself into the Springbok hotel, near Hyde Park, and gummed up the door locks of the Springboks' bedrooms so they had to break out in order to get to the match on time. So we did that kind of thing and, yes, it did shade over into potentially illegal activity though not on the scale which I subsequently found myself in at the Old Bailey.[14]

The reason Hain found himself in the Old Bailey was because of the opposition to his illegal protests, in particular the forthright opposing views of a barrister, Francis Bennion. Bennion had also been a wartime pilot, before going up to Oxford, qualifying as a barrister and then becoming a legislative draftsman. He had had an interesting career in the law: as well as drafting domestic English statutes and regulations, he was prominently involved in creating the post-independence constitutions for Ghana and Pakistan. His expertise in tax law had secured him a lucrative contract advising the Jamaican government.

Bennion was incensed by Hain's activities, because to him they offended a basic legal principle, which he explained in a pamphlet at the time:

> There's only one point, and it's quite simple. Agitators must not be allowed, however good or bad their cause may be, to stop the lawful activities of others. I don't care whether it is Peter Hain stopping lawful cricket matches (and all the other innocent activities associated

---

[14] '1972 Peter Hain Trial', *Politically Charged*, BBC Radio 4, 11 December 2005. Transcript available at www.francisbennion.com/pdfs/fb/2005/2005-066-hain-transcript.pdf (retrieved 17 April 2014).

with a sporting tour), or a handful of extremists shouting down the Foreign Secretary in the Oxford Union, or a gang of students occupying the administrative buildings at Southampton University, or – most heinous of all perhaps – Welsh language militants bringing the work of the High Court itself to a standstill. It is quite irrelevant what the reason is. No cause can justify the lawless disruption of a lawful activity. Freedom under the law is the proud boast of the British Constitution. The law, and nothing else, must determine what activities are forbidden.[15]

In 1971 Bennion founded an organization named Freedom under Law to promote the viewpoint expressed in the pamphlet and to facilitate the private prosecution.

The prosecution

Bennion's tactic was to employ the long-established – if seldom used – legal weapon of a private prosecution. The justification for the ability to bring a private prosecution is that police and prosecutors do not have the resources to pursue every single transgression of the criminal law. Sometimes they take the view that there is not enough public interest in a particular putative prosecution. The ability to bring a prosecution privately ensures that an individual who feels sufficiently strongly can ensure that a case is brought anyway.

The same requirements to secure a conviction – proof beyond reasonable doubt being the most obvious – apply to a private prosecution as to a normal prosecution by the state. Also, the Director of Public Prosecutions has the power to take over and discontinue a private prosecution if he or she considers the public interest requires it, although that did not occur in Bennion's case.[16]

The prosecution Bennion brought alleged criminal conspiracy, a charge which seems to have slipped from use in recent years. It alleged that Hain was involved in organizing illegal activities, even if he had not actually taken part in them. The nature of the charge meant

---

[15]   Francis Bennion, 'Why I Am Prosecuting Peter Hain', 27 May 1970, available at www.francisbennion.com/pdfs/fb/1970/1970-009-why-prosecuting-peter-hain.pdf (retrieved 17 April 2014).

[16]   See *R (on the application of Gujra) v Crown Prosecution Service* [2013] 1 All ER 612.

that the cumulative effect of a large number of minor offences could result in a substantial prison sentence, if it was proved that Hain had conspired to bring about each of the minor offences.

Bennion set about building his case. He went to South Africa to raise funds. While there he refused to have dinner with Prime Minister Vorster, because of Vorster's wartime record as a Nazi sympathizer. He also declined to set up a branch of Freedom under Law in South Africa, on the ground that South Africa was not a democracy.[17] Those actions were consistent with Bennion's insistence that although he opposed apartheid, he did not consider it relevant to the issue at stake in the case.

One important factual point of difference between Bennion and Hain concerned whether Hain's campaigners employed any violent means. Bennion alleged that in Hain's campaign, actions such as distributing tacks on playing surfaces and shining mirrors into players' eyes were commonplace. Hain countered that he was only ever involved in non-violent activities. Proof of violent methods used by Hain and his associates would have greatly assisted Bennion's case (as they would have been *ipso facto* unlawful), though it was not the decisive point, since obviously enough it was still possible to interfere unlawfully with sporting matches without the use of violence.

It was while compiling evidence against Hain that Bennion became most unwittingly stitched up. A journalist by the name of Gordon Winter came forward with a dossier on Hain's activities. The dossier included many photographs, and seemed to provide more than sufficient material for Bennion to secure a prosecution. Bennion was delighted – right up to the point when Winter entered the witness box. For the truth (not divulged until years later) was that Winter was actually an agent of the South African Bureau of State Security, known by the blunt acronym of BOSS. Winter's instructions initially had been to assist Bennion's prosecution, hence the compilation of the dossier. Just before he was due to give evidence, however, he received instructions to the opposite effect. Apparently BOSS had decided at the last minute to keep its powder dry, and wanted Hain let

---

[17]   See Derek Humphrey, 'Francis Bennion: the director of private prosecutions', *Sunday Times*, 3 September 1972.

off while it went after bigger targets, in particular Jeremy Thorpe MP (an outspoken opponent of apartheid). After Winter gave evidence, Hain's supporters congratulated him and expressed their relief that contrary to their suspicions he was not a BOSS agent after all...[18]

Bennion's case had therefore been severely undermined. It was further troubled by Hain's clever tactic part way through the trial of abandoning his representatives and acting in person. Anyone who has experienced litigants in person knows the tiresome delays that almost always result: irrelevant tangents being pursued, bad arguments being advanced and numerous pauses as the judge tries to explain legal concepts and procedure. But the move enabled Hain to play the victim card and present himself as a downtrodden moral campaigner being crushed by the system, or so Bennion saw it.[19] One former member of Hain's legal team, Geoffrey Robertson (later a Queen's Counsel and an eminent human rights lawyer), said that it had the double advantage of (i) sparing Hain from cross-examination, and (ii) leaving the jury (thanks to Hain's 'decent and earnest' testimony) distinctly bored.

After a trial lasting ten days, a conviction was only secured on one count relating to a Davis Cup tennis match, for which Hain was fined £200. The jury could not agree on the remaining counts. Technically, therefore, Bennion had secured a victory, in the form of the single conviction, but it was of the Pyrrhic variety. Ordinarily Hain would have been retried on the counts on which the jury had been unable to agree (as distinct from any on which he had been formally acquitted), but Bennion did not have the money or the energy for a second round. Not long after the trial, he separated from his wife and was compelled to move from a large house in Surrey to somewhat more modest accommodation. The Jamaican government ended its contract with him, and he went back to work in the Parliamentary Counsel office. He was, however, made a member of MCC in recognition of his attempts to promote cricket, and he went on to become a respected legal author.[20]

[18]   See Gordon Winter, *Inside BOSS: South Africa's Secret Police* (Penguin, 1981), ch 27.
[19]   '1972 Peter Hain Trial', op cit.
[20]   Bennion's collected works – and a good deal of material relating to the Hain

Hain appealed unsuccessfully against his conviction, the Court of Appeal stating that it had been "fully justified". Thereafter, he continued to be bothered by BOSS in one form or another, before setting out on his mainstream political career, which began in earnest in 1991 when he was first elected to Parliament. Among other things, he went on to serve as Secretary of State for Northern Ireland.

In retrospect

Looking back in 2005, Hain was in no doubt about whom history had judged the winner:

> I am proud I took part in those events. Perhaps one of the most significant things I did in my political career, in stopping those sports tours because, as Nelson Mandela told me when he got out of prison, they were decisive blows against apartheid. He thought perhaps the most decisive ...

> I just look back at it and I think he [Bennion] was absolutely wrong. I think that when you look back at what happened, and the miracle of South Africa's transformation, he was on the wrong side of the argument, and without being arrogant about it, I was on the right side of the argument and history has been the judge of that.[21]

Bennion was similarly intransigent, though less triumphalist:

> The way a civilized society conducts itself is by reasoned debate and decision on whether to change the law, and until the law is changed in that way you do not allow crude force to have its effect. That is a defeat for democracy ... It seemed right to me at the time. Now it seems an act of folly, but I can't say I regret it because I still think it was right. I still have very strong views about the rule of law and direct action.[22]

It was also put to Bennion that he might have inadvertently started Hain's political career, by 'putting him on the map' with all

---

prosecution – are set out in his website, www.francisbennion.com (retrieved 17 April 2014). These include extracts from Winter, op cit and also an interesting book, Derek Humphry, *The Cricket Conspiracy* (National Council for Civil Liberties, 1975).

[21] '1972 Peter Hain Trial', op cit.

[22] Ibid.

the publicity surrounding the case. He responded: 'I wouldn't like to leave this interesting conversation with that thought in my mind.'[23]

Right or wrong?

The interesting point about the case is that the popular view would be that Hain was right to oppose sporting relations with South Africa, but on the other hand Bennion's position about protests being confined to lawful means was more intellectually sound, at least in the abstract. As to whether the jury reached the right result in the case, nothing is offered here, since I did not sit through the trial and review all the evidence. Instead, I will consider the matter as one of general principle.

The issue of whether direct action (breaking the law to prevent or compel something) is ever morally justifiable is certainly not confined to cricket, or sport in general for that matter.[24] Some of the more emotive issues where it has arisen include abortion, testing of drugs and medical procedures on animals, fox-hunting, GM crops, and the building of new coal-fired power stations.[25]

There are two basic objections to unlawful protests. The first is that most issues are not as clear cut as protestors might like to think. Those who try and shut down power stations to prevent carbon emissions, for example, often reveal themselves not to be experts on the extremely complex subject of climate change – and, more to the point, rarely factor in the external costs of their actions (for the avoidance of doubt, I am expressing no opinion on the matter, merely highlighting some of the competing arguments). And there were certainly cogent

[23]   Ibid.
[24]   The literature on the subject is voluminous, to put it mildly. Some of the more interesting pieces I found in the course of researching this book included the BBC *Moral Maze* episode 'Protest by Any Means?'.
[25]   By way of another example, the group PETA (People for the Ethical Treatment of Animals) wrote to the ICC asking for a ban on leather balls, in advance of the 2015 World Cup. They argued that cows endured unnecessary suffering when being slaughtered for leather, and that chemicals used in the tanning process poisoned the water supply. PETA's views were delivered in a lawful fashion. But suppose some of their members developed a taste for extreme protest, formed a splinter group, and tried to disrupt matches along the same lines as Bennion alleged Hain and his supporters had done?

arguments in both directions on fox-hunting. Ultimately, the point is who, other than the lawful authorities, is supposed to decide who is right in all of these debates?

That leads to the second objection, which is that it is normally not necessary to break the law to register one's views in a free society. Bennion put it in these terms:

> Hain's direct action campaigns were conducted in Britain on the pretext that minority rights were threatened. In an enlightened democracy such as Britain, where justice and tolerance flourish, there can be few genuine instances of the oppression of a minority. Disagreement must never be mistaken for oppression; for disagreement is a distinguishing feature of free human societies. Where in a democracy the majority does seek to oppress a minority the latter are morally, if not legally, entitled to resist. However to be in conflict with the established order is not necessarily to be an agent of enlightenment ... In a democracy, a minority is not entitled to use illegal force where no force is used against it. To use such force in the promotion of a private opinion related to affairs in a distant country is tyrannous. The fact that the opinion is altruistic compounds the tyranny by making it plausible to the unthinking ...
>
> Freedom under democratic law is inviolate. Unlawful force deployed to advance an opinion is to be rejected. The place to advance an opinion is the assembly.[26]

It is true that having the law changed can be an arduous and expensive process. Moreover, the line between lawful and unlawful protests can also be unclear, as any number of cases can attest.[27]

---

[26]   Francis Bennion, 'The Old Bailey Conviction of Peter Hain' (2002), unpublished, available at www.francisbennion.com/pdfs/fb/2002/2002-008-hain-prosecution.pdf (retrieved 17 April 2014).

[27]   See for example those concerning the late Brian Haw's encampment in Parliament Square. Haw lived in his encampment for several years protesting about various causes including the Iraq war, and became well known to the courts due to the various attempts to get rid of his protest, including *R (on the application of Haw) v Secretary of State for the Home Department and another* [2006] 3 All ER 428; *DPP v Haw* [2008] 1 WLR 379; and *Mayor of London v Haw and others* [2011] All ER (D) 194 (Mar). Other well-known examples are the 'May Day' protest cases such as *Austin v United Kingdom* [2012] Crim LR 544, or the 'student fees' protest cases such as *R v Gilmour* [2011] EWCA Crim 2458.

But the problem is that once illegal activity is permitted – because the authorities decline to act due to political expediency, or because politically-minded juries decline to convict, or for any other reason – then there is no limit to the number or the extent of illegal actions which might take place. Even the worst terrorist atrocities are usually accompanied by various apologias in which the perpetrators or their supporters try and portray themselves as glorified political protestors.

Hain said in 2005 that were he 30 years younger, he would have been tempted to launch some more direct-action protests against cricket contact with Zimbabwe, on the basis of the Mugabe regime's abominations. While there is no question that apartheid should have been opposed at every turn, as should Mugabe's regime in the present day, there should be no need in free countries to break the law to register one's opinion and compel the authorities to act against rogue regimes elsewhere. It was certainly possible in the United Kingdom in 1970 to register protests in a variety of forceful fashions within the law, as indeed many did. The verdict on Hain's actions is accordingly that he helped achieve the right result for the right cause, but perhaps on occasion by using the wrong methods.

AFTERMATH

The D'Oliveira affair and Hain's prosecution took place during some interesting political times. Nineteen sixty-eight was also the year of Enoch Powell's 'Rivers of Blood' speech on immigration (whose critics included Alec Douglas-Home), a new Race Relations Act (which Powell opposed in his speech), Martin Luther King's assassination (and hence the height of the US Civil Rights movement), the Tet offensive in the Vietnam War, the Paris riots and the Prague Spring, to name just a few events which brought to public attention race relations, immigration and foreign affairs. So it is not surprising that cricket followers increasingly started to feel that the apartheid regime in South Africa could no longer be ignored.

The D'Oliveira affair and the voices of political agitators such as Peter Hain put paid to the scheduled tour of England by South Africa in 1970. The tour was replaced by a series between England and a Rest of the World XI (a team which included some South Africans).

Australia did go to South Africa in 1970, but shortly afterwards South Africa's cricketing purdah began.

In Australia's case the decision to cease sporting relations with South Africa was made partly on the basis of Sir Donald Bradman's actions as a member of the Australian Cricket Board, which had the added gravitas resulting from Bradman's unparalleled status in the game. Bradman had not opposed South African contact in his playing days, though no-one else had either.[28] When the issue came to prominence, following the D'Oliveira affair, Bradman decided in his usual thorough manner to go to South Africa to learn more about the situation. There he met John Vorster:

> Bradman asked questions in his direct way about why blacks were denied the chance to represent their country. Vorster suggested they were intellectually inferior and could not cope with cricket's intricacies. Bradman asked Vorster: 'Have you ever heard of Garry Sobers?'

> Vorster's racist attitudes – Bradman thought them 'ignorant and repugnant' – contributed to his change of mind .... Bradman flew to Britain to meet Harold Wilson and Ted Heath, British political leaders who had dealt with the protest problem in England. Bradman returned to Australia with his mind made up. He reached agreement with Cricket Board fellow members, called a media conference and announced the tour's cancellation. Bradman made a simple one-line statement: 'We will not play them [South Africa] until they choose a team on a non-racist basis.'[29]

In 1971 the Commonwealth Heads of Government made the Singapore Declaration, which set out founding principles for Commonwealth membership. The principles included a specific denunciation of racial discrimination.

In spite of the end of official relations, several tours took place involving top cricketers supposedly playing in an individual capacity.

---

[28] Strictly speaking apartheid was introduced in 1948, the year of Bradman's retirement, but its precursors were in place during his career.

[29] Roland Perry, 'The day apartheid was hit for six', *Sydney Morning Herald*, 23 August 2008. Perry was the author of a Bradman biography and his article was published on the 100th anniversary of Bradman's birth.

Four were organized by a wealthy former county cricketer, Derrick Robins. The tours attracted some mutterings but nothing like the protests which official tours might have done, and no disciplinary measures were taken against the players involved. The tours dried up after the Soweto uprising and associated incidents in 1976, which also led to the informal sporting boycott being set out in writing the following year in the form of the Gleneagles agreement.

By the Gleneagles agreement, the Commonwealth nations reiterated that they would not play matches against sides from apartheid nations. The signatories to the document stated that they 'accepted it as the urgent duty of each of their Governments vigorously to combat the evil of apartheid by withholding any form of support for, and by taking every practical step to discourage contact or competition by their nationals with sporting organisations, teams or sportsmen from South Africa or from any other country where sports are organised on the basis of race, colour or ethnic origin.'

It is right to acknowledge that in those days, international treaties (and public international law generally) were viewed rather more cynically than at present; an old saying was that they were disagreements reduced to writing. The Gleneagles agreement was therefore not expected to have force in the domestic law of individual countries. As a result, although no official test cricket sides played South Africa after the Australian series of 1970, rugby union was able to maintain official contacts for much longer, amid substantial controversy.[30]

Two interesting legal challenges were mounted in New Zealand against planned rugby matches with South Africa. In advance of the 1981 Springbok tour to New Zealand, an application was lodged in the High Court objecting to the decision of the Minister for Immigration

---

[30] The 1974 Lions tour to South Africa gave rise to an interesting legal side issue, with the infamous '99 call'. Expecting violent confrontations and biased refereeing, the Lions created a strategy whereby if the call '99' was made, every member of the team was expected to join the assault on the opposition, irrespective of where they happened to be on the field at the time. It would be difficult to maintain in response to a charge of criminal assault that the implied consent to physical contact that rugby necessarily entails extended to being on the receiving end of unprovoked 99-induced punches.

to grant visas to the Springbok players. It was argued that the minister would be in breach of international obligations in doing so. The case[31] failed because the court applied the then-orthodox rule that it was not incumbent on the minister to act in accordance with the international obligations. The 1981 tour thus went ahead, and gave rise to some of the worst civil disturbances in New Zealand's history. A few years later, a successful legal challenge[32] was made to the intended 1986 All Black tour of South Africa. On that occasion the plaintiff sued the Rugby Union, arguing that the tour would breach the union's own rules, which among other things required the union to promote rugby in New Zealand and act for the benefit of the sport. The plaintiff's case was that the image of the game would be considerably damaged by the tour.[33]

It is a moot point whether any similar challenge would have succeeded in cricket had any official tour been attempted at the same time. I suspect it would not have done so in England at least, because the courts would have regarded the cricketing authorities as a private organization which, in the absence of formal economic sanctions, was as entitled to trade with South Africa as other businesses were at the time. Instead, rebel cricket tours were undertaken by English, Australian, Sri Lankan and West Indian teams. The authorities in each country reacted by imposing bans on the players, three years in the case of the English and Australian teams, 25 years for the Sri Lankans and lifetime bans for the West Indians.

Kim Hughes brought a successful challenge[34] in the Australian courts against his ban from club cricket, on the ground that it amounted to an unlawful restraint of trade. The judge stated that the ban went 'beyond a restraint reasonably related to the objects of the

---

[31] *Ashby v Minister of Immigration* [1981] 1 NZLR 222. Subsequently the New Zealand Court of Appeal appeared to 'jump ship', by taking a more inclusive view of international treaties, in *Tavita v Minister of Immigration* [1994] 2 NZLR 257.

[32] *Finnigan v New Zealand Rugby Football Union Inc* [1985] 2 NZLR 159.

[33] A rebel 'cavaliers' tour took place instead, amid much controversy. Light bans were implemented by the Rugby Union.

[34] *Hughes v Western Australian Cricket Association Inc* (1986) 69 ALR 660. The English ban did not extend to domestic cricket, though the Sri Lankan one did, while the West Indian players were banned not just from cricket but in many cases from their home islands, *de facto* if not *de jure*.

Cricket Council and those who comprise its membership ... That consideration is reinforced by reference to the public interest which lies, I think, in having every opportunity to see first class cricketers in action.'

England had to cancel a tour of India towards the end of the 1980s because of the presence of a number of players from the first rebel tour (the planned series was before the second English rebel tour). Just as in D'Oliveira's case, the TCCB maintained that it could not have another country influence its selection choices. Pakistan objected to England's attempt to organize an alternative series (even though at the time they were playing in Australia against at least one former rebel, Terry Alderman). The TCCB then decided to avoid further trouble by announcing that in future anyone having sporting contact with South Africa would be ineligible for national selection. Graham Wright, then editor of *Wisden*, doubted the wisdom of that last move: 'It can be argued that a freedom which allows trade with an unjust society is not so valuable a freedom. None the less it is a freedom within British law. If it is expedient to accept restrictions on legal freedoms, how simple it will be to restrict freedom legally.'[35]

In January 1989, the ICC formalized the situation by issuing a resolution of its own providing that no-one who had had sporting contact as an adult with South Africa would be eligible for national selection for any country. Jack Bailey complained in *Wisden* that 'within a few months of its 80th birthday, ICC for the first time in its history admitted to its constitution a rule which made political considerations part of the process of qualification by which individuals would be eligible to play cricket in their country'.[36] Not that Bailey was unaware that political considerations had long been *de facto* part of the process...

Once South Africa was readmitted to the fold, the extant bans on English cricketers were lifted, a decision which seems contrary to the rule of law. If it was wrong to tour South Africa at the time they did it then the original punishment should have stood, regardless of what changed in South Africa afterwards. It was not a situation such

---

[35]   *Wisden* 1989, pp 48–9.
[36]   *Wisden* 1990, pp 51–2.

as the homosexual law reform legislation, where social attitudes had changed towards the relevant conduct. In those circumstances, the consensus was that no-one should ever have been convicted in the first place. With the South African bans, by contrast, the rationale was that it was wrong to play with apartheid South Africa. It became acceptable to play South Africa when apartheid was removed from cricket. That did not change the validity of the original punishment, unless it was thought that the rebel tours were somehow a good thing in retrospect. One could make a case for the West Indian rebel tours being an engine of change in South Africa,[37] but not the English ones, whose participants, it can be assumed, were in it purely for the money.

Happier endings

One may record three happy outcomes to the D'Oliveira saga. First, it acted as the catalyst for the reforms – which admittedly took more than two decades to come to fruition – to South African cricket, which was declared non-racial before apartheid itself had fallen. Much of the pressure to reform from within came from Dr Ali Bacher, who had been scheduled to captain South Africa in the aborted tour all those years ago. Though it would be going too far to suggest it was a decisive factor, it is generally accepted that sport has always been central to the South African way of life, and thus sporting boycotts had more effect than they might have done with some other oppressive regimes.

Secondly, D'Oliveira came to be recognized throughout the cricketing world for the honourable and dignified individual that he was. He was still alive when South Africa hosted the World Cup in 2003. He was invited along with Graeme Pollock to lead the teams out in the opening ceremony at what should have been his home ground of Newlands Park. Pollock graciously and correctly invited D'Oliveira to go in front.

---

[37]   See for example Daniel Schofield, 'Franklyn Stephenson argues that rebel West Indian tours helped to end apartheid in South Africa', *The Times*, 21 March 2013. The point is that black West Indian players competing with white South Africans on level terms in otherwise whites-only grounds demonstrated to all South Africans the folly of apartheid. The Sri Lankans also should be mentioned in this context, although their players were no match for the South Africans of the day.

Finally, in a rare moment of great sagacity, the English and South African authorities agreed that the trophy for test matches between their two countries should be known as the Basil D'Oliveira Trophy. Most bilateral cricketing trophies are named after great players from the respective nations, such as the Border–Gavaskar Trophy between Australia and India, or the Chappell–Hadlee Trophy between Australia and New Zealand. Without diminishing the cricketing significance of those great names, it should be obvious that the D'Oliveira Trophy has meaning far beyond anything that occurs over 22 yards with a bat and ball.

Chapter 8

THE REVOLUTIONARY:
MR PACKER GOES TO THE HIGH COURT

THE BACKGROUND

The story of Kerry Packer's dispute with cricket's governing bodies in Australia and abroad is one of the most dramatic off-field battles in cricketing history. It has been the subject of many books and, in recent times, a television miniseries.[1] For lawyers it is of especial interest since one of the important chapters was played out in the High Court in London. The saga led to a number of aspects of international cricket being changed forever.

In the mid-1970s, Kerry Packer was a young businessman who had obtained the helm of a number of his late father's media interests, including the television station Channel 9. As a cricket lover, the younger Packer decided that he wanted the rights to cover test matches held in Australia. The Australian Cricket Board, whose ranks at the time included Sir Donald Bradman, was unimpressed, despite Packer offering far more money than the traditional broadcaster. One imagines that the men of the board's generation were not used to brash and presumptuous youngsters demanding to get their way just because of the size of their chequebook.

After they rebuffed Packer's offer, it seems likely the board thought they were rid of him for good. They would then have turned their minds to forthcoming fixtures including the Centenary Test in Melbourne, a one-off match between England and Australia to mark 100 years since the 1877 contest between James Lillywhite's XI and the Combined Australian XI which Ted Pooley had the ill-fortune to miss. The 1977 match was a hugely successful occasion, played in a great spirit in front of a capacity crowd. The highlights of the match

---

[1] *Howzat! Kerry Packer's War*, Channel 9 (2012). As this is a book partly about law, it is necessary to throw in some legal pedantry and point out that in the programme Mr Justice Slade, as well as obviously not sitting in the Royal Courts of Justice, is depicted with a gavel – something never used in English courts. He would not have delivered the judgment orally either, though that was the most common method in the 1970s and is still used in a number of cases today.

were probably Derek Randall's tremendously gallant but ultimately unsuccessful rearguard action, and his duel during the course of that innings with Dennis Lillee. The match concluded with the remarkable outcome that the same team won by the same margin – Australia by 45 runs – as the 1877 match it was held to celebrate. The Australian team then set off for England in what would have seemed to outsiders a buoyant mood.

One can imagine therefore the shock which would have hit the Australian board – and all other cricket authorities for that matter – a few days into the tour, when they discovered what Packer had been up to since they last saw him.[2] He had taken his chequebook away from them and waved it directly under the noses of the players instead. He was proposing to set up his own rival competition, to be called World Series Cricket (WSC). By the time the news broke he had managed to secure no fewer than 34 leading international players. Possibly the greatest shock of all was when his chief recruiting officer turned out to be none other than the incumbent England captain, Tony Greig, who it transpired had been hard at work behind the scenes of the Centenary Test winning other players over to the cause. Also prominent among the players was Dennis Lillee, whose manager, John Cornell, had been partly responsible for the whole affair when he approached Packer with the idea of non-traditional exhibition cricket matches being organized at the end of the season.[3]

The immediate response of the governing body of English cricket at the time, the TCCB, was to decide that all players contracted to Packer would be banned from county cricket. The ICC followed suit at the international level. The effect of both proposed bans would be

---

[2] The story was broken by two Australian journalists, who had attended a party for both teams given by Tony Greig at his Sussex home. It seems quite extraordinary that everyone involved had stayed silent for so long, only for tongues to be loosened by a dash of *in vino veritas*. See Christopher Lee, *Howzat! Kerry Packer and the Great Cricket War* (Old Street, 2013), Kindle location 426ff. It is right to record that Ian Chappell later scoffed at the shock the board claimed to have suffered, reasoning that they had had fair warning of rebel competitions: see *Flying Stumps and Metal Bats: Cricket's Greatest Moments by the People Who Were There* (Aurum, 2008), p 242.

[3] Cornell's motivation was his belief that players of Lillee's calibre were seriously undervalued by the traditional authorities. Their subsequent conversation led to the idea for WSC, and Cornell played a leading part in the organization.

to limit players' earning potential significantly. For most players it would be career-ending, given that no-one would have known how long the gift of Packer's cash would keep on giving, and English county cricket was one of the few places for professional cricketers to earn a living.

Packer flew to London to negotiate a truce. He was prepared to concede virtually everything in exchange for the rights to broadcast Australian matches, but found that the ICC was prepared to concede nothing. Packer therefore packed up and left, announcing on his way out that it was every man for himself and the Devil take the hindmost.

The litigation

To counter the playing ban, Packer's recruits (with his backing) issued proceedings in the Chancery Division in London. Packer's approach to choosing his advisers mirrored his cricketing strategy: hire the best, with money no object. His leading barrister was Robert Alexander QC (later Lord Alexander), described by Lord Denning as the best advocate of his generation.

Two separate actions were filed, which were heard together. The first action was brought on behalf of the players, with Tony Greig and two other players chosen as representative plaintiffs. The defendants were the chairman and the secretary of the TCCB, who were sued on behalf of all members of the TCCB; and the chairman and the secretary of the ICC, who were sued on behalf of all members of the ICC. The chairman of the TCCB at the time was Doug Insole, who probably thought he had experienced enough controversy already, given that he had been chief selector at the time of the D'Oliveira affair.

The players sought a declaration from the court that the changes of rules by the ICC and the proposed changes of rules by the TCCB were *ultra vires* and an unlawful restraint of trade. They argued further, or in the alternative, that the rule changes were void on the ground that they denied the players the 'right to work', in other words the freedom to practise their profession when, where and how they pleased. In the second action, WSC itself issued proceedings against the same defendants, seeking a declaration that the proposed rule changes (i) were *ultra vires* on the same grounds advanced by the players, and (ii) constituted an unlawful inducement to the players contracted to WSC to break those contracts.

The TCCB and the ICC resisted all of the applications. As well as denying that their respective actions were *ultra vires*, they argued that the WSC agreements with the players were themselves inducements to breach of contract with their own agreements. Both the TCCB and the ICC also mounted a technical defence, contending that they were an 'employers' association' within s 28(2)(b) of the Trade Union and Labour Relations Act 1974, part of the complex labour legislation passed during the decade of some of Britain's worst industrial unrest. If they were able to bring themselves within the definition of 'employers' association' they could claim statutory immunity from any action in tort.

Section 28(2) defined 'employers' association' as

an organisation (whether permanent or temporary) which either – (a) consists wholly or mainly of employers ... of one or more descriptions and is an organisation whose principal purposes include the regulation of relations between employers of that description or those descriptions and workers ... or (b) consists wholly or mainly of – (i) constituent or affiliated organisations which fulfil the conditions specified in paragraph (a) above...

The case was heard by Mr Justice Slade over three months in the second half of 1977. Not surprisingly he reserved judgment rather than delivering it at the conclusion of the hearing.

The decision

Slade J's judgment[4] was an emphatic victory for Packer and the players. He held that both the players and WSC itself were entitled to declarations that the changes of the rules of the ICC and the new or proposed new rules of the TCCB were *ultra vires* and void as being in unreasonable restraint of trade.

WSC was entitled to a declaration that the changes of the rules of the ICC and all the resolutions of the ICC referred to and set out

---

[4] The decision is reported as *Greig v Insole; World Series Cricket Pty Ltd v Insole* [1978] 3 All ER 449.

in the ICC's accompanying press statement constituted an unlawful inducement to the players contracted to WSC to break those contracts. The proposed rule changes of the TCCB also amounted to an unlawful inducement to the players contracted to WSC to break those contracts. The contracts made between WSC and its players were not void on the ground of public policy as being in unreasonable restraint of trade or any other grounds, because there was an obligation on World Series Cricket to promote each year a tour for the contracted players in Australia. If necessary, such a term would be implied in the contracts for the purpose of giving them business efficacy. The ICC and TCCB could not, therefore, rely on the defence that it was not a tort to induce the breach or termination of a void contract.

The attempt by the TCCB and the ICC to hide behind the statutory immunity conferred by the 1974 Act failed, because neither was an employers' association. Under its rules the members of the ICC were the member countries themselves rather than their governing bodies for cricket. In any event, neither the member countries nor their governing bodies had been shown to be employers of cricketers. The ICC had thus failed to show that it was an organization which consisted 'wholly or mainly of employers' within s 28(2)(a) of the 1974 Act. As for the TCCB, although it was an organization which consisted 'wholly or mainly of employers' it also was not an employers' association within s 28(2) because its principal purposes did not include 'the regulation of relations between employers … and workers', within s 28(2)(a). For an association to have power to regulate relations between employers and workers it had to be responsible to the members who had associated themselves for such purposes. The TCCB was responsible not to its members (the MCC and the first-class county clubs) but to the Cricket Council in the exercise of its functions.

A parting shot

Slade J finished with the following observations:

> Counsel, in his opening speech for the defendants, generously but correctly, acknowledged five positive beneficial effects which, on the evidence, have already been produced by the emergence of World Series Cricket as a promoter of cricket. First, as he said, it has offered the promise of much greater rewards for star cricketers. Indeed, it

has gone further than this; it has offered secure, regular remunerative employment in cricket to more than 50 cricketers, in most cases for three English winter seasons, at a time when most of them would otherwise have had no guarantee of regular employment in the game. Secondly, it has already stimulated new sponsors for traditional cricket. Thirdly, it has brought back to the game in Australia several talented players. Fourthly, it, or the group of companies of which it forms part, has initiated a useful coaching scheme for young players in New South Wales. Fifthly, it has increased public interest in the game.

For all these acknowledged benefits, the defendants have held the strong opinion that the effective monopoly of the ICC in the promotion of first-class cricket at international level has been good for the game and that the emergence of World Series Cricket into the promotion field is bad for it. However, whether or not this opinion is correct has not been the question for this court. The question for decision has been whether the particular steps which the ICC and the TCCB took to combat what they regarded as the threat from World Series Cricket were legally justified. This long investigation has satisfied me that the positive demonstrable benefits that might be achieved by introducing the ICC and TCCB bans and applying them to players who had already committed themselves to contracts with World Series Cricket were at best speculative. On the other hand there were, as has been mentioned, a number of demonstrable disadvantages if the bans were to be applied in this way. They would preclude the players concerned from entry into important fields of professional livelihood. They would subject them to the hardships and injustices of essentially retrospective legislation. They would deprive the public of any opportunity of seeing the players concerned playing in conventional cricket, either at test or at English county level, for at least a number of years. By so depriving the public, they would carry with them an appreciable risk of diminishing both public enthusiasm for conventional cricket and the receipts to be derived from it. Furthermore, the defendants by imposing the bans, in the form which they took and with the intentions which prompted them, acted without adequate regard to the fact that World Series Cricket had contractual rights with the players concerned, which were entitled to the protection of the law. The defendants acted in good faith and in what they considered to be the best interests of cricket. That, however, is not enough to justify in law the course which they have taken.

It is not terribly surprising that the defendants thought that their stranglehold on the game was a good thing. It calls to mind the late Screaming Lord Sutch's question as to why there was only one Monopolies Commission. At all events, Packer had won a resounding victory in both actions and, once it was known that the defendants did not intend to appeal, he was free to proceed with his rebel competition. There were some legal wrinkles with individual players. Jeff Thomson and Alvin Kallicharran, senior players for Australia and West Indies respectively, had signed contracts with a Queensland radio station that required them to play for the state. As a result both pulled out of their WSC contracts and assumed leading roles for the patchwork official teams that the authorities fielded for the traditional matches which ran more or less in parallel with WSC. Thomson was later able to play for WSC after some renegotiation.

The matches and the truce

Although they had lost the main part of the cases before Slade J, the traditionalists had won a series of minor victories which became thorns in Packer's side. The Australian board was able to exclude Packer from the traditional cricket grounds and to prevent him from calling his contests 'test matches'. Packer countered the former by hiring rugby and other stadia and dropping in prepared pitches. He offset the latter by many innovations that have long since become an established part of the game: coloured clothing for limited-overs matches; multiple cameras at the ground; day/night matches; and in general the sort of snappy coverage that distinguishes television of the present day from that of the 1970s and before.

Some gravitas was added to the WSC contests not only by the presence of many of the best players of the day but also the likes of Richie Benaud as a commentator and organizer. Benaud was joined in the former capacity by Greig and in the latter by perhaps the greatest post-war cricketer of all, Sir Garfield Sobers. The sight of all three would have dispelled any suspicion on the part of the traditional authorities that they were facing only a maverick businessman with no cricketing credibility. Both Benaud and Greig would go on to become part of a team of commentators whose voices became among the most recognizable in any sport (the publicity from the Australian comedian and voice mimic Billy Birmingham's matchless imitations will have done no harm in this respect, at least if one takes Birmingham's word for it).

It is generally considered that the standard of WSC cricket was high, with the players deriving extra motivation not just from the money but from the career risk they were taking. Despite a slow start with the public, as more and more established players went to WSC the matches started to upstage the traditional contests (which had continued in direct competition with WSC). Packer was therefore winning the ultimate battle for the public's interest. After three seasons, a compromise was reached with the Australian Cricket Board (and with it the rest of the cricketing community, since Packer was only ever interested in the rights to broadcast matches in Australia). The terms involved Packer being granted a considerably better deal than he had asked for originally, and a continuing say in the domestic schedule in Australia. The settlement did not result in the WSC matches being granted the status of test matches, and despite the occasional mention by the players involved there has never been a suggestion on the authorities' part that the matches should be elevated in status retrospectively.

The legal legacy

Slade J's decision was not of great legal significance, because it did not deal with novel points or set out a new principle of law, but one of his observations about inducement to breach of contract was considered in *Proform Sports Management Ltd v Proactive Sports Management Ltd and another*.[5] The case concerned the contractual machinations of the well-known footballer Wayne Rooney. Rooney's contract was unusual because he was only a minor when it was signed. In essence, the judge in *Proform* said he agreed with Slade J's assumption that it was not a tort for a third party to induce a person to exercise a lawful right to rescind a contract. It followed that it was also not a tort to procure the breach of a voidable contract, at least where the person induced was the person who enjoyed the right to rescind. Moreover, the inability of the traditional authorities to stop the matches going ahead (as well as Packer's overall victory) would certainly have been

---

[5]   [2007] 1 All ER 542.

drawn to the attention of their modern counterparts when the different 20/20 tournaments started in the twenty-first century.

The verdict

Despite considerable opposition at the time,[6] most writing on the affair in recent years has been favourable to Packer,[7] chiefly for three reasons: (i) the traditional authorities of the day were a consignment of reactionary conservatives, with a hopeless lack of imagination; (ii) players were woefully underpaid; (iii) Packer's innovations were not just desirable but necessary to make the game more enjoyable and better suited to television.

Certainly the authorities fatally underestimated Packer, and can properly be called naïve in that respect. Moreover, major changes would have been inevitable to cricket whether Packer came along or not, if one considers how every other sport has changed in the past 30 years or so. Even Bradman later admitted that increased commercialization of cricket had been necessary and even desirable.[8] It follows that if cricket had not been changed by Packer, it would have had to have been changed by someone else, and the somewhat desiccated boards were unlikely candidates for changing anything. Alternatively, the game might have died a slow death as both players and spectators turned to more dynamic and better-funded alternative offerings.

Claims that the players were underpaid look valid now, but should also be seen in the light of professional sport generally in the 1970s. Greg Chappell, Australian captain at the time of Packer, had remarked in his autobiography just before the saga broke about how much conditions for players had improved – not that that stopped him joining Packer and trumpeting the parsimony of the *ancien régime* as justification. Afterwards Chappell was none too pleased with the

---

[6]   Much of this is set out in Richard Cashman, 'The Packer Cricket War', in Anthony Bateman and Jeffrey Hill (eds), *The Cambridge Companion to Cricket* (Cambridge University Press, 2011), p 100.

[7]   There are countless statements to this effect, easily found on the major cricketing websites and in the books already cited to this point, but see for example the interview with Bill Lawry shortly after Tony Greig's death, available at www.youtube.com/watch?v=wXO3ovKFif4 (retrieved 17 April 2014).

[8]   Sir Donald Bradman, 'Whither Cricket Now?', *Wisden* 1986.

greatly inflated playing schedule imposed as part of the Packer truce, as will be seen later with the underarm incident.

As mentioned, Packer's broadcasting innovations have long become a settled part of the game, and have been developed further in parallel with general advances in technology. Robert Alexander QC later became president of MCC, an appointment which has occasionally been cited[9] as evidence of how quickly the revolution became normality. This is not much of a point, however, as barristers are wholly independent from their clients: they are not permitted to take a case if they have any financial or other personal interest in it beyond getting paid their professional fees. (Otherwise, I expect criminal lawyers would not have many friends in wider society.)

Interestingly, nearly two decades after Packer an even more damaging civil war was fought in Australia over the sport of rugby league. On that occasion the rebels were led by Packer's great media rival, Rupert Murdoch, who sought to grab control of the broadcasting of the domestic Australian Rugby League club competition. It is hard to imagine that Murdoch was not emboldened by Packer's earlier success. Murdoch lost the first round of resultant litigation with the traditional rugby league authorities[10] but won on appeal,[11] though he was somewhat less successful overall with his planned revolution for the sport than Packer had been with cricket.[12]

---

[9] Michael Henderson, 'It's not cricket? W G Grace would disagree', *Daily Telegraph*, 19 April 2008.

[10] *News Limited v Australian Rugby Football League Limited and New South Wales Rugby League Limited and Others* No. NG 197 of 1995 FED No. 72/96.

[11] *News Limited and Others v Australian Rugby Football League Ltd and Others*; *Brisbane Broncos Rugby League Football Club Ltd and Others v Australian Rugby Football League Ltd and Others*; *Cowboys Rugby League Ltd v the Australian Rugby Football Club Ltd and Others* (1996) 870 FCA 1 (4 October 1996).

[12] It would be difficult to argue that rugby league benefited significantly from Murdoch's attempt to gain control of broadcasting matches. His stated aim of a globalised sport did not really come to anything much, and the present Australian domestic competition is not radically different in any respect from before. In fact, one could make a case that the threat posed by Super League played a part in forcing rugby union to go professional around the same time. As well as making union a greater commercial threat generally, professionalism meant that players could be enticed for the first time to change codes in the other direction (from league to union) – not exactly a positive outcome for league...

Finally, whatever one's view of WSC or its legacy, one thing is for certain: had he lost the court action in 1977, Packer would have been run out without facing a ball.

Chapter 9

THE LIBELS, PART I: THE PLAYERS

Introduction to libel

In *Othello* Cassio despairs: 'Reputation, reputation, reputation! O, I have lost my reputation! I have lost the immortal part of myself, and what remains is bestial. My reputation, Iago, my reputation!' It is the preservation of reputation that is the basis of the long-standing cause of action of libel.

The classic definition of libel in English law was set out by Lord Atkin in 1936, in *Sim v Stretch*: '[The question is] would the words tend to lower the plaintiff in the estimation of right-thinking members of society generally?'[1] There has been the occasional coat of varnish applied to Lord Atkin's wording in subsequent cases over the years, but it remains the basis of any libel suit. Much libel litigation – often heard at a preliminary stage – concerns the meaning of the disputed words and whether they would satisfy Lord Atkin's test. The defendant might dispute that the words at issue would be interpreted pejoratively. Or the defendant might assert that, although the words would technically mean something libellous, no reader would take them seriously because of the context.

If it is established that the impugned words do satisfy Lord Atkin's test, there are still a number of possible defences. It might be argued that the words were subject to privilege. Anything said in Parliament, for example, cannot be the subject of litigation even if it was outrageously slanderous. It might be argued that the words were mere opinion, not statement of fact. More colourfully, it might be argued that the plaintiff had no reputation worth preserving: a serial killer wrongly accused of a particular murder would likely have no case in libel because he would have no good name to protect (at most he might get a libel verdict in his favour, but only receive nominal damages, as a way of the court showing its opinion of his action).

Two of the more common defences to libel are 'justification' and 'fair comment'. In the former case, the defendant essentially argues

---

[1]   [1936] 2 All ER 1237.

that the words complained of were true. In the case of fair comment, the impugned statements have to be comment rather than statements of fact, and must be honestly held.

Several of the different defences can be seen in the libel actions considered in this and the next three chapters. The first concerns a case brought by Sid Barnes, an outstanding cricketer but a troubled man, who sued someone for libel after he was left out of the team on non-cricketing grounds. Many players since Barnes must have wished they had a similar opportunity to put disobliging selectors or administrators in the witness box and have them torn to shreds by a brilliant barrister. But, as will also be seen, a victory in court could not rescue Barnes from his personal demons.

Barnes is followed by another great batsman, the West Indian Clive Lloyd. Lloyd brought a claim against an Australian newspaper in the early 1980s arising out of allegations about a limited-overs match in the World Series Cricket tournament, which was such a feature of the Australian domestic calendar in the early post-Packer days. Lloyd's action was a good example of how fine the line can be between what is and is not libellous. The Privy Council was adamant that it was, though with the greatest respect it seems to me that the opposing view was at least arguable.

The next chapter deals with probably the best known of all cricketing libel sagas, the two cases in the 1990s involving England, Pakistan and the ball-tampering allegations that have never really gone away. The first case was brought by the former Pakistani fast bowler Sarfraz Narwaz, and the second by the recently retired England stalwarts Ian Botham and Allan Lamb.

Critics of the legal system have often said that libel is a plaintiff's tort, in which all one has to do to win in practice is to issue a writ. Such criticism is not entirely without foundation, but in both Sarfraz's case and that of Botham and Lamb, it was the plaintiffs who ended up with an expensive defeat. As a result, they inadvertently proved a different adage about litigation in general, namely that it always ends in failure for someone.

Following the discussion of the ball-tampering libels, Chapter XI surveys the modern law on ball-tampering, to place the libel actions in context. Then in Chapter XII libel is considered again, with two cases involving Lalit Modi, the Svengali of the 20/20 revolution. In the first case, concerning fallout from negotiations over a possible English equivalent to the IPL, he was the claimant. In the second case he was the defendant in an action which serves as a legal landmark of sorts, because it was the first-ever libel case based on a tweet. The following section begins with another libel case brought by several England players over an article in *Wisden Cricket Monthly*. The case raised the general issue of players' eligibility for test cricket and is therefore included as part of a general discussion about nationality, eligibility and integration.

Sid Barnes: 'A good deed not a bad one'

By a curious coincidence, one of the lowest-ever test bowling averages is held by Syd Barnes of England, while one of the highest sub-Bradman test batting averages is held by Sid Barnes of Australia.[2] S F Barnes the English bowler knew a bit about controversy, usually where his expenses were concerned. S G Barnes the Australian batsman knew quite a bit more, and on one memorable occasion found himself in the New South Wales High Court as a result.

Early years

Much of Barnes's story reads like a classic Australian tale: a youngster overcoming a tough upbringing (his father died before he was born) to become a great sportsman, regularly sticking it to authority and the opposition in equal measure. Unfortunately, it is also a clichéd tale in other respects, with a combination of misfortune and his personal issues leaving him having played far fewer games than his talent deserved, and with his life ending in tragic circumstances.

Barnes ran into bad luck in England in 1938 on his first tour for Australia. He fractured his wrist on the voyage over and so missed the first half of the series. He was not selected for the test team until the final match at the Oval. He acquitted himself satisfactorily with the bat in what remains the worst defeat in test cricket history (England won by an innings and 579 runs), but then the Second World War

---

[2]   Taking a qualification of ten matches, Barnes at the time of writing was in third place behind Bradman (obviously) and Stuart Dempster of New Zealand.

intervened and ruled out all international cricket for the following six years. After the war Barnes played in the 1946 Ashes series, his personal highlight being a 405-run partnership with Bradman in the second test, where both scored 234.

The 1948 tour

Barnes managed to gain selection for the 1948 'Invincibles' tour, where he averaged 82 in the tests despite encountering a few difficulties on and off the pitch. He was injured when fielding in his customary extremely close-in position. During one of the tour matches a stray dog ran on the pitch. Barnes picked it up and offered it to the umpire, telling him all he needed was a white stick to go with it. He attracted controversy among his teammates because his wife was living in Scotland and was therefore more accessible than was usual on tour at the time. His off-field entrepreneurial activities also required him to leave the boat at a different Australian port to the rest of the team when they returned, so as not to engage the interest of customs officials.

The comeback

Barnes retired after the 1948 tour, and spent a couple of years writing deliberately controversial newspaper columns. In time, he found life away from test cricket rather unfulfilling. He attempted a comeback in the 1951/2 season, and played well enough to earn selection for the third test against West Indies. When the team sheet was passed by the selectors to the board of control, however, the latter vetoed him, exercising a hitherto unused power they had granted themselves after some player misbehaviour on the 1912 tour of England.[3]

The selectors responded by delaying naming a replacement, realizing the backlash that Barnes's omission was bound to cause (clearly they did not want to stop a bullet for the board). The story soon leaked to the press and garnered a fair share of headlines. Still the board would not budge. Barnes seemed powerless to do anything,

---

[3] Maybe the board should have been more bothered about selectors than players in those days: in January 1912 a fight occurred between Peter McAlister and Clem Hill during a meeting in Sydney to choose the touring side. It went on for about 20 minutes, after which Hill went back to his hotel room and the meeting resumed.

but then he was gifted a legal full toss in the form of a letter to a national newspaper by one Jacob Raith, a master baker by trade and therefore perhaps not the obvious choice for the last word on the board's predilections. Raith claimed that the board would never have excluded Barnes for capricious reasons, 'but only for some matter of a sufficiently serious nature'; in other words, since the board was composed of distinguished gentlemen Barnes had to be a *bona fide* troublemaker for them to have left him out. Barnes responded by bringing proceedings against Raith for libel.

The litigation

Though the claim would not give Barnes an actionable remedy against his real enemy of the board, it gave him a very effective way to attack its members, since Raith had to call them as witnesses to support his defence. Moreover, the board could be subpoenaed to produce written records that would otherwise have been confidential. Barnes instructed a leading barrister, Jack Shand KC, who spent the first day of trial mercilessly cross-examining the board members.

Keith Johnson, a board member who had been Barnes's manager on the 1948 tour, turned out to be the chief villain. He stated that he would not have included Barnes in the next match 'even if his average was 200'. He produced a litany of offences Barnes had supposedly committed on the 1948 tour. He claimed the worst offence was Barnes taking unauthorized pictures of the Royal Family, though it turned out that Barnes had had permission after all. He said that Barnes had twice applied for permission to travel apart from the team (to see his wife in Scotland). He further alleged that Barnes had broken some sort of rule by taking the twelfth man to play tennis at a court 300 yards from the cricket field (David Gower and his Tiger Moth[4] would presumably have threatened Johnson's sanity). He added that Barnes was 'unsuited temperamentally' to captain a side, even though he himself had been partly responsible for Barnes being chosen to captain New South Wales.

---

[4] Gower got himself in trouble with the management during the 1990/91 Ashes series, when he and another player hired a Tiger Moth and buzzed the ground where England were playing a tour match. The fact that Gower had been the leading run scorer on the tour to that point seemed to cut little ice.

There was one major problem. Johnson had written a report at the conclusion of the 1948 tour, circulated to all of the state cricketing authorities, stating that all the players had behaved impeccably. When confronted with the report's conclusion, Johnson protested that he had verbally complained about Barnes at the time. That was the legal equivalent of shouldering arms to a straight ball, and Shand duly knocked over all three stumps. Shand pointed out that since they were inconsistent, either the written report or the alleged verbal report had to be a lie. He demanded to know which was which. Johnson squirmed, but could not escape. By standing by his view of Barnes as the recalcitrant, he was forced meekly to concede that the written report had been misleading. His credibility was therefore left in tatters.

Shand also exposed the fact that the board members were not united: three of the twelve had actually supported Barnes. He ridiculed the majority nine's cricketing credentials and successfully depicted them as motivated by pettiness, spite and the sort of tedious pomposity that the average Australian jury might be expected to disdain.

One day of Shand's salvos was enough. Raith conceded the case early on the second day. His own barrister, J W Smyth KC, agreed a settlement in which Raith withdrew his allegations and paid all of Barnes's costs. Smyth told the court that 'all decent citizens' should feel contempt for the nine members of the board who had voted against Barnes. Shand then added an acerbic parting shot by stating that Raith, in withdrawing his criticism, had shown the sort of courage that was 'markedly absent elsewhere'. The judge observed that when all was said and done Raith had done Barnes 'a good deed instead of a bad one'.

Perhaps it was all too neat for Barnes. Had the whole thing been a stitch-up between him and Raith, so that Barnes could humiliate the board? Bradman thought so, calling it a 'put-up job' to get the board in front of the bench.[5] Barnes denied ever having met Raith, but little seems to be known of the latter and so the possibility cannot be eliminated entirely. Or perhaps it was a put-up job in the other direction, which had gone spectacularly wrong. The board had limited

---

[5]   See David Frith and Gideon Haigh, *Inside Story: Unlocking Australian Cricket's Archives* (News Custom, 2007), p 109.

chances to advance its case publicly – it was not the done thing for it to be issuing public explanations – and thus it is possible that it found a way for Raith to act as its proxy. Once again, however, that is nothing more than speculation.

No happy ending

Barnes said after the litigation: 'I am completely vindicated. I am very happy with the verdict in my favour, and I feel that my name, which was besmirched by the action of the Australian Board of Control, has been completely restored. I will be ready to play for Australia again, if selected, and, of course, approved as a good citizen by the Board of Control.' But there was not to be a happy ending. Barnes never did play for Australia again. Just a few weeks after the trial he felt compelled to act the fool in a Sheffield Shield match: he came on as twelfth man in a grey suit, offering not simply drinks but also cigars, a radio and some scented spray. Initially the crowd found it funny, but then became bored with the delay, and afterwards the administrators did not go along with the joke.

Barnes continued writing on cricket, including an autobiography,[6] but after a while his tone became perceived less as controversial and more as tedious whinging (he would not be the last ex-player to attract that charge). Then, as his behaviour became increasingly erratic, he was diagnosed with bipolar disorder. Reflecting a less sympathetic age, his treatment included not only drugs but also electroconvulsive therapy. It all became too much: at the end of 1973, aged only in his 50s, Barnes committed suicide.[7]

Sid Barnes left behind an extraordinary record in the few tests that he played, but also substantial regrets, in the form of his tragic end and the fact that through wartime, officialdom and his own personal difficulties, he never had the career his talent deserved.

---

[6]   Sid Barnes, *It Isn't Cricket* (William Kimber, 1953).

[7]   See David Frith, *Silence of the Heart: Cricket Suicides* (Mainstream, 2001). The *Australian Dictionary of Biography*, vol 13 (Melbourne University Press, 1993) states that Barnes died 'from barbiturate and bromide poisoning, self-administered; the coroner was unable to determine intent'.

'COME ON, DOLLAR, COME ON…'

At the start of the 1980s, Kerry Packer was firmly in charge of Australian cricket, having had much the better of the settlement agreement with the Australian Cricket Board, as seen earlier in the book. One of the terms he laid down was that the new domestic programme had to include substantially more one-day internationals. There was a simple reason: one-day matches drew bigger audiences, both at the gate and on television.

One early result of Packer's treadmill was the Australian captain, Greg Chappell, becoming fed up to the point where he resorted to the underarm ball. Another result was cynicism in various quarters that the game had become ruled by Mammon. One journalist wrote an article saying as much, which brought his publishers face to face across a courtroom with the man at the helm of the most formidable cricket team of the day.

The tournament

In the early 1980s, no team was a bigger draw card than West Indies, with their seemingly never-ending supply of intimidating fast bowlers and a phalanx of indomitable batsmen, led by the imposing and patrician figure of Clive Lloyd. All cricketing promoters, Kerry Packer foremost among them, were anxious to host them as often as possible. Packer was especially keen to have West Indies feature in Australia's annual three-team limited-overs World Series Cricket tournament.

The early versions of the World Series tournaments involved a preliminary round of fifteen matches, with the top two teams then playing a best-of-five finals series (later reduced to best of three, after even Packer accepted that overkill was possible in limited-overs cricket). West Indies won the inaugural event in the 1979/80 season. They returned to take part in the 1981/82 series along with Pakistan and the Australian hosts. Naturally the hope of the organizers was that the finals would be played between Australia and West Indies, and preferably run to all five possible matches.

The first phase of the tournament turned out to be quite competitive. West Indies were the first to qualify for the finals, and the other two teams were close enough for the last preliminary match to be the decider. The match was between West Indies and Australia. If West Indies won, Pakistan would join them in the finals. If they lost, Australia would do so instead. In the event, West Indies, missing Lloyd through illness, were all out for 189. Australia reached 168/7 in reply after 43 overs before the match was rained off, leaving them the winners on the basis of comparative run rates, the standard pre-Duckworth–Lewis method of resolving limited-overs matches foreshortened by rain. The promoters therefore had the result they wanted.

The article

In a stark illustration of the lower scoring rates prevalent in limited-overs matches at the time, most commentators thought Australia would not have managed the last 22 runs had the match been completed.[8] The journalist David Thorpe of the Melbourne *Age* then weighed in with an article which took a somewhat darker view. Thorpe began with some slightly bizarre purple prose before making a pessimistic assessment of cricket in what he saw as the new commercial era. The article is short enough to reproduce in full:

1. **Come on, dollar, come on.**

2. 'I remembered, of course, that the World's Series had been fixed in 1919 … it never occurred to me that one man could start to play with the faith of 50 million people – with the single mindedness of a burglar blowing a safe.' – *The Great Gatsby* by F Scott Fitzgerald.

3. The only crises of conscience America has suffered this century have concerned President Nixon's blatant indiscretions, the Vietnam War and the fixing of the World Series baseball championship in 1919. All three events, to borrow Scott Fitzgerald's thought, played with the faith of the people.

---

[8] No side in those days had reached a score of 300 off 50 overs (60 overs was the norm in England at the time); it is not hard to imagine what players and commentators would have thought had they been told that one day Australia would fail to defend 431 runs in a 50-over match. It is probable that the commentators in the 1981/2 match were thinking more of the calibre of Australia's lower order facing the West Indian fast bowlers, rather than the difficulty of the run rate.

4.   In Australia, it is an article of faith that while the lower echelons of sport may be tainted with the 'taking the dive' concept of the prize-fighting booth, our main gladiatorial contests are conducted on the principle that the participants, be they teams or individuals, compete in good faith, ie, they are both trying to win.

5.   On this premise of good faith, no contestant wants to lose, but there are degrees of wanting to win that must be considered. A football team assured of top place on the ladder playing a lowly placed team in the last home and home game of the year is missing a vital cog in its incentive machine.

6.   On the other hand, its opponents may well have its incentive machine supercharged by the underdog's desire to topple the champion, a recurrent theme not confined to sport. Often that missing cog makes the champion team malfunction.

7.   For the same reasons in cricket, the team that has already lost the Test series often reverses form to win the last match. In both of these cases, the precepts of sporting honesty are being strictly observed. Nobody is playing with the faith of the people.

8.   Let us consider the delicate, unfathomable, mechanism that gives one team a moral edge over another in the context of the current Benson and Hedges World Cup Series.

9.   In last Tuesday's game, the West Indies, certain of a berth in the finals, lost to the underdogs, Australia, thus making it a West Indies–Australia finals series.

10. If my argument is correct, the West Indians were missing the vital cog in the incentive machine. Unfortunately the argument becomes muddied by material and commercial factors.

11. Had the West Indians won on Tuesday they would have played a best-of-five finals series against Pakistan. It is estimated that the West Indies–Australia finals will draw three times the crowds a West Indies–Pakistan series would have.

12. These figures will be reflected in television audiences, with a corresponding difference in advertising revenue (rival stations would counter-attack had Channel 9's flanks been so exposed). So while cricket-loving Australians were barracking for their country out of normal sporting patriotism, Mr Kerry Packer's

cheers had a strident dollar-desperation note about them. Come on dollars, come on.

13. One wonders about the collective state of mind of the West Indians. Was it sportingly honest, this incentive to win? Or did the factors just mentioned – commercial pressures of crowds, gate money, sponsorship – bring about an unstated thought: 'It doesn't matter if we lose'?

14. This thought edges perilously close to the concept of taking a dive.

15. It is conceivable that the same pressures will influence the thinking of both teams in the imminent finals series. Mr Packer would prefer a thrilling fifth match decider to a three-nil whitewash, for commercial reasons. So would the crowds, for obvious reasons.

16. But if both sides want a five-game series (intrinsically not a bad thing to watch) for Mr Packer's reason or any other reasons then the game of cricket is not being made as a contest but as a contrived spectacle with unsavoury commercial connotations.

17. Two opposing teams with a common goal cannot be said to be competing in good faith to win each game as it comes, but rather indulging in a mutely arranged and prolonged charade in which money has replaced that vital cog and is running the incentive machine.

18. Somebody is playing with the faith of the people – with the single mindedness of a burglar blowing a safe.[9]

The litigation

Lloyd, even though he had not played in the game, was enraged at the slight against his team's professionalism, to the point where he sued the publishers of the *Age* for defamation.

---

[9] The paragraph numbers have been added, as they were by the Privy Council later. The text of the article is taken from the report of the case: [1986] AC 350, 359–60. The title 'Come on Dollar, Come on' was a play on a popular song used to promote Australian cricket, coined (if the pun be excused) during the Packer revolution and retained as an 'official anthem' after the settlement.

The case was first heard in the Supreme Court of New South Wales. Lloyd contended that the article had made four imputations defamatory of him: (i) that he had committed, or (ii) was suspected of having committed, a fraud on the public for financial gain in pre-arranging in concert with other persons the result of a World Series match; and (iii) that he was prepared, or (iv) was suspected of being prepared, in the future to commit frauds on the public for financial gain by pre-arranging in concert with other persons the results of cricket matches.

The publishers denied that they had made any such imputations in the article, and confirmed in their pleadings[10] that they had not intended to do so. On the hearing of a preliminary issue, it was held that the article was nevertheless capable of bearing the defamatory imputations alleged by Lloyd. The case therefore proceeded to trial, where the jury found that Lloyd had been defamed as alleged. He was awarded the very substantial sum of A$100,000 in damages.

The publishers appealed to the New South Wales Court of Appeal. The majority of the judges allowed the appeal, primarily on the ground that they did not think that the article was capable of bearing the meaning alleged. Lloyd appealed to the Privy Council. The right to appeal to the Privy Council from the Australian High Court had long been regarded as spent,[11] but Lloyd was able to exercise a residual and somewhat anomalous right to appeal from a state court.

The Privy Council's judgment

The Privy Council's judgment[12] was given by Lord Keith of Kinkel. He began by expressing firm agreement with the judge and jury at the initial trial:

> The whole tone of the article seems to [the Privy Council] to suggest or imply that the West Indies were not only not keenly inspired to

---

[10]   In answer to interrogatories served by Lloyd's representatives.

[11]   The Privy Council (Limitation of Appeals) Act 1968 had ended appeals to the Privy Council in matters involving federal legislation. The Privy Council (Appeals from the High Court) Act 1975 abolished appeals from the High Court. In practice such appeals had been non-existent for a long time anyway: *Whitehouse v Queensland* (1961) 104 CLR 635.

[12]   *Lloyd v David Syme & Co Ltd* [1986] AC 350.

win the match in question because they were already assured of a place in the final, but also motivated to lose because that would have financially desirable results for them. Paragraph 14 appears clearly calculated to put the idea into the mind of a reader that the West Indies did 'take a dive', ie that they lost the match on purpose, necessarily involving a concerted plan. Paragraph 16 clearly implies that the West Indies, as one of the sides, did want a five-game series and therefore for commercial reasons would make the final series not a contest but a contrived spectacle, again involving a concerted plan. Paragraph 17 plainly implies that the West Indies as one of the opposing teams would not be competing in good faith, but, since money was running the incentive machine, would be putting on an arranged charade. In the circumstances the article contained ample material capable of supporting the pleaded imputations.

Lord Keith pointed out that the Court of Appeal seemed to have thought that the thrust of the article was directed at Packer alone, and would be so taken by the ordinary reader, having regard to the reference to 'one man' in paragraph 2 and to 'somebody' in paragraph 18. According to Lord Keith, however, an ordinary reader 'might well be disposed to wonder whether one man could fix either the World Series in 1919 or the World Cup Series in 1981/2 without the co-operation of some at least of the players. Their Lordships therefore consider the reasons given by [the Court of Appeal] for allowing the defendant's appeal on this branch of the case to have been unsound.'

Brushing aside a point raised by the publishers that Lloyd should have been excused from the article's scope because he had not played in the match, Lord Keith then turned to the final plank of the defence, which was that the article was 'comment'. In the law of New South Wales, that was covered by s 33 of the Defamation Act 1974, which provided:

Comment of servant or agent of defendant.

33(1) Subject to sections 30 and 31, it is a defence as to comment that the comment is the comment of a servant or agent of the defendant.

(2) A defence under subsection (1) as to any comment is defeated if, but only if, it is shown that, at the time when the comment was made, any person whose comment it is, being a servant or agent of the defendant, did not have the opinion represented by the comment.

Here the problem for the publishers was that they had said in their pleadings that neither they nor Thorpe himself had intended to make the imputations which Lloyd claimed were contained in the article. Section 33(2) provided that a defence of comment would fail if the person did not actually have the opinion represented by the comment. And so the publishers' argument fell away, leaving Lloyd the winner, as the jury had found in the first place. Since the article had been about the teams in general and not Lloyd in particular, it followed that all the other players involved had been libelled as well – all the more so given that Lloyd had not even played in the match. As they lined up to sue, the publishers were forced to settle out of court, at a total cost estimated at A$2 million.[13]

Right or wrong?

If the article had contained an express allegation that Lloyd and his team either had been bribed or were prepared to be bribed to throw the match, then clearly it would have been libellous. But had Thorpe made such an allegation? Earlier in the piece he had made a fairly uncontroversial observation, namely that it is a regular occurrence in all sports for a team which has already finished top of the table to lose an inconsequential match at the end of the season to the bottom-ranked side. It would not be defamatory to suggest that that had occurred between West Indies and Australia, any more than it would be defamatory to level the standard criticisms one finds on the sports pages every day along the lines of a team being underprepared, or unable to cope with pressure, or unable to adapt to new conditions.

A more serious situation is the Machiavellian practice whereby a team which has already qualified for the next round of a tournament deliberately loses a match so that the side it wants to face in the next round will get through. There have been a few unsavoury examples of that practice in cricket and other sports over the years,[14] and it is

---

[13]   See the obituary of David Thorpe, *The Age*, 5 October 2007.

[14]   In cricket there was Australia's attempted manipulation of the net run rate in the first round of the 1999 World Cup – ironically against West Indies – so that the latter would progress instead of New Zealand. There was the odd suggestion that the Australians were putting in some petty retaliation for New Zealand having lost to Pakistan in the 1992 World Cup first round – their only loss of that stage of the competition – so that Australia would be out of the tournament and New Zealand

now explicitly banned (subject to difficulties of proof) by the laws of cricket. But Thorpe was careful to say that the particular match in question was not lost because of a conscious decision by West Indies. Instead, he suggested that West Indies would have subconsciously underperformed because gnawing away at the back of their minds would have been the thought that there would be far more money involved should Australia make the finals instead of Pakistan.

Slackening off for the promise of more money has a more unsavoury flavour than doing so simply because a team has already made it to the next round or is cynically trying to maximize its chances with the schedule. On the other hand, with the actual match having already been played, Thorpe's allegations should be seen against the background that most thought West Indies would have won had it not been for the conspicuously unfair net run rate rule.

It seems to me that there were three respects in which the article might be said to cross the line from legitimate opinion or analysis and into libellous territory. The first was the fact that Thorpe had begun the piece with the quotation from Fitzgerald, which placed squarely in readers' minds the out-and-out fraud that was the infamous 1919 Baseball World Series. Secondly, Thorpe made a clear inference that both teams might manipulate the finals to ensure that all five matches were played, when he wrote: 'Two opposing teams with a common goal cannot be said to be competing in good faith to win each game

could play a home semi-final. Given that Pakistan won that semi-final and then the final in convincing style, there seems little substance to such an accusation, and the Australian captain, Allan Border, explicitly rejected it.

In football there was the much criticized 1982 World Cup match between West Germany and Austria in Gijon, where both teams appeared content to play out a 1-0 West German victory, which ensured that both progressed to the next round. West German fans denounced the match as the *Schande von Gijón*, or 'Disgrace of Gijón'. Fans from Algeria, the victims of the contrivance, came up with the funnier but distinctly more insulting label of *Anschluss*.

In both cases the organisers could do nothing since the teams were acting within the rules (the 1999 Australian cricket plot failed anyway since New Zealand scored enough in its final match to get through, though Australia went on to win the tournament). By contrast, when several badminton players tried to throw matches in the 2012 Olympics so they could then face easier opponents, they were all disqualified, the IOC having more powers in that regard than their cricketing or footballing counterparts.

as it comes, but rather indulging in a mutely arranged and prolonged charade in which money has replaced that vital cog and is running the incentive machine.'

And yet, Thorpe was not making a direct accusation. He said it would be a 'mutely' (not 'mutually') arranged charade if both teams were so intimidated by the money involved that their incentive was subconsciously lessened. He also used phrases such as 'one wonders', 'perilously close' and 'it is conceivable' – all of which suggest that he intended to stop short of an outright allegation of fraud. Ironically, the argument most oft repeated about Packer's rebel series is that the money on offer spurred the players on to greater heights than 'ordinary' matches would have done.

The third respect in which Thorpe possibly crossed the line was in paragraph 18, when he said without any qualification that 'somebody is playing with the faith of the people', which suggested a deliberate action, though he did not say who that 'somebody' was or the precise actions involved. But it would not take many steps on the reader's part to infer that he meant that the players might abdicate their duty to give 100 per cent at all times.

Part of the problem is the context of the article – a short comment piece in a daily newspaper. The tone on a first reading (and not many would give daily papers more than one read) was more a classic example of an old buffer complaining that it was all about the money, rather than an explicit allegation of match-rigging. Cricketing writers have long excelled at complaining about things not being what they were, and there was no shortage of them doing so during and after the Packer affair. To subject the piece to a line-by-line analysis to determine if the words could technically bear one meaning is perhaps not as appropriate as if the document was, say, a review of the series for *Wisden* published a year after it had taken place.

Then again, it would not be practical to try and fashion the law around esoteric distinctions. Instead, the nature of the publication is more a factor to take into account in borderline cases, both in determining whether a libel has occurred, and, if so, the damages to be awarded. It seems to me that Lloyd's action was indeed a borderline case, as reflected by the difference of opinion between the majority of the Court of Appeal and the other judges involved – as well as the fact that a preliminary issue had to be tried to determine whether a libel was even possible in the first place. In those circumstances, it could be argued that the importance of a free press should have prevailed and the case been dismissed.[15]

Whatever view one takes, the case serves to illustrate that as long as a technically permissible interpretation of an article is established which meets the requirement of lowering the plaintiff in the eyes of right-thinking members of society generally, the plaintiff will almost certainly win, even if the defendant had intended to say something different. And hence libel is known as a plaintiff's tort.

The forum

Two side questions arise about the how the case was decided. The first is that it was heard in the first instance before a jury, something highly unusual for non-criminal cases nowadays. The case did not turn on any technical legal point (or any particular knowledge of cricket for that matter); instead, the key question was the impression that an average reader would gain from reading Thorpe's piece. One could argue that a panel of ordinary citizens was actually more appropriate in those circumstances than a judge. On the other hand, jury trials are far more expensive than judge-only trials; they exist virtually nowhere else in non-criminal cases, and a judge-only hearing was still held to determine whether or not it was linguistically possible for the impugned passages to carry the meaning Lloyd said they did. I shall return to this point when discussing the libel cases of Sarfraz and Botham and Lamb, in both of which the losing parties predictably blamed the jury.

The Privy Council

The second issue about how the case was decided is that the final judgment was delivered by the Privy Council in London, rather than an Australian court. That point caused great annoyance in Australia at the time, with not a few parochial politicians incensed that a group of foreigners had overturned Australian judges in an Australian case.

---

[15] A straw poll I conducted (involving both lawyers and non-lawyers) actually returned a unanimous verdict in favour of the defendant.

There was a touch of irony about their indignation, given that the supposedly distant and out-of-touch foreign judges had actually sided with the most demotic judicial panel in the case by reaffirming the decision of the jury of ordinary Australian citizens. Nevertheless, the patriots had a point as a matter of principle, and shortly afterwards they won the day when all remaining possibilities for appeals to the Privy Council were removed by the Australia Act 1986.

The size and sophistication of Australia's legal system, and the perhaps greater republican sentiment in that country, made the severance of the Privy Council relatively uncontroversial. It survived for much longer in smaller Commonwealth jurisdictions such as New Zealand, and still exists for one or two others including some Caribbean islands. New Zealand eventually did away with the right to appeal early in the twenty-first century. There were various arguments in both directions, but the key point seemed to me to be that whatever benefits were offered by the system,[16] it made no more sense for judges in London to be supervising New Zealand courts than it would have done for the United Kingdom Parliament to be vetting New Zealand legislation – the same applying for all other sovereign nations (as opposed to leftover colonial territories such as Gibraltar or the unusual jurisdictions such as the Channel Islands).

Coda

A decade later, Lloyd won another libel case in London, albeit on a rather smaller scale. In December 2003, a Sri Lankan newspaper published an article entitled 'When Hussain threatened match referee Clive Lloyd' with an accompanying cartoon. The article concerned a disciplinary hearing conducted by Lloyd in his capacity as a match

---

[16] The benefits included the international respect accorded to the Privy Council, which was an incentive for overseas businesspeople to invest in New Zealand – knowing that if there was a major dispute, it might be resolved finally by an internationally renowned court. Also, the Privy Council cost New Zealand taxpayers nothing, and while the cost of appeals was prohibitive for most private litigants, the same could be said for most domestic litigation. Lack of knowledge of local conditions was a major objection advanced, though this could be overstated – the rules about judicial notice had been formulated over the years precisely because most judges would not have knowledge of the ways of any particular litigants. Moreover, local conditions would not usually be relevant in commercial cases.

referee, following an incident involving the England captain, Nasser Hussain, and the Sri Lankan spin bowler Muttiah Muralitharan in a test in Kandy.

Lloyd sued the paper in London. He argued that the article represented (i) that he had failed to act impartially as match referee; (ii) that he had breached the ICC's Code of Conduct for Players; and (iii) that he had thereby disgraced the ICC and the whole game of cricket. The paper took few steps to defend the proceedings and Lloyd was therefore able to enter judgment by default, in January 2005. Damages were then assessed in the High Court under the summary disposal procedure. The judge declared that the newspaper's allegations were defamatory and false, and ordered the defendants to pay the maximum sum available under the summary procedure, which at the time was £10,000.

Chapter 10

THE LIBELS, PART II: THE BALL-TAMPERING CONTROVERSIES

INTRODUCTION

' Pakistan is the sort of country to send your mother-in-law to' was one of Ian Botham's more infamous quotes. On the field he had a few occasions on which to regret his words, particularly in 1992 when England lost to Pakistan in the World Cup final in March and then lost what turned out to be his final test series a few months later.

Pakistan's success at the time was due in no small measure to the phenomenal fast bowlers at its disposal, primarily their elder cricketing statesman, Imran Khan, and their intimidating youngsters Wasim Akram and Waqar Younis. Wasim famously dismissed Botham in the World Cup final, the umpire's decision not being one with which Botham happened to agree. He went on to dismiss Allan Lamb and Chris Lewis later in the same match with consecutive deliveries. 'Let me put it this way: I've never seen a ball behave like those two did,' Botham later wrote, not entirely in admiration.[1]

Imran, who captained the side in the World Cup, was one of Botham's great on-field rivals, and an equally strong contender for the finest all-rounder of the era. He retired before the test series in England, but at least his bowling was not much missed since Waqar was able to return after missing the World Cup through injury.

The accusations fly

During the test series, as Waqar and Wasim sent a procession of the home side's batsmen back to the pavilion, mutterings started about how they were managing the then-new phenomenon of reverse swing.[2]

---

[1] Ian Botham, *Botham: My Autobiography* (Willow, new edn, 2000), p 407.
[2] It may not have been so new. Was reverse swing S F Barnes's secret weapon? Or does it even exist? Over a decade after the 1992 series, in the 2005 Ashes, as the English bowlers finally overcame Australia, Ian Chappell was still puzzled by talk of reverse swing, much as Dennis Compton had been at the time of the Pakistani controversy. Both Chappell and Compton reasoned that either the ball swung one way, in which case it was an in-swinger, or it swung the other way, in which case

Suggestions were made that some unorthodox or even unlawful tampering of the ball was involved. The comfortably retired Geoff Boycott disagreed, explaining that it was less a case of good bowling on Pakistan's part and more a case of bad batting on England's. For once Boycott's was about the least controversial voice.

The ball-tampering allegations started to mount, with the tension between the two sides rising in parallel. Matters were not helped by the odd cultural misunderstanding. The journalist Martin Johnson inadvertently caused offence by calling the Pakistani captain, Javed Miandad, a 'streetfighter'. He had intended to praise Javed's resilience at the crease, but his words were translated too literally, so that Pakistanis thought their batting genius was spending his off-days roughing up hooligans. Johnson's Fleet St colleague Mike Langley had less of an excuse when he likened Javed to 'a wild man you might spot crouched behind rocks in ambush along the Khyber'.

Javed probably felt he had had enough compliments from the English after that. Pakistan's manager, Intikhab Alam, complained that his players had been made to feel very uncomfortable. The former England player Trevor Bailey offered a strange sort of olive branch by saying he had nothing against Pakistanis: 'I buy my newspapers from them,' he reassured Channel 4. Imran Khan, who had become something of an *éminence grise* for Pakistani cricket in his retirement, doubted whether his countrymen would ever return to England. Few could have blamed him after English supporters at Headingley threw a pig's head in a plastic bag at Pakistani supporters.

After the series had concluded, however, an expatriate South African, Allan Lamb, ignited a still-combustible mix by writing in *The Mirror* that a former Pakistani fast bowler, Sarfraz Narwaz, had told him how to doctor the ball when they were teammates at Northamptonshire in the 1980s. According to Lamb, Sarfraz claimed to have invented reverse swing. 'Yes Lambie, I am the king,' he had supposedly said.[3] Sarfraz's response was to sue Lamb and *The Mirror* for libel.

---

it was an out-swinger, neither of which was remotely new. Billy Birmingham was similarly confused, and started describing dropping the ball as a 'reverse catch'. The difference seems to be the means by which swing is generated.

[3]   David Hopps, *Great Cricket Quotes* (Robson, 1998), p 221.

SARFRAZ V LAMB

A confrontational sort

Anyone familiar with the playing career of Sarfraz Narwaz would have known he had a particularly confrontational manner. He clearly did not pay his subscriptions to the fast bowlers' union, being known to bounce Jeff Thomson (unwisely) and Joel Garner (improbably). He once walked out of a test series because of a dispute about his pay. He was also the bowler who appealed for 'handled-the-ball' when the Australian batsman Andrew Hilditch innocently returned it to him. Aside from all that, he was a good opening bowler who formed an effective partnership with Imran Khan for much of his career, even if his statistics do not place him in the top echelon of his era. His personal highlight was probably a spell of seven wickets for one run (in total he took nine in the innings) in a test against Australia.

The case

Sarfraz's case was straightforward: Lamb had accused him of admitting doctoring the ball, an action which would be a clear breach of the laws of the game. There was no real doubt that Lamb's statement was libellous, unless he could establish it was true.

The case came on for trial in November 1993 before a jury and Mr Justice Otton. Sarfraz was represented by Jonathan Crystal QC, while Lamb was represented by David Eady QC, who would later become the head libel judge for England and Wales. Otton J and Eady made no secret of their enjoyment of cricket, trading puns and, in the former's case, reportedly keeping one of the balls admitted in evidence as a souvenir at the end of the trial. Crystal, on the other hand, perhaps betrayed a preference for other sports when he asked Chris Cowdrey if he knew about bowling. 'I once took a wicket for England,' replied the slightly wounded former all-rounder, son of one of England's greatest ever players.[4]

---

[4] Stephen Ward, 'Are the Pakistani bowlers cheating?: After the 'ball tampering' case, a question remains unanswered', *Independent on Sunday*, 21 November 1993. In fairness, Crystal was and remains a distinguished sports lawyer, and since the Sarfraz–Lamb trial he has represented no less a cricketer than Brian Lara.

Cowdrey was one of a number of past and present players called to give evidence during the trial, which ended up lasting four days. When Lamb himself entered the witness box, he stated that he had never actually seen Sarfraz cheat in a match. Shortly afterwards, however, Crystal brought a dramatic halt to proceedings when he told the court that Sarfraz was withdrawing the claim. Inevitably the reason for that sudden ending was the subject of much conjecture. Sarfraz himself offered the following insight:

> The court didn't understand all this. There were nine young girls on the jury who didn't know the difference between a football and a cricket ball. We should have had a multi-racial jury, instead we had 11 English people. And most of those were women who kept looking and smiling at Lamby and Robin Smith and Botham. That's understandable, but it was not a serious court case – that's why we stopped it.[5]

The English far-right political parties would have agreed with Sarfraz's ethnic classification of the members of the jury, though they would have approved of rather than complained about its composition. As to whether the female jurors could have understood the game, the question of any lay jury's ability to understand a complicated matter in any specialist field is a valid one, but not on the ground of Sarfraz's rather outdated gender stereotypes. In fairness, Sarfraz also played a more orthodox defensive shot when he declared: 'Whatever I have done in my life, playing for Northampton and around the world, and inventing reverse-swing, was within the law.'[6]

A costly action

Some thought Sarfraz would have felt sufficiently vindicated by Lamb's concession in his oral evidence about not observing any actual cheating, and might have halted proceedings for that reason.

Another explanation might have been the costs involved. Sarfraz had to pay all of the costs (both his own and the other side's), though in the event Lamb and *The Mirror* waived their £130,000 entitlement, leaving Sarfraz 'only' having to pay his side's total of £75,000.

[5] David Hopps, Op Cit.
[6] Ibid.

Immediately after the case he returned to Pakistan and embroiled himself in a dispute with the Cricket Board of Control over who was going to pay. He argued that the board had used him as a 'stalking horse'[7] in anticipation of other libel actions; the board disagreed.[8]

At all events, the dramatic collapse of the case should have served as a warning for others in general, and Lamb in particular, against the risks and costs of High Court litigation. Instead, Lamb seems to have drawn the opposite conclusion and assumed that because he had won once he would win again. A year after Sarfraz's case, when Imran made his comments about match-fixing, Lamb and his former teammate Ian Botham went to their lawyers for another round of writs.

BOTHAM AND LAMB v IMRAN

Wickets and accusations

After the 1992 series, Waqar and Wasim continued to build on their reputation as the most feared fast-bowling combination in world cricket. Some commentators expressed relief that pitching the ball up and moving it had come back into fashion, after nearly two decades of dominance by the relentless barrage of West Indian short-pitched deliveries. But the ball-tampering insinuations did not go away.

By 1994, Imran's patience had run out. In an interview in London with *India Today*, he said: 'Why did the umpires not question [Waqar and Wasim]? The only two cases where players have been caught tampering involved Derek Pringle and Phil Tufnell, a spinner who was doing it for the fast bowlers. Remember that John Holder, the umpire who caught them, has never stood in a test match again. You know why? Because he is black.'

That was inflammatory enough, but in cricketing terms it was only a gentle loosener given what was to follow. Imran then bowled a searing verbal bouncer:

---

[7]   In liquidation proceedings, a stalking horse is the company or individual that first bids for the insolvent company's assets.

[8]   As reported in a somewhat self-congratulatory tone by Sarfraz's successful opponents: see 'No way, Sarfraz', *The Mirror*, 25 May 1996. The paper also reported that, in happier news for the unsuccessful litigant, Sarfraz had been appointed to a position as sports adviser to the Prime Minister, Benazir Bhutto.

There is a lot of racism here. When Bob Willis or Fred Trueman were tearing the heart out of Indian or Pakistani batsmen we never heard an outcry about short pitched bowling. How come the noise started when the West Indian and Pakistani bowlers started winning matches with their fast bowlers? How come we never heard about slow over rates until the West Indies fast bowlers came along? Australians can get away with anything because they are white. There is a lot of racism in this society. A lot of people such as Lamb and Botham making statements like 'Oh I never thought much of him anyway and now it's been proved that he's a cheat'.

He finished with another nasty short ball: 'Look at Tony Lewis, Christopher Martin-Jenkins and Derek Pringle. They are all educated Oxbridge types. Look at the others, Lamb, Botham, Trueman. Differences in class and upbringing makes [*sic*] a difference.'

To add to all that, in a later interview for the *Sun* newspaper in England, Imran said:

[I have] seen all the leading bowlers of the last 20 years interfering with the ball in a way that would today be considered illegal ... there is TV footage to prove it. [I] watched senior county bowlers lift the seam of the ball after [I] arrived in England as a teenager – and copied them because it was seen as an accepted practice ... The biggest names of English cricket have all done it. And, when I say big names, I mean as big as you can get.

Enter the lawyers

Botham and Lamb were incensed. They instructed solicitors, who complained to Imran in a threatening tone. Imran's initial response was diplomatic. He wrote Botham a private letter claiming that he had been misquoted in the *India Today* article and that he had only been trying to defend himself after admitting that he had once tampered with a ball in a county match 18 years previously. He dismissed talk of the class system, saying he did not believe in it. He finished by saying that he was sad that the issue had brought unpleasantness between two cricketing nations, and that he hoped to bury the hatchet.

Mollified Botham was not. His solicitors wrote a stern response, demanding a fulsome public apology;[9] Imran showed them the draft of a letter he had intended to send to *The Times* explaining his position, but Botham was still not satisfied. He and Lamb issued proceedings for libel.

The litigation

Botham and Lamb relied upon the second and third passages quoted above from the *India Today* article to establish that a libel had been committed. The pleaded meaning was that Imran had suggested in the second passage that they were racist, and in the third passage had said that they (along with Fred Trueman, who did not bother suing[10]) were different in some way from three named individuals because of their inferior 'class and upbringing'.

As to the *Sun* article, Botham argued that its meaning was that the leading bowlers in England over the previous 20 years (of whom he correctly regarded himself as one – at the time he had taken the most test wickets in English history) had interfered with the ball in an illegal fashion; in other words, they had cheated. In his statement of claim, the allegation was phrased in the following terms: 'In their natural and ordinary meaning the words … meant and were understood to mean that the plaintiff had cheated at cricket by tampering with the ball and had been caught doing so on television.'

Before the trial, Imran's team argued that the impugned words in the *Sun* article were not libellous. That argument was heard as a preliminary issue. The judge ruled in Botham's favour and Imran appealed. Imran relied upon the following passages in the *Sun* article to set the disputed words in context:

> I don't consider either to be cheating. [Imran was there referring to lifting the seam and scratching one side of the ball]. To me, they are within acceptable limits.

---

[9]   Botham, op cit, p 414.

[10]   Trueman was later quoted as saying he preferred to settle disputes over a pint, and that he wasn't going to 'sit on my arse waiting for some court' to resolve anything. I suspect he might have had in mind that the leading barristers and judges at the time would have been drawn from the same pool as (and may even have included some of) the Oxbridge amateurs he so despised in his early playing days.

It is only when an outside agent, such as Vaseline to shine the ball or a bottle top to scratch it, is introduced that I regard it as cheating.

But I'm not condemning them [he was referring to bowlers in particular] – because I believe it to be within acceptable bounds.

Laws are only laws if they are enforced.

It was an accepted practice.

The Court of Appeal gave Imran's argument short shrift. Lord Justice Russell explained:

> In my judgment the important point in this appeal is what Mr Botham is said to have done, not what Mr Khan thinks is the true quality of the act. It may be that the reader will agree with Mr Khan and say that, although the activity of lifting the seam is contrary to the rules, the activity is not cheating. If that is so then the defendant will be entitled to a verdict. On the other hand, the reader may say – and this is a matter for the jury – 'I do not accept what Mr Khan says as to whether this activity amounts to cheating. I think it does; it gains an unfair advantage for the bowler which he is not entitled by the rules to have. I think it is not proved that Mr Botham did engage in this practice' and accordingly, if that is right, he will succeed.

His Lordship then reminded himself of the classic libel test, namely that a statement would be libellous if it would tend to lower the plaintiff in the estimation of right-thinking members of society generally, or be likely to affect a person adversely in the estimation of reasonable people generally.[11] He concluded that the words were capable of bearing a defamatory meaning and that the jury should decide whether or not they in fact bore such a meaning. Accordingly, the appeal should be dismissed. Lord Justice Hutchison agreed, and so the case proceeded to trial.

The trial

The trial began in the middle of July 1996, in front of a jury and presided over by Mr Justice French. Botham was represented by Charles Gray QC, a libel specialist who would go on to become a judge. Imran was represented by the late George Carman QC, perhaps

---

[11] Russell LJ quoted *Gillick v the British Broadcasting Corporation* [1996] EMLR 267, but the test derives originally from *Sim v Stretch*, as mentioned above.

the only 'celebrity advocate' of his generation: the sort of lawyer who attracted headlines for the brilliance and theatre of his advocacy as much as the public profile of his clients or the notoriety of his cases.

Carman began by pointing to Imran's efforts to settle the case. 'Remember this,' he told the jury: 'who offered the hand of friendship and who spurned it?' But Carman's advocacy involved anything but offering the hand of friendship. 'No-one can deny that this case is emotionally charged,' he went on, with a certain amount of understatement. 'Issues of race, class and country move in and move out of it like black clouds.' When Botham entered the witness box, Carman stepped up a notch – or down, depending on one's point of view – by raking over the substantial coals of Botham's colourful public and private lives. Even the state of his marriage did not go unexamined, to Botham's (understandable) fury.

Botham and Lamb generally stuck to their guns throughout Carman's searching cross-examination. Botham stated how proud he was of his background and mentioned his friendship with Viv Richards as a refutation of the charge of racism. Lamb for his part pointed out that he had left South Africa precisely to get away from the racism that was apartheid. He admitted using his thumb on a ball during the 1982 Lord's test against Pakistan, but maintained that he had been trying to push the ball back into shape rather than damage it. Footage from the Oval test in the same series showed the wicket keeper Bob Taylor vigorously rubbing the ball after Botham threw it to him, but Botham argued that Taylor was only drying it and that the keeper's gloves were incapable of removing the lacquer from it as had been alleged.

The trial lasted two weeks, during which a parade of past and present cricketers gave evidence. Imran called Geoffrey Boycott, who had not always been on the best of terms with Botham. He spent more time talking about Brian Close (one of his old foes from Yorkshire, who had given evidence for Botham) and other irrelevant subjects than he did about anything material to the case. Unsurprisingly, he earned himself a reprimand from the judge. David Gower, called by Botham, assumed the relaxed air of a man at a cocktail party, much as he had at the crease during his playing career. (At least he did not cut short his evidence to go to the theatre, as he had in 1989 when giving a press conference as England captain in a losing Ashes series.) Gower confirmed Botham's stance that he had only tried to preserve rather than alter the condition of the ball.

On the ninth day of the trial, Imran rather dramatically withdrew his allegation about cheating, stating that he was happy to accept Botham's assertion that he had only 'squeezed' the ball. He still maintained that Botham had been technically guilty of ball-tampering, but his defence of justification (that he had been justified in calling Botham a cheat) no longer stood.

With a sizeable wink, fate decreed that the trial should coincide with the Lord's test during another series between England and Pakistan. Some of the witnesses had to come straight from the field (or, in Boycott's case, straight from the commentary box, not in his usual immaculate suit but wearing some sponsor's garb which he openly displayed in court...). England's captain, Mike Atherton, and coach, David Lloyd, both had to come just before the test began, which cannot have helped their preparation (they lost the match, but commendably offered no excuse).[12] Meanwhile, Lamb had not exactly done his bit to help smooth things over: before the trial he had released a ghosted autobiography in which he sought to refight all the old battles. Just to make sure no-one missed the point, the juicier parts of the book were serialized by a newspaper while the tour was in progress.

Nevertheless, fears of on-field acrimony proved unfounded: the series was played in a good spirit throughout by both sides. It helped a great deal that the opposing captains, Atherton and Wasim, had been Lancashire teammates for years and were on excellent terms. Wasim did not perform to his usual standard on the field – perhaps reflecting the strain he was under trying to keep the peace – but with Waqar and

---

[12] Prior to the test series, England had visited Pakistan as part of their hapless 1996 World Cup campaign. Atherton got things under way with a faux pas when he remarked *sotto voce* 'Will someone please remove this buffoon?' in respect of a Pakistani journalist. Microphones unfortunately removed the *sotto* aspect. Something of an overreaction followed on the journalist's part when England returned in 2000: he threatened to sue Atherton for having 'ruined his life', though the precise cause of action he had in mind remained unclear.

others firing on all cylinders it made no difference, since Pakistan still won the series convincingly.

Across town at the Royal Courts, Imran emerged the winner as well, when all of Botham and Lamb's claims were dismissed. The jury's verdict was by a majority, meaning that it was split either 11–1 or 10–2 (any lesser majority is insufficient for a verdict and would be classed as a hung jury). Botham and Lamb were stunned, and it has to be said that the defeat was more surprising than that of their former teammates on the field. Given that the Court of Appeal had held that Imran's comments were undoubtedly capable of being libellous, and that Imran had abandoned one of his primary defences, it is not easy to understand why the jury rejected the claim.

No reasons are ever given by juries and neither the judge nor anyone else may inquire into what happened during the jury's deliberations. Both sides could therefore only guess as to the reasons for the result. The judge delivered his own verdict, which was lacking in charity: 'A complete exercise in futility,' he declaimed. Perhaps that was the key: the jury may have accepted that there had technically been a libel, but had decided not to award anything to Botham or Lamb on the ground that they should have taken any insults on the chin and replied, if at all, through the media rather than the law courts. With that view I would have some sympathy.

The costs linger

The case might have come to a shattering end for them, but Botham and Lamb strung things out for several years afterwards. The judge had ordered them to pay Imran's costs, save that Imran was ordered to pay the costs of his plea of justification, which had been withdrawn during the trial.

After the expiration of the three-month time limit for commencing assessment proceedings (by which the court determines the exact amount of costs payable if the parties have not been able to agree), the parties agreed a general extension in order to negotiate. Those negotiations broke down and, as a later judge put it, 'matters were allowed to drift'. Finally, in 2003, Imran's solicitors began detailed assessment proceedings. Botham and Lamb responded with an application that Imran's costs be disallowed because of all the delay.

The judge dismissed Botham and Lamb's application.[13] He ruled that, although the period of delay was regrettable, it would not prevent a fair assessment of Imran's costs. Both sides were responsible for the delay, and it would not be proportionate or just to deny Imran the chance to recover assessed costs to which he was entitled. Imran therefore won in court a second time.

Aftermath

And so, eight years after the trial had concluded, the matter finally spluttered to a halt. 'Time heals most wounds, but every so often Kath and I think back to the case and we both get depressed by the memories,' Botham later wrote.[14] Not that the affair got in the way of his successful career in the media, chiefly as a commentator for Sky television. He also continued with the charitable works which had been an important factor in his award of a knighthood. Lamb did some media work with Botham and otherwise found a living working in the corporate hospitality business.

Imran worked as a commentator on and off for different channels, but spent much more time and energy away from cricket on his political career and charitable activities. He showed no more fear in opposing his rival politicians or even the US military (taking issue with its drone strikes in northern Pakistan) than he had when facing the fastest bowlers of his cricket career.

It was Sarfraz who had the least happy-ever-after. His experience convinced him to switch tack and start making allegations instead of waiting to be on the receiving end. He became particularly known for his grape-shot conjecture about match-fixing. In 1999, for example, live on Indian television, he offered the following about a test which had taken place as far back as 1980:[15] 'I have been saying this from 1980 when things started from India. Asif Iqbal and Gavaskar were openly involved ... The match in Bombay where the wicket and outfield were wet ... that pitch was not fit to play. And many of the

---

[13]   See [2004] All ER (D) 222 (Nov).

[14]   Botham, op cit, p 424.

[15]   See Abdul Waheed Khan and Rohit Brijnath, 'Silly Point', *India Today*, 22 March 1999, indiatoday.intoday.in/story/sarfaraz-nawaz-says-sunil-gavaskar-involved-in-fixing-matches-claim-finds-few-takers/1/253539.html (retrieved 18 April 2014).

Pakistani batsmen complained, they didn't want to bat on a wet wicket. But Asif and Gavaskar agreed. So what (does) this mean? I mean this inquiry should start from the beginning.'

Asif initially declined to comment, saying he did not want to dignify the allegations with a response. Then he bowled the verbal equivalent of a Waqar Younis toe crusher by pointing out that Sarfraz had not even been on the tour in which the match in question took place. Gavaskar responded by calling Sarfraz 'the scum of the earth'. Two days later he added, in a slightly more measured tone, 'Looking at his credibility I should have laughed at the matter rather than react the way I did.' Elsewhere Sarfraz apparently called Imran 'a Jewish agent'.[16] Imran unsurprisingly did not bother replying. More than a few others in all the ball-tampering controversies might have been advised to follow the same course.

[16]   Ibid.

Chapter 11

BALL-TAMPERING AND LAW 42

A MOST UNUSUAL OCCURRENCE

I would have liked to say that ball-tampering controversies were confined to the two libel actions just reviewed. Regrettably, that was very far from the case, and in fact neither of the libel actions came close to the last word about the two questions of (i) what amounts to ball-tampering and (ii) who has been guilty (or innocent) of it over the years.

As it happens, a much more blatant round of accusations had been made a couple of years before Sarfraz's action, following a series played between New Zealand and Pakistan. In November 1990, the New Zealand captain, Martin Crowe, and team manager, Ian Taylor, told the *New Zealand Herald* that they had used a doctored ball in Faisalabad that year,[1] in a series in which Imran Khan had refused to play because he rather uncharitably (though not wholly inaccurately) thought the opposition would be unworthy. Crowe decided while he was batting that the ball had been damaged in a manner that was simply not possible without artificial assistance. Tired of being routed by Waqar and his cohorts, and with complaints to umpires and officials falling on deaf ears, Crowe decided his team would retaliate by using a bottle top on the ball themselves in the third test. The journeyman medium pacer Chris Pringle promptly took seven wickets as Pakistan were bowled out for 102 in their first innings. Pringle finished with 11–152 in the match. By way of comparison, his other 19 test wickets were taken over the course of 13 matches at 65 runs apiece. Not that the plan changed anything: Pakistan still won the match.

Over the past 20 years a number of players from (but not limited to) India, South Africa, New Zealand, Australia and Pakistan have had

---

[1]   Kishore Bhimani, *Director's Special Book of Cricket Controversies* (Allied, 2nd edn, 1996), p 195. Richard Hadlee had just retired, at once reducing New Zealand's bowling resources to the negligible, and a few other senior players did not tour either. See also Martin Williamson, 'As old as the hills', Cricinfo, 16 September 2006, www.espncricinfo.com/magazine/content/story/259676.html (retrieved 18 April 2014). Note that Williamson quotes Wasim's verdict on the New Zealanders' allegations: 'bullshit'.

accusations levelled against them, though not many have involved the sort of blatant confession coupled with excuse offered by the New Zealanders after the 1990 tour. Rather than try and list all of the incidents worthy of note, I shall look instead at what the laws of the game actually say about ball-tampering, with reference to some of the well-known controversies to see how the laws should be interpreted. The laws have been revised since some of the incidents occurred, and thus any references to actual events are for illustrative purposes rather than to reargue whether they were correctly resolved according to the laws of the day.

The law

Ball-tampering is covered by law 42(3):

3. The match ball – changing its condition

(a) Any fielder may

(i) polish the ball provided that no artificial substance is used and that such polishing wastes no time.

(ii) remove mud from the ball under the supervision of the umpire.

(iii) dry a wet ball on a piece of cloth.

(b) It is unfair for anyone to rub the ball on the ground for any reason, to interfere with any of the seams or the surface of the ball, to use any implement, or to take any other action whatsoever which is likely to alter the condition of the ball, except as permitted in (a) above.

I will take each of the subsections in turn.

Law 42(3)(a)(i): 'no artificial substance'

There are two issues under law 42(3)(a)(i): first, what constitutes 'artificial', and second, whether the use of an artificial substance has to be intentional before an offence is committed.

In 1994, England captain Mike Atherton was seen putting his hand in his pocket before rubbing the ball. Atherton initially told the match referee that there was nothing in his pocket but later accepted that it had contained dirt which he used to keep his hands dry.[2] Among the excuses offered on Atherton's behalf was the argument that dirt was not an 'artificial' substance. It is true that dirt is not artificial in the usual sense of being man made, but that is not necessarily decisive. If a player happened to find a broken stick with a jagged edge on the boundary then that too would be no more 'artificial' than the dirt on the ground, but not many would assume that he could then use it under the guise of polishing the ball with a 'natural substance'.

Rather, 'artificial' has to mean any substance other than that found on a player's body – essentially, his saliva, sweat and skin, and not dirt or anything else even if it is ordinarily found on the field of play. This still leaves room for argument. What of saliva that has been altered by a cough lozenge? Or sweat mixed with sunscreen which a player has legitimately applied to his face? Or dirt that has found its way onto a player's hands in the ordinary course of fielding rather than being pocketed for the purpose? The answer is that there has to be some room at the margins, if only for the usual *de minimus* rule (or 'the law does not concern itself with trifling things'). That aside,

---

[2] Critics were quick to argue that Atherton's wrongdoing was exacerbated by the fact he was England captain and therefore someone from whom a higher standard of conduct was expected. Atherton was resistant to the idea in his autobiography, *Opening Up* (Hodder & Stoughton, 2002), but the concept of the holder of high office being held to a higher standard than ordinary citizens is not unknown in the general law. The Official Solicitor, for example, is an officer of the High Court. In *R v Tower Hamlets London Borough Council, ex p Chetnik Developments Ltd* [1988] AC 858 at 876–7, it was held that the court would only allow its officers to act in a 'high-principled' manner. Even where an ordinary person might lawfully act in a morally dubious way, officers of the court could not.

Atherton admitted being foolish; he was young, naïve and out of his depth, especially when it came to dealing with the media storm which followed. At the same time, it should be noted that he was an experienced cricketer and an intelligent, well-educated man who had voluntarily assumed the responsibility of captaining his country. That said, and with the benefit of hindsight after almost 20 years, I would suggest that Atherton genuinely did not think he had done anything wrong on the field at the time, even if when called to account he probably started to suspect quite quickly that he had. I disagree with the legal academic David Fraser (see Fraser, *Cricket and the Law: The Man in White Is Always Right* (Routledge, 2nd edn, 2005)) that no Pakistani would have been rehabilitated as quickly as Atherton under the same circumstances: it seems to me that several top Pakistani players have not gone without stains on their character over the years but have still received due praise in England for their cricketing skill and achievements.

sunscreen, lozenges, mints or anything equivalent constitute artificial substances which are banned by law 42.

Is it necessary that the substance is applied intentionally? On tour in India in 1976/7, the England fast bowlers John Lever and Bob Willis started wearing strips of gauze soaked in Vaseline on their foreheads to stop sweat from going into their eyes. The Indian captain, Bishen Bedi, complained that the bowlers had been rubbing the Vaseline on the ball, thereby generating the swing that had done for the Indian batsmen. England countered that any offence had been unintentional (they also bluntly pointed out that India had been losing long before the gauze strips had been employed – this would not disprove the allegation of itself, but would mean that Bedi would struggle to prove the allegation if there was no discernible change in the run of play after the gauze had been applied).

Normally, criminal law requires two elements – the act of doing the crime (or omission), known by the Latin phrase *actus reus*, and the mental element, or *mens rea* in Latin. The mental element requires the offender to be of sound mind, and to have done the act or omission either intentionally or recklessly. But it is not always required: many environmental offences, for example, do not require any intention or recklessness on the part of the perpetrator; polluting a river might incur a fine even if it was by accident. Such crimes are called 'strict liability' offences.

Does law 42(3)(a)(i) set out an offence of strict liability? It does not say in terms that the application of artificial substances has to be intentional. And it is easy to see how it could be grossly unfair to the batting side if the fielding team was able to benefit from a very happy accident, if after a substance accidently was smeared the ball suddenly proceeded to swing as though it was in the hands of Bob Massie at Lord's in 1972. Equally, however, it is easy to imagine circumstances in which a player inadvertently applies the substance with no intention of breaching the law, in which case it might be thought unfair to punish him – as seems the verdict of most (if not that of Bishen Bedi) regarding the 1976/7 England Vaseline controversy.[3]

---

[3]   Another point about that incident is that the amount of Vaseline which found its way onto the ball would have been trifling; thus the *de minimus* rule would have precluded any finding of a breach of the laws by England. See Mike Selvey (who

In more recent times, India's Rahul Dravid was found guilty of using a lozenge on the ball. The match referee, Clive Lloyd, expressly stated that he had found the action to have been intentional, though the Indian team had been adamant that it was not. Lloyd said that the footage showed clearly that something had been applied to the ball that was not sweat or saliva, and it could not have been there by accident.[4] Lloyd (who was not purporting to give a technical analysis of the laws) was applying something akin to a different Latin maxim, *res ipsa loquitur*, or 'the thing speaks for itself'. In other words, if something could not have been in the wrong place by accident, the person who was responsible for it had to be found liable, even if there was no direct evidence as to how it got there. Suppose, for example, a surgical tool was found in a patient's abdomen after an operation (and they had never had a previous operation) – even if no-one saw the surgeon use the tool, there could be only one explanation and therefore the surgeon might be found liable.

In criminal law, it is not normally necessary for a criminal statute expressly to provide that intention is required; the courts will imply it unless there are express words rejecting it.[5] If there is any ambiguity, it will usually be resolved in favour of the defendant, given that the criminal law is the ultimate sanction society applies to its members. Since ball-tampering is cricket's equivalent of a criminal offence (a level 2 offence under the laws), the better reading is that it is not an offence of strict liability and that some degree of intention is required. That would include being reckless – a player could not expect to be able to coat himself with various substances in the manner of a cross-Channel swimmer and then protest that he never intentionally applied anything to the ball. Equally, ignorance of the law is no excuse,[6] and therefore a player who deliberately altered the ball without realizing it was wrong to do so (if such a player could be found) would be guilty all the same.

---

played in the match), 'The rankling history of our Vaseline Incident', *The Guardian*, 11 December 2008.

[4] Alex Brown, 'Ball tampering was deliberate, says Lloyd', *Sydney Morning Herald*, 22 January 2004.

[5] See *Bennion on Statutory Interpretation* (LexisNexis, 5th edn, 2008), s 334 (pp 1077–86).

[6] Ibid, pp 40–44.

Law 42(3)(a)(ii) – removing mud under the umpire's supervision

The key point about law 42(3)(a)(ii) is that it refers to an action being taken 'under the umpire's supervision'. Obviously, the law would be breached if a player pretended to show the umpire the ball but deceived him with some sleight of hand. More importantly, since the law specifically provides for removing mud under the umpire's supervision, it has to follow that it is unlawful to remove it under any other circumstances (this point is confirmed by law 42(3)(b), as will be seen).

It is for that reason that Sachin Tendulkar was found guilty of a ball-tampering offence in South Africa in November 2001.[7] Not surprisingly, given Tendulkar's status even then as the most famous Indian player in history, there was umbrage from Indian quarters, with BCCI president Jagmohan Dalmiya calling for the match referee, Mike Denness, to be removed from the following test. The controversy was all the greater because other Indian players were censured during the same match for other offences, leading to the not unfamiliar allegations of racism and colonialism.

It is not my intention to discuss any of those allegations. Instead, I will assume in Tendulkar's favour that he had no intention to cheat, and that he had only intended to remove mud from the ball as permitted by law 42(3)(b). It did not matter that Tendulkar did not realize he was committing wrongdoing – ignorance of the law is no excuse. Nor did it matter that he was doing something which would have been legal had he showed the umpire. However, both those factors would go to the appropriateness of the penalty: since Tendulkar had not set out to cheat and had done something that would have been acceptable had he followed the correct procedure, his actions were more akin to, say, forgetting to register his car (no doubt the cursed Ferrari, if that had happened in real life) rather than a more serious offence such as a hit-and-run.

It should also be noted that, just as with his taxation troubles, Tendulkar's undoubted genius and unrivalled standing in the modern game was no reason to make an exception from the rules which

[7] See Martin Williamson, 'The Denness affair', Cricinfo, 15 January 2011, www.espncricinfo.com/magazine/content/story/496743.html (retrieved 18 April 2014).

applied to everyone else. Quite the opposite: Tendulkar's status was all the more reason to apply the rules rigidly, since no-one should be above – or seen to be above – the law. And that is precisely how he conducted himself throughout his unique career, which places the 2001 controversy properly in context.

Law 42(3)(a)(iii)

Law 42(3)(a)(iii) seems self-explanatory: a cloth may be used to dry the ball but nothing else – presumably not even normal cricket gear such as wicket keeper's gloves, as was done in the past (and I should stress that it was done innocently) by Bob Taylor and others. Even that strict construction still leaves room for someone to invent a type of cloth that could damage a ball. New Zealand's outfitters feared they had done just that before the 2008 tour of England: the bowlers' outfits included a patch made of a chamois-like material, on which they could shine the ball. The outfitters had intended to put an abrasive material on as well, but it was thought such material might contravene law 42(3)(a)(iii). The tour went ahead with the only disagreement being from those who felt the New Zealanders looked slightly camp in their gleaming microfibre gear compared with the traditional jerseys of the English (though the Kiwi players themselves would probably have been more concerned with the fact that they lost the series).

Law 42(3)(b) – the 'catch-all'

Law 42(3)(b) specifically rules out rubbing the ball on the ground, interfering with the seams and using 'any implement', and then adds what in legal terms is called a 'catch-all' provision – a broadly worded sentence designed to sweep up anything not specifically outlawed by any of the other provisions.

Rubbing the ball on the ground is a reasonably unambiguous rule, as is 'using any implement' – which would catch out the hypothetical stick of wood mentioned earlier. 'Interfering with the seams or the surface of the ball' also seems straightforward – and would rule out the actions Imran admitted having done in his career. There would be a possible grey area when it comes to polishing the ball, which is permitted, and 'interfering with the surface', which is not. Finally, the 'catch-all' section proscribes 'any other action whatsoever which is likely to alter the condition of the ball, except as permitted in (a) above'. That would rule out any try-on attempts such as arguing about 'natural' substances found on the pitch, or any similar actions.

As ever, some ambiguity will always remain: one thinks for example of the old practice whereby bowlers would warm up by slamming the ball into an adjacent playing strip and the fielders would return the ball by the same method. If such actions were thought to constitute a cynical ploy by the fielding side to rough up the ball, then the umpires could invoke law 42(3)(b) and demand they move elsewhere.

An overview

Looking at law 42 overall, the intention of the drafters seems clear: the ways in which a player may interfere with the ball are to be limited to those expressly allowed. If an action is not expressly allowed it is not allowed at all. There is no use trying to come up with a way of altering the ball not mentioned in law 42, for that would be caught under 42(3)(b) as 'any other action whatsoever'. The permissible methods are in essence polishing the ball on one's whites in the time-honoured method, spitting on it as part of that process, removing mud as described or drying the ball with a cloth, and that is about it.

The strictness of the rules means that a few players might be found in breach here and there without much in the way of moral transgressions. It might seem harsh in those circumstances for them to be labelled a cheat. But it should be seen as the same as in real life when someone breaks a minor law such as marginally exceeding the speed limit: technically they might be a 'criminal' but hardly of a piece with an armed robber or a murderer.

A few players over the years have expressed the feeling that since the practice of ball-tampering is so widespread, the rules should at least be loosened, if not wholly abandoned. The arguments here run in parallel with those regarding the legalization of drugs: everyone does it; the authorities cannot stop it; the game is not much ruined by it; and so the authorities should bow to the inevitable and end prohibition. There are even those who also feel it would be a positive step, not just acquiescing in the face of difficulties of enforcement. The former

England player Mark Nicholas, for instance, argued that the odds have become so stacked against bowlers in modern times with heavy bats, short boundaries and fielding restrictions, that allowing them to tweak the ball (provided no artificial substance is used) would be a welcome innovation.[8]

It is a plausible argument, but if top-level bowlers suddenly become able to make a ball swing or turn square at any point in any innings, then I suspect the liberalizers might have cause to regret. Again, this is a common argument against legalizing drugs – it is feared that severe social consequences will follow (or the 'slippery slope' argument if one prefers). Rather, it seems to me that the current strictly drafted laws, added to the fact that there are now in excess of 20 high-definition cameras at some test grounds, should remove most of the problems regarding tampering, though it has to be acknowledged that human ingenuity and foibles will always leave some room for controversy.

As for the advantage to batsmen which Nicholas mentioned, that seems fair enough in theory but is not always borne out in reality. As this chapter was being written, for example, England were going down to the worst defeat (statistically measured) in Ashes history, having failed to reach 200 six times in five test matches, and with only a solitary hundred across the entire side. They had won the previous Ashes series primarily because Australia's top order had obligingly failed at every critical juncture. Prior to that, both sides had beaten India in a clean sweep at home but, in Australia's case, had also lost a clean sweep to India away. In none of those series would the batsmen on the losing side have felt the bowlers to have been conspicuously disadvantaged.[9]

[8]   Mark Nicholas, 'A little ball-tampering will do cricket good', Cricinfo, 31 October 2013, www.espncricinfo.com/magazine/content/story/684129.html (retrieved 18 April 2014).

[9]   Admittedly, limited-overs cricket, particularly of the 20/20 variety, might be a different story, with the severe restrictions on bowling and field placings that are required, along with shortened boundaries in many cases. But the simple answer would be to remove some of those restrictions, rather than the altogether more risky strategy of allowing ball tampering, particularly if it is not to be allowed in other forms of cricket such as test matches.

Chapter 12

THE LIBELS, PART III:
THE TRIALS OF LALIT MODI

INTRODUCTION

In the late 2000s, Lalit Modi became one of cricket's best-known administrators. As one of the founders of the Indian Premier League (IPL), his influence may yet be judged by history to have been greater than that of Kerry Packer. Perhaps with an eye to how comprehensively Packer succeeded in his revolution, the traditional authorities generally sought to be more accommodating of Modi's proposals – not surprisingly, given that the sums of money involved dwarfed those of Packer, even adjusting for inflation. Reflecting the official accommodation, Modi became an officer of the Board of Control for Cricket in India (BCCI) and of International Management Group (UK) Ltd (IMG), a company which represented the BCCI and various other international sports governing bodies. At that time he was probably the single most important person in world cricket.

But it was not all plain sailing. On two occasions early in the twenty-first century, Modi's forceful nature impelled him into the English High Court on libel actions, in one case as claimant and in the other as defendant.

MODI V CLARKE

The facts

By 2010 the IPL had become an established tournament, or at least had made sufficient money to ensure it would not be going away in a hurry. In England it had been perceived as enough of a threat for the England and Wales Cricket Board (ECB) to rush into the ill-advised adventure with the American billionaire Allen Stanford, which ended in complete farce when Stanford was sentenced to a lengthy jail term in the United States for fraud. No doubt drawing the conclusion that it was better to join the IPL than try and oppose it, three individuals involved in county cricket, including Yorkshire's chief executive, Stewart Regan, met Modi and some IMG representatives in Delhi. At the time Modi was a vice-president of the BCCI and also an alternate director on the board of the ICC.

The meeting considered whether a franchise for a 20/20 cricket league should be established in the Northern Hemisphere, mirroring the IPL. The idea was for 10 new English franchises, with the owners of the existing Indian franchises being offered the first refusal to buy them.

A report of the meeting was emailed to a number of others interested in English county cricket. In May 2010, Regan sent a copy to Giles Clarke, the chairman of the ECB. Clarke evidently did not like what he read. He fired off the following email to Shashank Manohar, president of the BCCI:

Dear Shashank

I attach an email detailing minutes of a meeting called by Mr Modi, held with IMG and 3 English Test grounds. A whistleblower provided this.

The minutes are self-explanatory.

It sets out a plan to destroy world cricket's structure and especially that in England, and create a new rebel league.

The plan seeks to remove all Boards' powers, and involve players in a fashion unheard of.

I am certain BCCI had no knowledge of this meeting nor of these proposals, but Mr Modi clearly represents that [IPL] and its Governing Council are offering financial inducements to English counties.

*We have already commenced legal action with regard to the English officials and counties involved.

*We also wish to take action against IMG for promoting this along with Mr Modi and to seek their banning from world cricket.

*ICC Regulations are very clear concerning contacts of this nature which are forbidden.

Your help and support in eradicating this threat and dealing with the miscreants will be greatly appreciated. The ECB believes under your leadership the BCCI/ECB relationship has become very strong.'

The attachment contained the report of the March meeting with Modi and the IMG. Some days later, Clarke wrote a letter to Manohar in the same terms as the email above, save that he omitted the paragraphs marked by an asterisk. Clarke's email was copied to the secretary of the BCCI and the chief executive of the ECB. Inevitably the details were leaked to the Indian press, which gave the matter a substantial amount of publicity and comment.

The action

Both IMG and Modi issued proceedings in England in libel against Clarke. IMG sued in respect of both the email and the letter; Modi only sued in respect of the email.

A preliminary hearing was held before Mr Justice Tugendhat, a very experienced libel judge, to determine whether anything in Clarke's email could actually be considered defamatory. IMG argued that the words meant that it was

complicit in the promotion of a plan to destroy the structure of world cricket and especially that in England by the creation of a new rebel cricket league so as to subvert the legitimate powers of all national and world cricketing boards ... in a manner forbidden by the ICC regulations and such as to merit the banning of the miscreant [IMG] from any role in world cricket as well as the institution of legal proceedings.

It also alleged that the email and letter had accused it of gross professional misconduct justifying not only it being banned from world cricket but also the institution of legal proceedings against it. Modi's case was that the email meant that he had been secretly orchestrating a plan to destroy world cricket; that his conduct had been unlawful; and that his conduct justified legal action against him and a ban from world cricket.

Tugendhat J rejected those arguments and held that nothing in the impugned emails was defamatory. He therefore struck out the action.

Modi and IMG appealed to the Court of Appeal, contending that the words were in fact capable of bearing a defamatory meaning.[1]

The law

There was no dispute as to the applicable law. The parties chose as usual a restatement of the classic *Sim v Stretch* test, choosing *Skuse v Granada Television Limited*,[2] in which Sir Thomas Bingham MR said: 'A statement should be taken to be defamatory if it would tend to lower the plaintiff in the estimation of right-thinking members of society generally or would be likely to affect a person adversely in the estimation of reasonable people generally.' In determining what meaning the words complained of were capable of bearing, the court referred to the summary in *Jeynes v News Magazines Limited*:

> The legal principles relevant to meaning ... may be summarised in this way: (1) The governing principle is reasonableness. (2) The hypothetical reasonable reader is not naïve but he is not unduly suspicious. He can read between the lines. He can read in an implication more readily than a lawyer and may indulge in a certain amount of loose thinking but he must be treated as being a man who is not avid for scandal and someone who does not, and should not, select one bad meaning where other non-defamatory meanings are available. (3) Over-elaborate analysis is best avoided. (4) The intention of the publisher is irrelevant. (5) The article must be read as a whole, and any 'bane and antidote' taken together. (6) The hypothetical reader is taken to be representative of those who would read the publication in question. (7) In delimiting the range of permissible defamatory meanings, the court should rule out any meaning which 'can only emerge as the produce of some strained, or forced, or utterly unreasonable interpretation' ... (8) It follows that 'it is not enough to say that by some person or another the words might be understood in a defamatory sense'.[3]

It was also accepted that there was a distinction between 'people generally' and a section of people.[4] That is to say, even if words damaged someone in the eyes of a section of the community, they

---

[1] Clarke raised other defences, but they did not fall for consideration on the appeal.
[2] [1996] EMLR 278 at 286.
[3] [2008] EWCA Civ 130 at para 14.
[4] See Greer LJ in *Tolley v Fry* [1930] 1 KB 467 at 479.

would not be defamatory unless they would also damage him or her in the eyes of right-thinking people generally. That had been the key point for Tugendhat J below: he had struck out the action in large part because Clarke's views of Modi's plans and the structure of world cricket in general would not bother society at large.

The Court of Appeal defined its task according to the words of Lord Phillips MR in *Gillick v Brook Advisory Centres*:

> The court should give the article the natural and ordinary meaning which it would have conveyed to the ordinary reasonable reader reading the article once. Hypothetical reasonable readers should not be treated as either naive or unduly suspicious. They should be treated as being capable of reading between the lines and engaging in some loose thinking, but not as being avid for scandal. The court should avoid an over-elaborate analysis of the article, because an ordinary reader would not analyse the article as a lawyer or accountant would analyse documents or accounts. Judges should have regard to the impression the article has made upon them themselves in considering what impact it would have made on the hypothetical reasonable reader. The court should certainly not take a too literal approach to its task.[5]

In other words, it was necessary to try and apply some common sense to the wording and not fail to see the wood for the trees.

The Court of Appeal's decision

The court returned to Tugendhat J's point that most people would frankly not be interested in the structure of world cricket:

> Actions designed to destroy cricket's structure or which could be viewed by the cricketing authorities as requiring banning a person from cricket because of the desire to destroy its structure would only be considered defamatory by that section of the cricketing public which has faith in the current structure. It is difficult to see how saying of someone that he wishes to destroy the structure of world cricket would be considered by society at large as being disparaging; there may be all sorts of reasons why someone would wish to change the structure of cricket, but it would be only to that section that believed in the present structure that making such a statement would be

---

[5]   [2001] EWCA Civ 1263.

Eighteenth century cricket: elaborate costumes, elaborate betting transactions
(TopFoto)

WG Grace: genius, gamesmanship
and General of Victorian cricket
(TopFoto)

Lord Denning: village cricket's champion
(TopFoto)

Master cricketer with a master
advocate: Imran Khan and George
Carman QC outside the Royal
Courts of Justice (TopFoto)

"The line of the body": Harold Larwood bowls to Bill Woodfull with a full Bodyline field in place (TopFoto)

Modern protection: almost 80 years after Bodyline, a well-insulated Brendon McCullum dodges a bouncer against West Indies (TopFoto)

Rebels with a cause: Tony Greig and and Kerry Packer, just after announcing they are going to court over World Series Cricket (TopFoto)

Corruption exposed: former Pakistani captain Salman Butt on trial in London for spot-fixing charges (TopFoto)

disparaging. If, by way of example in another world sport, a person was seeking to undermine the existing structure and that person had meetings without telling the establishment, the view of that person's conduct would depend entirely upon the views of that section of the public interested in that sport on the current structure.

The court then went further. First, it pointed out that it could not be considered disparaging of someone that he had gone behind the backs of the ECB and entered into negotiations with the county cricket representatives without making that fact known. Negotiations in confidence that might undermine an existing commercial structure were the ordinary stuff of business life. Second, it could not be said to be disparaging of someone that an action was being brought against him for inducing breach of contract (and therefore acting unlawfully under the civil law). Third, someone could not be disparaged by the allegation that his or her actions were forbidden by the regulations of the ICC. Those cricket followers who accorded respect to the ICC might think so, but society as a whole would not. A person seeking to bring about change could not always abide by the rules of the activity he or she was seeking to change.

Common sense and a limited victory

The court's caveats seem, with respect, obvious common sense. Nevertheless, Modi and IMG did succeed on appeal on a limited basis. In respect of Modi, the Court of Appeal stated:

> The e-mail is capable of meaning that Mr Modi was acting dishonourably as he was breaking the rules to which he had subscribed. Given his position as a member of the Board of Control of Cricket in India and an alternate director of the International Cricket Council, the reader would know he had agreed to be bound by the rules and practices of those organisations that govern international and national cricket. The e-mail was capable of meaning that he had by his actions undermined those rules to which he was party whilst professing to be bound by them; he had engaged in secret meetings and was therefore acting dishonourably.

Hence, because Modi had signed agreements binding himself to the existing structure, it might lower his reputation in the eyes of the general public if he was known to be actively seeking to undermine that structure. He would not, as it were, be a man of his word.

IMG was in a slightly different position, since it was not a director of one of the governing bodies. Again, though, it might have its reputation lowered because it had signed contracts binding itself to the existing structure.

On that basis – much more restricted than the claims as pleaded – the court granted permission for the claims to proceed to trial.

The aftermath

The action was settled out of court on a confidential basis not long after the Court of Appeal's ruling. It has to be said that the Court of Appeal's ultimate decision seemed somewhat at odds with all that had led up to that point, including the decision of Tugendhat J, whose expertise and experience in the field (as the Court of Appeal was quick to acknowledge) is surpassed by few. What exactly was libellous about the comments? After all, Kerry Packer's reputation in the eyes of many was actually enhanced in the end by his going behind the backs of the authorities and seriously undermining them (though he himself did not have any executive role with the governing bodies or contractual arrangements with them of which he was in breach).

It is also necessary to bear in mind the importance of free speech in general and the dangers of allowing libel laws in particular to become too claimant friendly. Having said that, at least the Court of Appeal placed a reasonably tight restriction on what matters Modi and IMG could take to trial, and I should not be taken to be saying that their ruling was illogical or necessarily wrong at law – only that, on a finely balanced equation, I would be inclined to err on the side of free expression and opt for Tugendhat J's decision instead.

Not that Modi would have been complaining, after his partial victory. Having settled the case, no doubt he considered that he had finished with the English libel courts. But, as he was about to discover, they were not finished with him.

CAIRNS V MODI: A TWEET TOO FAR

A nearly great

When the New Zealand side took to the field against Australia at the WACA in 1989, supporters of both teams could have been forgiven for doing a double-take at one of the opening bowlers. Chris Cairns, making his test debut, was the spitting image of his recently retired father, Lance, once said to be the most recognizable person in New Zealand. Lance had achieved folk hero status just a few years earlier at the MCG, when he nonchalantly hit six sixes off an Australian attack including Dennis Lillee, using an almost comically large bat he had christened 'Excalibur'.

There were accordingly some substantial boots for Chris to try and fill. It soon became apparent, though, that not only was Chris just as physically strong as his father, he was actually quite a lot more talented with both bat and ball. He was somewhat more athletic as well, though in fairness that was as much a reflection of the era in which he played as anything else. The talent of the younger Cairns was such that he became the customary one New Zealand selection for the hypothetical World XI of his era.

Sadly, as with almost every other New Zealand World XI contender over the years, Cairns's career became a cause for frustration almost as much as celebration. Anyone capable of plundering a test hundred off McGrath and Warne at their peak, or taking 6 for 52 against a decent English batting line-up, for example, should have finished with better statistics than a batting average of 33 and a bowling average of 29, impressive enough though those figures are.[6] Moreover, in total Cairns missed exactly half of the test matches between his debut and his retirement, due in large part to injury but also the occasional differences with management.

It would therefore have been a pleasant surprise for Cairns following his retirement from international cricket to be able to keep playing in the get-rich-quick arena of the Indian 20/20 leagues. From

---

[6] They are on a par with Ian Botham's career averages, for example. Cairns was also the world record holder for sixes hit in test cricket at the time of his retirement – quite remarkable given he only played 62 tests.

the early days of the competitions, the sort of money being bandied about was enough for any recent retiree to shrug off any lingering aches and pains and send down a few more overs.

A revolution begins

The first big-money 20/20 competition in India was the rebel Indian Cricket League (ICL). It was a Packeresque competition, not recognized by either the ICC or several national boards, including India's own. Players who took part therefore risked a ban from official competitions. Unsurprisingly therefore most of the overseas participants were from the ranks of the recently retired, joining Indian nationals who were mostly just below international contention.

The ICL held three international tournaments, the first in late 2007 followed by two in 2008. Cairns played in all three as captain of the Chandigarh Lions. In the third tournament he was also their coach.

Seeing which way the wind was blowing, the BCCI decided to organize its own 20/20 tournament, which led to the creation of the IPL. For the first IPL tournament an auction of players was held, which attracted considerable media attention due to the wholly unprecedented amount of money that the players were reputedly going to receive.

Modi tweets, Cairns sues

At the time of the first IPL tournament, Lalit Modi was the vice-president of the BCCI and chairman and commissioner of the IPL, and thus probably the single most influential official in world cricket. On 5 January 2010, he tweeted the following: 'Chris Cairns removed from the IPL auction list due to his past record in match fixing. This was done by the Governing Council today.' On the same day a journalist from Cricinfo asked Modi to confirm the tweet. Modi replied: 'We have removed him from the list for alleged allegations [sic] as we have zero tolerance of this kind of stuff. The Governing Council has decided against keeping him on the list.' Cricinfo then published an article reporting the allegations, entitled 'There is no place in the IPL for Chris Cairns'.

On 8 January, again in response to a journalist's enquiry, Modi said: 'We know what we are doing and at the end of the day he is not going to be allowed to play and that's it. Let him sue us, then we will produce what we have in court.' Sue him is precisely what Cairns proceeded to do. He brought an action in libel in respect of the first two quotations above. He brought a separate claim against Cricinfo, who settled quickly by paying the relatively modest sums of £7,000 by way of damages and £8,000 towards Cairns's legal costs.

The trial

The trial began in March 2012, before a judge sitting alone rather than with a jury.[7] Although both sides had permission to call expert evidence, neither did, leaving it up to the judge to decide everything himself.

Modi's defence was that of justification: he had been correct to call Cairns a match fixer. The burden rested upon him to prove that defence. In most civil law cases Modi would only have to show that his version of events was more likely than that of Cairns in order to win the case (the 'balance of probabilities' test). Because he had alleged criminal conduct, however, he was forced to prove his case to something closer to the criminal standard of 'beyond reasonable doubt'.

There were no technical legal issues in the case; it was simply down to the factual question of who was telling the truth. The judge sensibly held that there was no distinction between spot-fixing and match-fixing. If Cairns was involved in either he was a cheat, and would lose. The judge also held that there would be a strict definition of cheating: as captain, Cairns would not have been guilty of any wrongdoing by giving instructions to bowl any form of legitimate delivery – short pitched, on off stump or whatever. Those were matters properly within a captain's discretion, even if someone took the view that a particular decision was a poor one to make (say, pitching it up to a batsman known to be vulnerable to the short ball, or conversely dropping short on a flat track when bowling to Ricky Ponting). By contrast, an instruction to bowl a wide or a no-ball would amount to

---

[7]   The judgment is *Cairns v Modi* [2012] EWHC 756 (QB).

spot-fixing, because a captain could never have a legitimate reason to order such a delivery. Therefore, for Modi to succeed in his defence, it would not suffice to criticize Cairns's tactics; he would have to go much further and prove that Cairns had blatantly demanded cheating of some sort.

Cairns spent eight hours in the witness box over the first two days of trial, and received prolonged and sustained cross-examination by Modi's barrister. At times he came close to losing his temper, slamming his glass of water on the bench in front of him and otherwise showing frustration. But he never wavered in his version of events, and instead consistently maintained that he had never been involved in any form of match-fixing whatsoever. In a widely reported remark, he added: 'It hurts me, too, that friends – many of whom are former cricketing foes – will question my integrity as a man and a sportsman and that all I achieved in the great game of cricket is dust.'

On the fifth day, Modi's counsel indicated that Modi himself would not give evidence, even though he was present in court. Cairns was apoplectic, and rose to his feet. Towering over all others in the room, he started to advance menacingly towards Modi, who would have been relieved that the security intervened and discreetly ushered Cairns out.

Judgment was handed down a few weeks after the hearing had finished. The result was an unqualified victory for Cairns. The judge concluded that, taking account of all the evidence, and especially the witnesses called by the respective sides, Cairns could be believed and Modi could not. He rubbished the evidence of Modi's most important witnesses and added that even if he had been applying a simple balance-of-probabilities test, Modi would still have lost. He finished the issue of liability with these forthright words: 'In my judgment Mr Modi has singularly failed to provide any reliable evidence that Mr Cairns was involved in match-fixing or spot-fixing, or even that there were strong grounds for suspicion that he was.' Modi was therefore liable to pay damages.

The damages

In calculating the damages, the judge took account of the low amount Cricinfo had paid to settle the case against them, and the fact that Modi had had very few Twitter followers in England at the material time. Counting in the other direction was the way in which Modi had run the defence. The judge held that the sustained nature of Modi's plea of justification warranted an increase of 20 per cent in the damages. He decided upon the sum of £75,000, and explained:

> The flavour of the way the defence was run at trial is most vividly conveyed by the closing speech on behalf of the Defendant. As [Cairns' barrister] submitted, [Modi's barrister] could hardly have pitched it higher. The words 'liar', 'lie' and 'lies' were used in all 24 times. One passage, as [Cairns' barrister] rightly says, stands out as particularly offensive to the Claimant: 'In our submission it was nothing short of a diabolical scheme that involved blackmailing young players of ability and integrity into match fixing when that was the last thing they wanted to do ... So they were prisoners. They were being abused. There was a breach of trust by the captain and the vice-captain. They were like children in an orphans' home who, abused by everyone around them, can trust no one, can report to no one.'

Because of that aggressive conduct by Modi's representatives, the judge added another £15,000. All told, therefore, Cairns received £90,000 damages. Modi obtained permission to appeal against the award of damages, but not against the finding of liability.

The appeal

Modi's appeal[8] made a number of criticisms of the judgment. In the event, all were dismissed by the Court of Appeal, and thus the damages of £90,000 stood. Among other things, Modi's barrister argued that the detailed rejection of all the allegations in the judgment should have been sufficient to restore Cairns's reputation, and a significant award of damages was therefore unnecessary. The Court of Appeal rejected that argument, pointing out that very few cricket fans would bother to download and read the full judgment. They would not consider Cairns to have been vindicated unless a substantial award of damages had been made in his favour, and therefore the £90,000 award had been

---

[8] The appeal was joined with another case which had nothing to do with cricket and which I will therefore leave out. It was joined with Cairns's appeal because both concerned the amount of damages to be awarded for libel.

appropriate. On top of that, Modi would have to pay the costs of the trial and the appeal.

Some commentators doubted from a non-legal perspective the wisdom of resorting to the courts.[9] Cairns won the case, but it brought Modi's tweet to far greater attention than it would have had otherwise. And, despite the outcome, there would remain some who would harbour suspicions based on the cliché of there being no smoke without fire, or who would gripe about the English courts being biased. Those points are fair enough, but given the judge's complete exoneration of him and the damages awarded, I doubt Cairns had many regrets.

Comment – Twitter and libel

There was some legal novelty in the claim, because it was the first libel case in English history based on a tweet. I am unsure that the libel laws will be able to police online social networks in the long run. At the time of writing, there were more than a billion posts globally every day on the various sites such as Facebook and Twitter, and anyone's guess as to how many comments were being posted below newspaper and blog posts. Those already substantial numbers can be expected to increase exponentially over the next few years, as smartphones and tablets become still more widely used. Any number of posts and comments might be libellous, so the potential exists for the courts to be completely swamped by all the possible actions.

Or perhaps it is not as new as all that. A former England manager once complained that, thanks to modern technology, cricketers could not even go about any of the most mundane daily activities without some intrusive bystander immediately reporting the fact to the other side of the world. He lamented: 'The ether simply buzzes with these asinine messages, and "private lives" have ceased to exist. What a sense of proportion, what a waste of money, and what complete rot!'

---

[9]　See for example Mark Reason, 'Cairns will be forever the loser from court win', Stuff.co.nz Sport, 28 March 2012, www.stuff.co.nz/sport/opinion/6648547/Cairns-will-be-forever-the-loser-from-court-win (retrieved 22 April 2014).

That was Pelham Warner in 1934, referring to wireless telegraphs.[10] A few years earlier, after the first live commentary of a rugby match had been broadcast on BBC radio, the Cambridge Union had debated the motion 'The listening-in habit is a menace to the sanity of England'. In favour was one R E Stevenson, who barked: 'Wireless is a stratagem for monstrous national inactivity.'[11] I leave it to readers to guess what Warner would have thought about selfies and Facebook, or what Stevenson might have said about wireless internet connections. Staying with social media and libel laws, however, there is no principled distinction between, say, a short note on a Victorian calling card (as founded Oscar Wilde's ill-fated action against the Marquis of Queensbury in the 1890s), a wireless telegraph in the 1930s, and a 140-character tweet in the twenty-first century. In that sense, tweets are business as usual for libel courts.

Libel tourism

In his closing submissions, Modi's counsel also complained that Cairns was engaging in 'libel tourism' by suing in London. He pointed out that Cairns was a New Zealander and Modi was Indian, and the tweet had been made in India regarding an Indian tournament. The judge brushed that objection aside: Cairns had played county cricket in England for years, and by the time of the trial Modi was resident in England. Modi had never made a formal application to stay the proceedings on 'forum shopping' grounds (which in any event should have been made before the trial started, not in the closing stages) and even if he had it would have failed.

The tweet had been received by English followers, who could also read the Cricinfo article online. That would satisfy the traditional test for libel of publication within the jurisdiction. Here is another aspect on which the internet poses a significant problem for traditional legal rules. In order to bring an action for libel the claimant has to prove that there was publication in the jurisdiction: there would be no basis to bring an action in, say, England over an Indian magazine article,

---

[10]   Pelham Warner, 'Australia and the Ashes', *The Spectator*, 20 April 1934.
[11]   From Matthew Engel, 'It's the Cat's Whisker', Second Oxford Lecture, 1 February 2011, www.matthewengel.co.uk/lectures/oxford/lecture2.html (retrieved 22 April 2014).

unless the magazine had also been sold in England. Even in the days before online publishing, that would occasionally prove problematic: the rule would be technically satisfied if even one copy had been sold in England, but objective observers would be entitled to raise an eyebrow if, say, 99 per cent of a publication's circulation was in one country but the claimant was able to bring an action in the country which received the 1 per cent. One way of compensating for that anomaly would be for the court in the 1 per cent jurisdiction to award much lower damages, since the damage to the claimant's reputation in that country would be less, but that would not avoid the expense and other costs of the trial being incurred in what would seem an opportunistic forum rather than the natural forum for the case.

Since nowadays in theory anyone in any country with an internet connection can read anything published online anywhere else, the possibilities for libel tourism are much greater. Perhaps some small jurisdictions might become 'libel fora of convenience' in the same way in international shipping one finds flags of convenience. We therefore have a situation where there are billions of communications on a daily basis that might or might not be libellous, and a choice of jurisdictions over the globe.[12] The potential for libel actions swamping courts is therefore manifest. The answer I imagine will be twofold. First, over time social media will be taken less and less seriously, and a consensus will emerge that no-one in a respectable jurisdiction will be able to sue on most tweets or blog comments, in much the same way that contract law has long had a filter of 'intention to create legal relations' to discount informal agreements. Libel law has already done so for many years by excluding things said at Speakers' Corner or in obviously satirical publications (though, as *Private Eye*'s proprietors might confirm, the definition of 'obviously satirical' is something of a shifting sand...).

Secondly, most countries will follow the lead of the United States and refuse to recognize libel judgments obtained overseas, thus

---

[12]   Again, all this is not entirely new. In the 1930s, thanks to wireless telegraphs of the sort that annoyed Warner, newspapers around the world freely published details of (and speculation about) Edward VIII and Mrs Simpson, while the more deferential English papers buried their heads in the sand and said nothing until rather later in what became the abdication crisis.

rendering worthless any damages award obtained outside the natural forum. By that means the US has already shown the proper disdain for the way in which British libel and privacy laws went out of control in the early twenty-first century.

Aftermath

Modi continued his wranglings with cricket's administrative bodies, and even claimed to have survived an assassination attempt. In September 2013, he was banned for life by the BCCI, though he indicated that he wished to challenge the decision.

When first drafting this chapter, I wrote that it was probably safe to assume that Modi's story had another chapter or two yet to come.[13] What was rather a shock was to find new accusations bandied about regarding Cairns in early 2014, though it was made clear that they were only speculation and Cairns himself issued a furious denial. Shortly before this book was going to press, Cairns had travelled to London to present his side of the story to investigators, following leaked testimony from other players that seemed to implicate him in some match-fixing activities; he maintained his strenuous denials.

Meanwhile, all signs suggest that the IPL and its clones around the world will become more significant in world cricket over time. As to how beneficial for cricket they will be, the answer is probably the same as the Chinese statesman Zhou Enlai reputedly gave when asked about the French Revolution: it is too soon to tell.[14]

---

[13] In early 2014, Cricinfo's profile of Modi only offered the cautious (and hence very sparse) note: 'Fifteen days after his initial indiscreet tweet Modi was served his suspension notice by the BCCI, ironically moments after an emotional closing ceremony to the 2010 IPL final. The fallout has been messy and prolonged, with Modi taking on his former bosses at various legal and institutional levels, ensuring he remains in the headlines.'

[14] A pedant would add that Zhou, who made the quote in the early 1970s when Premier of China, was probably speaking of the 1968 revolution, not the 1789 one, but that makes the quote less amusing.

Chapter 13

THE FIXERS

THE INTERNET AGE

One of the new features Matthew Engel introduced when he became the editor of *Wisden* in the early 1990s was a section on cricket and betting. In those days it seems to have been thought a luxury rather than a necessity, since it was not included in every edition for which Engel was responsible. In the 1997 edition, Paul Haigh was sanguine about the state of play: 'Cricket is split on betting. On the one side are people who think the excitement of gambling can only be beneficial to a sport which in Britain attracts a significantly older following than most. On the other side are the traditionalists …. [who] remain convinced that gambling can only corrupt and must eventually damage the spirit of the game – if it hasn't done already.'[1]

It is fair to say that in the present day there would not be much of a split. Anyone who still thinks gambling has not damaged the spirit of the game should be referred to men in white coats, by whom I do not mean umpires. It can be said without hyperbole that gambling has become the single biggest threat to the game in recorded history. The problem, it should be stressed, does not concern the traditional, legal bookmakers such as William Hill or Ladbrokes, whom Haigh had in mind, but the network of illegal bookmakers and match fixers found predominantly on the subcontinent.

Even at the time Haigh wrote his piece, there had been an ongoing match-fixing scandal for some time in Pakistan, involving senior players. In response, Pakistan established a commission of inquiry under Judge Qayyum.[2] In the course of his investigation came what might be called the Warne and Waugh affair, in which two great Australian players were found to have taken money in return for information about games, such as pitch conditions. It turned out that instead of a holding a public hearing, the Australian board had tried

---

[1] *Wisden* 1997, p 1391.
[2] His subsequent report has been published on Cricinfo: static.espncricinfo.com/ db/NATIONAL/PAK/NEWS/qayyumreport/qayyum_report.html (retrieved 22 April 2014).

to deal with the matter in secret. That strategy might have worked if word had not leaked out, but inevitably it did, and any student of 1970s American politics could have told the Australian board about the probable consequences of trying to suppress an embarrassing story.

The Australian mishandling seemed to spring from an underlying conviction that high-profile players from outside the subcontinent could not possibly have consciously involved themselves in the Hades of match-fixing. They were right in the particular case – there has never been any suggestion that Warne or Waugh took any money to underperform, only that they naïvely supplied some anodyne information about playing conditions, the sort of things that retired players make a living discussing in the commentary box before each match. As a general proposition, however, any assumption about the unimpeachable probity of non-subcontinental players was obliterated in 2000, when, to the astonishment of the entire cricketing world, the South African captain, Hansie Cronje, admitted taking money in return for which he and certain teammates would underperform. He had also taken money (and, with a certain amount of bathos, a leather jacket) for his dramatic decision to forfeit a test match innings in order to contrive a result. Cronje was revealed to have been so corrupt that he had short-changed his co-conspirators by not paying them the full amount he had negotiated with the illegal bookmakers on their behalf. There never was any honour among thieves.

From that point, all of cricket's authorities had to accept that feigning ignorance or giving pious utterances about dealing with illegal betting would not be enough. The ICC responded by establishing the Anti-Corruption and Security Unit (ACSU). Its founding head was Sir Paul Condon, a former senior police officer.[3] A decade later, not long after retiring, Lord Condon (as he had become) gave the press a gloomy picture of international cricket before the advent of the ACSU: 'In the late 1990s, Test and World Cup matches were being routinely fixed. From the late Eighties certainly through to 1999/2000

---

[3] See 'Anti Corruption Overview', International Cricket Council, www.icc-cricket.com/about/35/anti-corruption (retrieved 22 April 2014).

there were a number of teams involved in fixing, and certainly more than the Indian sub-continent teams were involved.'[4]

The Federation of International Cricketers' Associations strongly rejected that claim. Its spokesman Tim May stated: 'To suggest that a whole generation of cricketers knew what was going on is clearly without any foundation – to further claim that they should be feeling shamed by not doing anything about it is an excessive observation.'[5] For what it is worth, I suspect May had the better of the argument: few doubt there was some match-rigging going on in the 1990s, but I do not think 'Cronjerie' was universal at the time, so far as the truth can ever be known.

Lord Condon went on to say that the fixing of whole matches or series had dried up after the establishment of the ACSU, but had been replaced by the equally iniquitous menace of spot-fixing. He also said the beginnings of match-fixing lay in the gentlemen's agreements between county sides in the old Sunday leagues: 'If you're Team A and have a higher position in the Sunday league and I'm captain of Team B and my team have no chance in the Sunday league, I might do a deal to ensure you got maximum points in your Sunday league match. You would reciprocate in the County Championships. These friendly fixes quickly became more sinister, probably in the Eighties.'

I have to say that I also find that claim somewhat tenuous. There is a substantial difference between bartering in the old domestic programme, which captains did virtually in the open at times, and the rigging of more recent international matches, which all concerned knew to be a serious criminal offence. That is not to downplay the tawdriness of the old county practice, but it is hard to believe that present-day illegal bookmakers had 1980s English domestic cricket much in mind when building their criminal empires. It is true that both old county matches and modern international fixtures suffered from a bloated schedule involving too many matches in too many tournaments. An overblown fixture list in any competition has to

---

[4] 'Every international team fixed matches in 1990s: Condon', *Times of India*, 16 November 2011.

[5] 'FICA rejects Condon's fixing claims – Sir Paul Condon Match Fixing Scandal', Cricncric, 18 November 2011, cricncric.com/news/fica-rejects-condons-fixing-claims-sir-paul-condon-match-fixing-scandal-866.html (retrieved 22 April 2014).

lessen the meaning of individual matches and thus make unscrupulous players less bothered about throwing one here or there. But to suggest that the origins of the modern match-fixing scandals lie in long forgotten county matches of decades past is, with due respect to Lord Condon, drawing too long a bow.

The sting

For all the work it undertook, it was not the ICC and its ACSU but journalists who were responsible for probably the two most important steps in combating match-fixing at the time of writing. The first was when a reporter from the British newspaper *News of the World* (a paper later closed down in the wake of a phone-hacking scandal) secretly filmed a player's agent, Mazhar Majeed. Majeed promised that he had three of the touring Pakistani players in his pocket, captain Salman Butt and the fast bowlers Mohammad Asif and the brilliant 18-year-old Mohammad Amir. To prove it Majeed said that the two bowlers would bowl no-balls at specified times of the following day's play in a test against England, which they duly did, overstepping by huge margins. All three players along with Majeed were later convicted by the English courts of conspiracy to accept corrupt payments and conspiracy to cheat.[6]

I wrote about the case at the time[7] and, like most others, was concerned with the implications of spot-fixing. I argued that even an occasional no-ball bowled intentionally would be fatal to the integrity of a game, for two reasons: (i) single runs or no-balls can be decisive in close matches; and (ii) more to the point, spectators are entitled to believe that players are giving their all at all times. That is the essence of competitive sport. The judge took much the same view and imposed harsh sentences accordingly. It transpired, however, thanks to the second significant journalistic achievement of recent times, that that was a somewhat naïve analysis.

---

[6] See *R v Mohammad Amir and Salman Butt* [2011] EWCA Crim 2914; *R v Majeed and Westfield* [2012] EWCA Crim 1186.

[7] See *Cases, Causes and Controversies*, ch 38.

Bookies, gamblers, fixers and spies

Ed Hawkins's *Bookie Gambler Fixer Spy: A Journey to the Heart of Cricket's Underworld*[8] was chosen as *Wisden*'s book of the year in 2013, not because Hawkins was being hailed as a new Cardus, but because he as a lone journalist had managed to do more to expose the scale and the mechanics of illegal betting than the ICC had managed in a decade. He had travelled to India and worked his way into the cesspool of illegal gambling; his book presented his findings.

With respect to the *News of the World* sting, Hawkins explained that no bookie would accept a bet on a single delivery, because the odds are too great and foul play would therefore immediately be suspected. Thus, by ordering the spot-fixes, Majeed had simply been demonstrating that he had the players in question in his pocket (or that he knew nothing about how the illegal gaming market worked). Instead, Hawkins discovered that there are four principal markets for illegal bookies: (i) overall match odds; (ii) runs scored in each innings; (iii) bets on runs to be scored in a certain number of overs, known as 'brackets'; and (iv) 'lunch favourites', which are bets taken during innings breaks or, say, lunch in a test match – the equivalent of half-time bets in football.

The most-prized target for the fixers is naturally the captain, because he decides who bowls when and sets all the field placings. Hence, Hawkins warns, one sign that a match has been nobbled is a bizarre and unorthodox fielding choice at a critical stage of an innings. Behind the captain the next favourite targets are the opening batsmen and bowlers, because they can have a decisive influence on each of the four markets, especially (i), (ii) and (iv).

The fixers use a '*bhao*' line for each match, which consists of someone delivering odds into a microphone attached to phone lines. The location – usually hotel rooms – is always changing. Bets are taken throughout the match, based on shifting odds. The market is so large and sophisticated that, like the futures market in the City of London, traders buy and sell bets depending on how the odds are shifting as the game pans out. Because each syndicate knows that others may have influenced the match as well as them, they scrutinize

---

[8]   Published by Bloomsbury in 2012.

each game's progress, just like a trader watching the market. In particular, they are on the lookout for a shock event, which might reveal that someone else's fix is in play – say if a number of wickets fall in short order without any apparent brilliance on the part of a bowler or unpredictability on the part of the pitch.

Payment is by a system called '*hawala*'. It involves no money physically changing hands. Instead, it is sent by a telephone call or other electronic means, and no written contracts are involved. Recipients are given only a code or a token of some description. Over time, transactions between regular parties may cancel each other out, which eliminates or at least reduces the need for movement. Should a sizeable imbalance accrue, it might be settled by a courier taking money or jewels, or a normal bank might be employed for what will not necessarily look like a suspicious transaction. With a hefty dose of irony, the system works on trust (in which case it was just as well for those dealing with him that Cronje was a player rather than a fixer).

The problem

Hawkins's book sets out a damning case and his conclusions, despite commendable restraint, are appropriately pessimistic. In 2010, not long before the book came out, the Pakistani journalist Osman Samiuddin felt reasonably optimistic about cricket in general:

> India and South Africa made more or less clean breaks after their investigations in 2000. Sourav Ganguly and Shaun Pollock (and then Graeme Smith) immediately began new, successful eras for their sides as captain. Big existing fish such as Hansie Cronje and Mohammad Azharuddin were banned for life and smaller fish, such as Ajay Jadeja or Ajay Sharma or Henry Williams, were not only punished but never played for their countries again.[9]

He was, however, a good deal less optimistic about Pakistan in particular:

> That a politician, a president, a judge, a policeman, an army general or a bureaucrat is corrupt is, and long has been, inevitable. It is a

---

[9] Osman Samiuddin, 'Forever the shadow', Cricinfo, 9 July 2010, www.espncricinfo.com/match-fixing-anniversary/content/story/466539.html (retrieved 22 April 2014).

given. Cricketers used to be above this, but match-fixing simply dragged them down into this already well-built narrative. And once that transition happened, it became impossible to go back to being clean; of course a cricketer can be as corrupt as any of the above, for is he not from this land?

Hawkins has shown that corruption is anything but an exclusively Pakistani problem. With libel considerations properly in mind, he is careful about which individuals and games he names. But he claims that no international team has been entirely free from suspicion, and sometimes in games of the highest importance. For example, he offers a strong *prima facie* case that there was a serious problem with the World Cup match between India and Pakistan in 2011, and with a dramatic test match collapse by Sri Lanka at Cardiff in May 2011; if he was right about either of those, then the situation is truly dire. It is no wonder that Hawkins laments: 'I have caught the whispers and claims of too many teams, matches and players to be able to sit in a stadium or in front of a television and not, in the words of Lord Condon, exclaim "that must be moody".'

Anyone who reads his book will find themselves compelled to agree.

The obstacles

There are some parallels between combating match-fixing in cricket and the 'war on drugs' in general society considered earlier in the book. In both cases the network of criminals is so widespread, the amount of money is so large, and the communications and money trails so difficult to trace that the authorities face a near-impossible task. In cricket's case the problem is even worse since, unlike recreational drugs, there can be no argument for legalizing match-fixing.

The first suggestion which usually arises in combating any sort of crime is harsher penalties, for deterrent purposes. In the context of match-fixing I doubt there is much point – at least in England, where the existing offences and sentences are probably strong enough since match fixers of the scale of Majeed can be virtually certain of a prison sentence, and any player involved will face career ruin as well. The problem is that any potential criminal tends to be much more concerned with the chances of being caught, rather than the subsequent crime and punishment regime – unless the regime is particularly barbaric, which is not an option for a civilized nation.

Moreover, even if there is a strong punishment regime and a substantial chance of being caught, the incentive might still be enough for some players, if they happen to have sufficiently unfortunate personal circumstances. One would hope that none of the players who went on rebel tours to South Africa in the 1980s would have supported apartheid, but in many cases the money was enough for them to put aside personal principles and absorb the public opprobrium. Thus, the second suggestion which is usually made for combating crime is for living conditions to be improved, to remove the economic incentive. It is not always the case that professional cricketers are particularly wealthy. Some might start out that way and get into bad debts through bad investments, drugs or whatever. Or they might suffer misfortune through no fault of their own. In the Cardiff test of May 2011, which Hawkins identifies as questionable, many of the Sri Lankan players had been on the bus that was fired upon by terrorists in Pakistan in 2009, and on top of that they had apparently not been paid by their own board for many months. Though nothing has ever been proven in respect of the match, one can sense the strain the players would have been under.

Further, even well-paid players may succumb to temptation. No-one, including himself, thought that Cronje was short of cash, but he admitted to remaining obsessed with money however much he earned. In recent years, some successful professional snooker players, none of whom was conspicuously badly off, have been involved in match-rigging scandals as well.

One other lesson from the 'war on drugs' is that the authority's strategy of targeting the heads of syndicates – the 'Mr Bigs' of the crime world – is sound enough in theory but rarely has the desired effect. Apart from the fact that crime lords usually have greater resources than the state can spare, removing one crime lord will simply enable a rival to take over the territory. Drug lords also operate with enormous margins and so can withstand the loss of valuable consignments here and there (and the loss of a major consignment pushes up drug prices, encouraging others to invest in the trade), though the same may not yet apply to illegal gamblers.

Some solutions

Hawkins does not have a ready cure for his very bleak diagnosis, though he does offer some sensible suggestions. For a start, he argues for a better-resourced and more assertive ACSU, and a stronger approach overall by the ICC, and no-one could disagree on either count.[10] He is also correct to call for a better culture among players, and in particular a greater willingness to blow the whistle on their teammates (with suitable protection, including anonymity). Given the problems in tracing communications and money trails, having honest players informing on dishonest ones is one of the few ways one can imagine the authorities ever getting to grips with match-fixing. Here one enters the realm of game theory in behavioural economics, where players can be offered the incentive of anonymization and immunity from prosecution in return for giving Queen's evidence against their co-conspirators.

No-one, however, should underestimate how difficult it will be for players to report suspicions, even anonymously. Given Cronje's standing before he was caught, it would have taken a brave player indeed to have risked a confrontation with him. Cronje was also careful only to approach the more junior players, who were least well placed to challenge him. Maintaining anonymity would not be straightforward when the witness is going to be one of a squad of probably less than twenty players. And, even if anonymity could be guaranteed, there has to be a balance maintained between the protection of a witness and the right of an accused to know the case against him. The leaks of testimonies in May 2014 given by players to the ICC will have done immeasurable harm in this respect, whatever the outcome of the particular investigations.

Hawkins further submits that that having a legalized gambling market in India would reduce corruption by half, as well as providing a handsome return for the Indian revenue, since legal bookmakers would be subject to tax. I agree that gambling should be legalized

---

[10]   Shortly before this book went to press, some considerable controversy was under way concerning the governance of ICC (a wider subject than I wished to attempt) and its relationship with the ACSU. The competence of both institutions was brought into question by the leaking of confidential testimony given by players about alleged match-fixing activities.

in India – prohibition can hardly be said to have worked – but I am sceptical that it would have a major effect on match-fixing. The same amount of money would still be gambled and the same almost invisible mechanisms would remain available to the unscrupulous. Moreover, match-fixing aside, I can imagine the large syndicates will not be especially willing to surrender a percentage of their profits to the taxman, so legalization will not interest them much.

I have no ready answer either, and instead can only add a few modest points to Hawkins's proposals.

First, given that cricketers play according to private contracts with national boards, the latter can insist on fuller disclosure of personal information, and greater controls, than the state can with its citizens. Private contracts can also provide for discipline (in the form of suspension and financial penalties) for more minor infringements and with a lower standard of proof than the criminal law can. Thus, players can be compelled to disclose dealings with bookmakers, and can be fined for having contact with them, even if no money is shown to have changed hands. No such disclosure and sanction could be applied by the state to drug dealers, for example, in the ordinary course of events.

Secondly, even though the economic incentive can never be removed entirely, the amount of money players receive nowadays, not just for international matches but for 20/20 competitions, means that the incentive can at least be reduced.

Thirdly, although the state can never hope to rein in the net of illegal bookmakers fully, the possibility of being caught in a sting, either by undercover police or by journalists, might give players pause for thought. Investigative journalists stand to make a tidy sum of money should they pull off a coup like the one which trapped the Pakistani players in England, so there are economic incentives for positive actions as well as negative ones – though a note of caution should be added about the possibility of overzealous journalists entrapping innocent players. Some high profile convictions would go a long way in this respect.

Fourthly (and I am aware that I am grasping at straws on this count), illegal bookmakers might become a victim of their own success. If there are so many syndicates trying to fix the same matches they might find it is no longer worth the risk, since bribing one player might be trumped by someone else bribing several more.

Finally, given that the wretched hive of scum and villainy that was cricket in the eighteenth century died out more or less by the end of the nineteenth century, there is some positive precedent to be found in cricket's not always illustrious past.

Chapter 14
THE NATIONALS

INTRODUCTION

The multinationals

The very first ball bowled in test cricket was faced by an Englishman, Charles Bannerman, who went on to score the very first test century.[1] Except he scored it for Australia.

No-one thought anything of Bannerman's nationality at the time, doubtless because Australia was still a fledgling nation and one which still regarded England as the 'Mother Country'. Also, given the rate of immigration from England to Australia in the nineteenth century, it was only to be expected, as reflected in the fact that as well as Bannerman, five others in that first ever Australian side had been born overseas.[2]

In fact no-one in the Victorian era even seems to have been bothered about players turning out for more than one country. In a test in Cape Town in 1892, for example, Alec and George Hearne appeared on debut for England while their brother Frank appeared for South Africa, having previously played for England twice.[3] Later Australia selected the New Zealander Clarrie Grimmett in the 1920s,

---

[1] Most of the rest of the team failed, leaving Bannerman's eventual score of 165 comprising 67.34 per cent of Australia's total of 245. Quite remarkably, at the time of writing that remains the record percentage of a team's score in a single innings in test matches (Viv Richards holds the record for 50-over internationals and, just before this book went to press, Kane Williamson managed 70 per cent of New Zealand's rather modest 60 runs in a 20/20 match against Sri Lanka).
   Also of interest is the fact that it was Bannerman's only hundred in a first-class career comprising 84 innings between 1870/71 and 1887/8. He was handsomely rewarded for the effort too – a whip-round in the crowd netted him £165.

[2] B B Cooper was born in India and T P Horan in Ireland. Like Bannerman, J R Hodges, T K Kendall and M E Midwinter were born in England.

[3] There was also a rather entertaining clash between Australia and Gloucestershire in the late 1870s (and to no great surprise W. G. Grace featured prominently) over the services of the cricketer Billy Midwinter, who ended up playing for both Australia and England at different points in his career: see Geoff Tibballs, *No-Balls and Googlies: A Cricket Companion* (Michael O'Mara, new edn, 2013), pp 101–2.

who went on to become the first bowler in history to take 200 test wickets, though in fairness New Zealand was not a test side at the time of Grimmett's debut. Elsewhere three great Indian players – K S Ranjitsinhji, his nephew K S Duleepsinhji and the Nawab of Pataudi – played test cricket for England before the Second World War. In 1956, there was some irony when New Zealand finally won a test match at the 45th attempt. Their opponents were West Indies, whose last wicket fell when the batsman was stumped by the New Zealand keeper, Simpson Guillen – who was from Trinidad and had previously played five tests for West Indies.

In February 2005, the late Bill Frindall recorded that in all some 14 cricketers had represented two countries at test level.[4] He noted that under modern ICC regulations, a lengthy period of residential qualification was required before a cricketer could represent a second country, but in olden times the rules were far more lax, enabling a few players to act in what modern observers would see as rather a mercenary fashion.

The controversies

It was only in the post-war era that issues of race and nationality took on much significance in cricket, reflecting the wider global changes of the independence of former colonies, increased rates of migration, and international attention on the apartheid regime in South Africa as seen with the D'Oliveira affair. In the 1990s, as a result of those changes, it came to pass that a substantial number of England test cricketers had not been born there, or were the children of recent immigrants. One minor cricket writer, Robert Henderson, published a piece in a major cricketing magazine deprecating the trend. The result was a furious protest followed quickly by a brace of High Court writs. The story is told in the first article in this chapter.

The second article then considers what the rules should be for different nationalities. The definition of international cricket is cricket between different *nations*. It follows that there has to be some

---

[4] 'Stump the Bearded Wonder No 93', BBC Sport, 15 February 2005, news.bbc. co.uk/sport1/hi/sports_talk/stump_bearders/4268507.stm (retrieved 22 April 2014). See also Steven Lynch, 'One of us against us', Cricinfo, 28 October 2013, www. espncricinfo.com/magazine/content/story/682705.html (retrieved 22 April 2014).

definition of what constitutes a 'national'. Otherwise, the format of international cricket as it has existed for over 130 years might as well be abandoned, presumably to be replaced by fixtures such as Acme XI v Continent Bank XI – and it has to be acknowledged that the rise of independent 20/20 competitions such as the IPL constitutes a possible step in that direction. The third article looks at one side issue generated by modern migration and demographic patterns, namely how to deal with players who wish to be excused from certain of their contractual obligations on the ground of their religious beliefs, which might not be shared by a majority of their side. The final article arises from another major political development from the second half of the twentieth century, the European Union. A ruling by the European Court of Justice in 2003, intended to resolve a dispute between a Slovakian national and a German legal entity, had a drastic effect for English county cricket. It was a classic example of the law of unintended consequences – in that instance, well-meaning rules intended for Europe's trading arrangements having effects in the very different world of county cricket a few hundred miles from Brussels.

It might be said that the same argument about nationality applies at one remove to county cricket eligibility; too many foreign players will stunt the development of locals. On the other hand, a select few of the better foreign players will increase the standard of county cricket generally and provide some (usually much-needed) box office appeal. That is a debate which can be expected to continue.

THE HENDERSON AFFAIR

England's decline and fall

In 1990 the well-known British politician Norman Tebbit (later Lord Tebbit) famously coined his 'cricket test'. He explained it in these terms: 'A large proportion of Britain's Asian population fail to pass the cricket test. Which side do they cheer for? It's an interesting test. Are you still harking back to where you came from or where you are?' Tebbit's comments – which were controversial from the start – were made just a year after the fatwa imposed by the Ayatollah Khomeini on the British author Salman Rushdie and thus at a time of some tension surrounding Britain's minority communities. Cricket followers might not have appreciated their sport being made a byword for a controversial viewpoint in such loaded political matters. But the reality was that race and nationality were already issues in cricket by that time.

Just a few years after Tebbit's pronouncement, an article was published in a leading cricketing magazine that prompted not just outrage but High Court litigation. The saga ended in embarrassment for the editor responsible, substantial costs for the publishers and a great deal of embitterment for the author.

The background

From about the late 1980s, the English national cricket team began a steady decline, culminating in 1999 when they were the lowest-ranked test side in the world. Away from home they started to resemble the Washington Generals, the exhibition basketball side fated always to lose to the Harlem Globetrotters. For the whole of the 1990s England would not win a single test series overseas, except in New Zealand, whose national side in the post-Hadlee era had fallen even further and faster than England's. Predictably, as the rot started to set in, there was considerable consternation among fans and the press at England's predicament. Equally predictably, people went looking for scapegoats.

It also happened that in the early years of England's decline a number of regular English test players had either not been born or raised in England, or were of first-generation immigrant stock. The former included the South Africans Robin Smith[5] and Allan Lamb, who had qualified for England during the period when South Africa was banished from international cricket, the Zimbabwean Graeme Hick[6] and the New Zealander Andy Caddick, Those who had learned their cricket in England but who had been born overseas or were from

[5]   Robin Smith's older brother Chris also played for England a few times in the mid-1980s. He was the polar opposite in his playing style. His highest score of 91 was made against New Zealand at Eden Park in 1984; it took 459 minutes and 396 balls, and if he had just managed another half hour or so accumulating the remaining nine then he would have made England's slowest test hundred.
[6]   Hick provided another example of the usual short-sighted approach of cricketing authorities when the TCCB executive committee proposed that the qualification period be reduced so he could play for England sooner; the motion was rejected by the board.

ethnic minorities included Mark Ramprakash, Nasser Hussain, Devon Malcolm and Phil DeFreitas.[7]

Step forward one Robert Henderson. His day job was with the Inland Revenue, but he was also an avid cricket fan who had had several articles published in cricket magazines. In 1991, he sent a lengthy tract to several professional cricket writers complaining about the number of foreign-born players and what he saw as otherwise not full Englishmen in the side. According to Henderson, a team made up of multiple nationalities could not perform together as a side as effectively as one composed wholly of the same nationality, and would be better described as a team of 'All Stars' rather than a national team. He received a number of courteous replies offering varying degrees of support.[8] For example, Jim Swanton, one of the greatest of all cricket writers, gave a guarded but far from dismissive response. He wrote:

> Briefly, I have sympathy for your point of view, but, of course, its implementation is unattainable. A considerable body of men cannot suddenly be deprived of their livelihood.
>
> I think the integration of disparate groups is largely a matter of leadership. I would however include in Test teams only those who have been educated and learned their cricket here: for instance Lamb no, Ramprakash yes.[9]

Peter Deeley's response predicted the Kolpak affair of two decades later, by warning that European integration might preclude national sporting teams from discriminating on the ground of nationality.

---

[7] The first black English test cricketer actually born in England was David 'Syd' Lawrence. Malcolm and DeFreitas were born in the Caribbean, though they had spent almost all their lives in England. Lawrence had a short international career, which was foreshortened by an horrendous injury in New Zealand in the early 1990s.
[8] Henderson's version of events, including all the letters quoted from here, is set out in 'Is it in the Blood? and the hypocrisy of the media', England Calling, 15 February 2011, englandcalling.wordpress.com/2011/02/15/is-it-in-the-blood-and-the-hypocrisy-of-the-media (retrieved 22 April 2014). It goes without saying that if any attribution is incorrect then I apologise unreservedly to anyone traduced thereby.
[9] http://englandcalling.wordpress.com/2011/02/15/is-it-in-the-blood-and-the-hypocrisy-of-the-media

David Foot suggested publishing the letter as a column, which Henderson managed to do in the magazine *Wisden Cricket Monthly* (WCM) later that year.

Three years later, Henderson's views seem to have hardened. He attempted to raise the subject not only of nationality but also the ethnicity of players with a number of cricketing publications. He claims to have received the following from David Frith on 30 March 1994:

> Let me just assure you that I was one of the earliest to feel a sense of unease at the number of foreign players piling into the England XI. It's hard to separate oneself from the personal side of it all I know all of them – even the reclusive Caddick – and like them almost without exception. But the principle seems wrong, and I think that there has been some sort of dislocation in the national psyche. How can a true Englishman ever see this as his representative side despite all the chat about the commitment of the immigrant?

Frith had founded WCM at the end of the 1970s and was still editing the magazine at the time.

The article

After further exchanges between the two, Frith published another article by Henderson in WCM. Entitled 'Is it in the blood?' (Henderson has stated that it was submitted under the title 'Racism and National Identity'), it went much further than his earlier article by suggesting that ethnic minority players were effectively incapable of giving their all for England. Henderson mentioned Malcolm and DeFreitas in the course of the article and concluded:

> In summary, the essence of my case ... is that for a man to feel the pull of 'cricketing patriotism' he must be so imbued with a sense of cultural belonging, that it is second nature to go beyond the call of duty, to give that little bit extra. All the England players whom I would describe as foreigners, may well be trying at a conscious level, but is that desire to succeed instinctive, a matter of biology? There lies the heart of the matter.[10]

---

[10] Robert Henderson, 'Is it in the Blood?, Peter Oborne and the question of Englishness', England Calling, 29 August 2010, englandcalling.wordpress.com/2012/08/29/is-it-in-the-blood-peter-oborne-and-the-question-of-englishness

To no great surprise, a storm of protest followed. Frith initially defended his right to publish the piece, while conceding that some of it had not been acceptable, but went on to make an 'unreserved apology', in which he said: 'I now accept that it was an error of judgement to have accepted [the article] for publication in the first place. I had hoped that the article would be a springboard for beneficial debate, but have been deeply disappointed at distortions in certain sections of the media. To that end, *Wisden*'s legal advisers continue to monitor the position...'[11]

The litigation

Wisden's legal advisers had plenty to monitor, as proceedings were soon issued for libel by Malcolm and DeFreitas. They chose to sue only the publishers of WCM, and not Henderson personally.

There is always some speculation when a plaintiff makes a decision not to sue everyone involved in the alleged wrongdoing.[12] Sometimes the decision might be made because the plaintiff's motives are other than financial. In Henderson's case, it has been suggested that the reason is that the plaintiffs suspected that WCM would mostly likely settle the case fairly promptly to get rid of the bad publicity, whereas Henderson – with nothing left to lose – would fight his corner. The result would have been an expensive trial and, even if the plaintiffs won, Henderson as a private individual and presumably not of great wealth would probably not have been able to pay much towards any damages or costs awarded.

In those circumstances, one can imagine the plaintiffs being advised that the publisher would be the only one worth suing. Whatever the reason, however, the plaintiff has the right to sue whoever he or she chooses. If there is someone else who has committed the same wrongdoing, then the defendant can join them as a third party (or,

---

(retrieved 22 April 2014).

[11] Quoted in *The Independent*, 8 July 1995.

[12] See for example the case of *British Chiropractic Association v Singh*, where the plaintiff chose to sue the individual author Simon Singh rather than his publisher, the *Guardian* newspaper, doubtless because they were more interested in silencing criticism than recovering damages. I have discussed the case in *Cases, Causes and Controversies*, ch 21.

in the newspeak of the Civil Procedure Rules 1998, as a 'Part 20 defendant') and compel them to pay their share of the damages.

With the writs having been issued, the question then arose as to whether a libel had been committed. Once again, the question turned on the classic definition of libel and whether Henderson's words would tend to lower the players about whom he wrote in the estimation of right-thinking members of society generally. Henderson has since maintained that the Professional Cricketers' Association was advised that there was no libel,[13] and that WCM only settled to avoid bad publicity.

His general point about only 'unequivocally English' players playing for England would certainly have been offensive to many, though that does not necessarily mean the law should have become involved. The boundaries of what the law should police either by way of hate speech or defamation are hotly contested, as one of the traditional free speech battlegrounds. Banning 'offensive' material heads down a well-trodden dangerous path. Remaining with libel, however, the important point is that one cannot libel a group, only individuals. Therefore, it would not have been enough for Henderson to have denigrated all 'non-English' (as he defined them) as a group; he would have to have named names, or at least said enough to leave the reader in no doubt as to which individuals he had in mind. Then of course he would have to have made a statement about them that would lower their standing in the eyes of right-thinking members of society generally.

One might flippantly say that the article was more likely to result in Henderson himself being thought of less well in polite society rather than anyone he was writing about. More seriously, putting the case at its highest, since Henderson had questioned whether ethnic minority players were capable of giving their all for England, and specific individuals were mentioned in the article, he had arguably implied that those players had given less than 100 per cent commitment on the international stage. It might follow that he was arguing that the players he had mentioned in the article should never have been chosen and, effectively, had failed the public, who were entitled to

---

[13]   Henderson, 'Is it in the Blood? and the hypocrisy of the media', op cit.

expect players in a test match to be giving their all. Henderson might have responded that he did not say they were not consciously giving their all, but rather that he was questioning whether they were capable of doing so, but that would not exactly help his cause.

There was, accordingly, an arguable but far from conclusive case that Henderson had libelled the players in question. Added to the bad publicity that would only have been exacerbated had it chosen to try and defend the Henderson piece in court, WCM acted sensibly by settling the case before trial. The terms of the settlement involved the payment of substantial sums to Malcolm and DeFreitas (both then made donations to charity) and a statement being read out in open court on the magazine's behalf unreservedly rejecting Henderson's views. Chris Lewis also received an apology and a donation was made to charity on his behalf. Frith weathered a severe media storm for a while, before being removed from the board of the magazine.[14]

The fallout

In his subsequent autobiography, Frith went to some trouble to disown the article:

> Robert Henderson, the author who had previously had letters published in the *Sunday Telegraph* and, this very month, in *The Cricketer*, was all but invisible and inaudible through all the uproar. It would have been so different had a leading and accessible writer penned the article. Instead, I, as editor, was taking a double blast, and the perception eventually became so ludicrously blurred that I was considered by some of the more careless as having been the actual author. The *Telegraph Magazine* later gave me a 'Flying Duck Award' as Editor of the Year, stating that I 'cast doubt on the patriotism of black and Asian England players' and that *Wisden* subsequently attracted a flurry of writs and had to pay out undisclosed damages to Devon Malcolm. I suggested they should publish a correction and apology for this particularly sloppy piece of journalism, and they did so two months later. I now wonder whether I should have pressed for compensation.[15]

[14] See David Frith, *Caught England, Bowled Australia: A Cricket Slave's Complex Story* (Eva Press, 1997), pp 330*ff.*
[15] Ibid, p 334.

Two points in that passage were not entirely fair to Henderson. First, Henderson was 'all but invisible and inaudible through all the uproar' only because no-one was prepared to give him a forum to defend his views. Indeed Frith had specifically written to him saying that he could never accept another contribution. Henderson had in fact tried hard to respond to his critics, and he became highly embittered by his failure to be given a public hearing. Of course, whether he would have been successful in defending himself and thus restoring his reputation is another matter. He has since set out several lengthy defences on his website, England Calling,[16] so readers can judge for themselves. Secondly, Frith's hurried disowning of Henderson overlooked the fact that he had corresponded with Henderson before and, obviously, as editor had accepted the article for publication.

The story was later told fairly, if through gritted teeth, in *Wisden Cricketers'Almanack*,[17] which shared its publisher with WCM. Many years later, in 2012, after a feature appeared on a different website recalling the affair, Henderson accepted an invitation to respond.[18] Frith did not, but he did allow the site to reproduce a waspish article[19] from some years before in which he had been very critical of Malcolm's autobiography, while still distancing himself from Henderson and the article.

Comment

There were two objectionable aspects to Henderson's piece. The first was that his central thesis about ethnic minorities being unable to give their all for England was nonsense. The point should not need elaboration, but one might observe in passing that it was Nasser Hussain, a promising young player at the time of Henderson's piece, whose bulldog determination finally put a stop to England's losing

[16] englandcalling.wordpress.com.
[17] *Wisden* 1996, pp 11, 1371.
[18] 'Racial slur or misunderstanding?', Cricket Web, www.cricketweb.net/forum/cricket-chat/56373-racial-slur-misunderstanding.html (retrieved 22 April 2014).
[19] See Martin Chandler, 'A Delayed Response', Cricket Web, 17 April 2012, www.cricketweb.net/blog/features/401.php (retrieved 22 April 2014). For a different account of the Henderson affair, see Neil Farrington et al., *Race, Racism and Sports Journalism* (Routledge, 2012).

culture. He was considerably aided by the Zimbabwean coach, Duncan Fletcher. No-one who saw Hussain's reaction to one of England's customary Ashes drubbings in 2003 could doubt his commitment to the cause.

By the time Hussain had finished, England had put together a string of solid performances, including winning two test series on the subcontinent as part of a sequence in which they were undefeated in five consecutive test series. Most importantly, the groundwork – partly in terms of selection and strategy, but mostly in terms of the team ethos and commitment – had been laid for the 2005 Ashes success, arguably the greatest test series victory in English history.

Moreover, although no-one was to know it at the time, Mark Ramprakash (often considered the most naturally gifted of all England's 1990s batsmen) struggled at test level not due to a lack of commitment to the cause but because he was *over*committed – in the view of all who played with him – and thus the stress he put on himself did for him at the crease.

The fact is that England performed poorly in the 1990s for a variety of reasons, none having anything to do with the ethnicity or place of birth of anyone involved. One was substandard management, including selection and coaching. The selection policies can be judged by the Gower affair, or the fact that no fewer than 28 of the players who made their debut in the 1990s ended up playing fewer than five tests each.[20] As to the general management, many examples might be chosen, but I would single out the tour of India and Sri Lanka in 1992/3, brutally dissected by Peter Hayter in *Wisden* 1994, to show that something was very rotten indeed in the state of English cricket at the time.[21] In limited-overs cricket, England did not just go from

---

[20] John Morris, Neil Williams, Steve Watkin, Hugh Morris, Dermot Reeve, Tim Munton, Neil Mallender, Paul Taylor, Richard Blakey, Mark Lathwell, Martin McCague, Martin Bicknell, Joey Benjamin, Jason Gallian, Mike Watkinson, Alan Wells, Ronnie Irani, Min Patel, Simon Brown, Mike Smith, Adam Hollioake, Ben Hollioake, Steve James, Warren Hegg, Aftab Habib, Ed Giddins, Darren Maddy, Gavin Hamilton.

[21] The tour began with the Gower affair, which I mentioned in the section on D'Oliveira. Hayter describes in wincing detail how England prepared in the wrong conditions, chose the wrong players throughout, completely misjudged the opposition, and began their post-mortem report with a lecture on facial hair.

World Cup finalists in 1992 to slightly comical failures in 1996, but managed to insult their hosts in the latter while they were about it.[22] It is unarguable that England's administration was below par for almost all of the decade, and they managed that with very few people who had a background of which Henderson would have disapproved. In early 2014, after England's defeat in Australia, Henderson wheeled his old arguments out and once again demanded that England cease hiring 'foreign' players,[23] conveniently ignoring the fact that almost all of the players to whom he objected had played important parts in England's victories in the three previous Ashes series.[24]

The second and perhaps more lasting problem with the Henderson piece was that it served to confuse an entirely legitimate debate with an entirely illegitimate one. The legitimate debate concerned selecting players who are sporting passports of convenience, which I will consider in the next chapter.

THE PROPER DEBATE

Why does nationality matter?

Outside the sporting context the question of nationality matters little once someone is deemed to be in a country lawfully. Few would dispute the right of all legal residents to be treated equally, wherever they happen to have been born and whatever their ethnicity. Most Western legal systems have developed complex non-discrimination laws accordingly.

---

[22]   See Robert Winder, *Hell for Leather: A Modern Cricket Journey* (Phoenix, 1999), who has a lot of fun at England's expense describing the 1996 tournament. Incidentally, the less said about the 1999 World Cup from England's perspective the better.

[23]   See Robert Henderson, 'Mending English cricket', England Calling, 2 January 2014, englandcalling.wordpress.com/2014/01/02/mending-english-cricket (retrieved 22 April 2014).

[24]   He might have added that the only English player to advance his reputation on the 2013/14 tour was Ben Stokes, who was born in New Zealand and whose father had represented New Zealand at rugby league. Furthermore, history quickly put England's shattering defeat in context, when the Australians defeated South Africa in their first test series after the Ashes, thus demonstrating that the Ashes defeat was due less to England's supposed foreigners and more to Australia's bowlers. In particular, England had no answer to Mitchell Johnson's rejuvenation.

For sport, however, somewhat different considerations sometimes apply, because the point of international sport is exactly that – sport between 'nations'. International team sports such as cricket depend on there being nations to compete. In turn that means there has to be something about being a national of a country – Indian or South African or whatever – as distinct from anyone else. And that requires something more than a random grandmother on either side of a player's family or one or two years living somewhere.

At the outset it is necessary to deal with the anomaly that is West Indies. Their team is drawn from a number of separate sovereign countries, and is an exception therefore to the idea of test matches being between different nations. It is, however, the exception that proves the rule: there is enough tradition and cricketing unity among the constituent nations of the Caribbean that it would be wrong on many levels to split the side into Barbados, Jamaica and the others. It is true that inter-island politics still crosses over to cricketing circles from time to time, but it is unarguable that West Indies have long been established as a test cricket team with a heritage and tradition to equal any other.[25]

For a ringing example of why nations, and nationality, matter in sport, one only needs to consider the 'Supertest' debacle of 2005. Australia's ruthless dominance of cricket for most of the 1990s and through to the mid-2000s led those with short memories to cast around for some way of challenging them (those with longer memories knew that dominant teams have one thing in common – they always lose their dominance eventually). They came up with the idea of a match between Australia and a Rest of the World XI. All being well, it was hoped that a contest between the top-ranked test side and the rest of the world would become a regular fixture on the international calendar.

[25] Being pedantic, it might be said that England is also an anomaly, since it is not a sovereign state but part of the United Kingdom. The reality has always been that anyone from Scotland, Northern Ireland or Wales who has been good enough to play test cricket has represented England without any questions being asked. To the extent that England is an anomaly, it is in the name only, perhaps deriving from the fact that 'English' and 'British' were synonymous at the time international cricket began, and it was not until the 1930s and the rise of Scottish nationalism that they ceased to be so.

The ICC decided from the start that the 2005 series in Australia would be granted full international status (a decision clearly in breach of its own rules, and therefore objectionable regardless of any cricketing merit[26]). There were three limited-overs matches and one six-day 'Supertest'.

The short-sightedness of the ICC was exposed even before the series began, when England won the 2005 Ashes. Two things resulted: first, less polite English supporters taunted that the wrong side was facing the Rest of the World; and secondly, however good the cricket was going to be, no-one thought it would touch the just-completed Ashes.

And so it proved. Not only did the cricket fail to approach the Ashes, it did not even reach the level of the previous tour of Australia by Bangladesh. The Rest of the World XI lost all four 'international' matches by a huge margin and the experiment was deemed a resounding failure by all concerned. Matthew Engel, a year before the Henderson storm, had said: 'It cannot be irrelevant to England's long-term failures that so many of their recent Test players were either born overseas and/or spent their formative years as citizens of other countries. In the heat of Test cricket, there is a difference between a cohesive team with a common goal, and a coalition of individuals whose major ambitions are for themselves.'[27] The Supertest debacle was the perfect illustration.

---

[26]   The ICC's own rules stated specifically that tests could only take place between full members of the ICC. Obviously the 'Rest of the World' was not a full member and accordingly the ICC had unarguably breached its own rules. The fact that it might have found the rule inconvenient, because sponsorship would have been harder to attract, is not the point. In retrospect, almost everyone agreed that the rule should have been applied and that, from any perspective, the ICC's decision was a failure, but that too is not to the point (salutary lesson though it provides). The only point is that the rules for test matches were set out in advance, and the ICC should have either changed them by the usual methods or put up with them.

The ICC's behaviour throughout displayed a *de haut en bas* attitude – we are the masters and we know what is best for you.

[27]   *Wisden* 1995, p 11. In the 1990 edition, Graeme Wright quoted Allan Border (p 42) once saying that the problem with Australia was that 'they had forgotten the reason for playing Test cricket: the feeling of national pride'.

Spirit versus the letter

Lawyers will instantly recognize the issue as the classic question of the spirit of the law versus its letter. The letter of the law might say that a national of a country is someone who holds its passport; the spirit might require something more. Were Allan Lamb and the brothers Smith (Chris and Robin) English by any sensible definition? Not according to one of their most formidable on-field opponents, Richard Hadlee of New Zealand: 'In my opinion England should not have the right to pick players like Allan Lamb to play for England. As far as I'm concerned, he is South African and NOT English. He has evidently qualified to play for England because of his English relations. If that's the case, England will soon have a team of foreigners.'[28]

Lamb and the Smiths were following in the footsteps of another South African, Tony Greig, who was England captain at the time of the Packer saga. Upon hearing the news of Packer's plans and Greig's apparent role as chief recruiting officer, John Woodcock wrote in *The Times*: 'What has to be remembered, of course, is that [Greig] is an Englishman, not by birth or upbringing, but only by adoption. It is not the same as being an Englishman through and through.'[29]

It should be said that Woodcock's point looked rather incongruous given that Australia's captain at the time, Greg Chappell, was as Australian as Bondi Beach but that did not stop him joining the Packer circus and encouraging his teammates to do likewise. Similarly, lots of 'through and through Englishmen' (however Woodcock might have defined them) were just as keen as Greig to join Packer, and for that matter to take the rand on offer in South African rebel tours not long afterwards. It was obviously unfair that South Africa at the time of Greig, Lamb and the Smiths had an iniquitous domestic policy which prevented South Africans playing test cricket. But one could

---

[28]   Richard Hadlee, *Hadlee Hits Out* (Landsowne-Rigby, 1983), p 118. Not so very long afterwards, it might be observed, Hadlee was joined in the New Zealand team by Dipak Patel. Born in Kenya, Patel was of Indian ethnicity and had lived most of his life in England.

[29]   Quoted in Christopher Lee, *Howzat! Kerry Packer and the Great Cricket War* (Old Street, 2013), Kindle location 541.

equally argue that that was not England's problem, and logically nor should it have been England's gain.

No-one could doubt the commitment of Greig, Lamb or either Smith to their own professional standards or their determination to succeed in test cricket. So too in more recent times Kevin Pietersen, perhaps the most naturally gifted player to appear for England since David Gower.[30] Pietersen claimed to have been a refugee from the post-apartheid regime, which, he argued, discriminated *against* him as a white South African by imposing affirmative action quota systems – in other words, the opposite problem to that faced by Greig or Lamb. After he qualified, Pietersen was quite outspoken about his loyalty to England. He performed sensationally in South Africa at the start of his career, hitting three extraordinary limited overs centuries in early 2005 and giving an animated response to the fairly hostile South African crowds while he was about it. Throughout his career he scorned any question about his allegiance and openly challenged anyone who offered contrary opinions, including, towards the end of his international career, the footballer Jack Wilshere[31], who had argued in the press against foreign-born and bred players turning out for England. And yet, when playing South Africa in 2012, he famously sent texts to the opposition in Afrikaans, apparently critical of his captain (Andrew Strauss, who had also been born in South Africa, though he had lived in England since the age of six).

Pietersen's vicissitudes, of which injudicious use of his *selfoon* was only one example,[32] not only raised the question about his own belief in the England cause (as opposed to the Kevin Pietersen cause), but once again called into question how 'national' the English national

---

[30]   Note that I have been writing about Pietersen's career in the past tense: he was rather dramatically removed from England contention a few weeks after the disastrous 2013/14 Ashes. As with Parliament, however, the England selectors cannot bind their successors, and so new management could not be debarred from choosing Pietersen just because of a declaration by the former regime.

[31]   See for example 'Kevin Pietersen and Jack Wilshere in Twitter row over eligibility', Sky Sports website, 10 October 2013, www1.skysports.com/football/news/12173/8965397/kevin-pietersen-and-jack-wilshere-in-twitter-row-over-eligibility (retrieved 22 April 2014).

[32]   See Patrick Collin, 'It's tough being Kevin', *Wisden* 2013, p 67.

team actually was.[33] Between 1989 and 2003 England did not field a single test side in which every player had been born in England.[34]

The journalist Peter Oborne put the matter in the following terms:

Is it possible to be born and brought up as a South African and give your full loyalty to England? I believe not. Nationality is not just a matter of convenience. It is a matter of identity. Kevin Pietersen may have chosen to come to Britain. But his attitudes and his cast of mind were formed in South Africa. Ultimately, Pietersen has not much idea of what it means to be British.'[35]

Matthew Engel stated:

My own view is simple: those who come to Britain as genuine migrants and are educated in the country should count, which would include the Somali-born Olympic champion Mo Farah, but not the likes of Pietersen or Januzaj, who move as professionals to advance their career. Without genuine allegiance, international sport becomes meaningless, and Pietersen, a great player, has always given the impression of representing Kevinland above all.[36]

Having said all that, I might throw a spanner in the works by asking rhetorically who would not be glad in retrospect that Basil

---

[33] There was also the Darren Pattinson farce. Born in England, he had grown up in Australia, where he had played most of his first-class career. In 2008, he happened to be playing county cricket in England and was having a decent season. Out of virtually nowhere he was selected for England to play South Africa. As late as the morning of the match Cricinfo listed him as an Australian player. He played one test before being discarded, with a cacophony of protest about his selection coming from former players, along with a suggestion that he had only been chosen by England to cut down Australia's options in the forthcoming Ashes. Irony was added when his brother James was later selected for Australia and played in the 2013 Ashes, leading a few comedians to suggest that England should recall Darren so that he could threaten to give James a Chinese burn or a headlock if he dismissed any of the top order.

[34] The period ran from the third Ashes test at Edgbaston in July 1989, when Allan Lamb and Robin Smith were unavailable through injury, to the first test against Sri Lanka at Gaulle in December 2003, which Nasser Hussain missed. The run would obviously have been even longer had those three players had been available to the respective sides.

[35] Peter Oborne, 'England's South Africans are on a sticky wicket', *Daily Telegraph*, 15 August 2012.

[36] Matthew Engel, 'If only all national heroes were as clear-cut as Tendulkar', *Financial Times*, 11 October 2013.

D'Oliveira was allowed to play for England and thus turn the tables on the despotic regime in his country of origin. Oborne, D'Oliveira's biographer, confined the article quoted above to criticizing white South Africans such as Greig, Lamb and Pietersen for playing for England. Partly his criticism was based on his argument that they ought to have remained in South Africa to assist in and be part of the rebuilding of that country, whereas the reverse was true in D'Oliveira's case: he assisted South Africa by moving to England and exposing the hypocrisy of the Pretoria regime. But Oborne was not simply arguing that Pietersen should have remained in South Africa, he was also arguing that he should not play for England because he was not English. Neither, by Oborne's criteria, was D'Oliveira.

A circuitous conclusion

Now to the legal problem. It is necessary to draft a set of rules specifying who can qualify to play for which team. How does one define nationality in a substantive rather than formalistic sense? How is a legislative draftsperson to spell out what makes an Englishman, a Sri Lankan or a Pakistani?

As to the first of those, the anthropologist Kate Fox concluded after an entire book on the subject: 'Englishness is not a matter of birth, race, colour or creed: it is a mindset, an ethos, a behavioural "grammar" – a set of unwritten codes that might seem enigmatic, but that anyone can decipher and apply, now that we have the key.'[37] Which is a nice definition, but not one that would pass muster for a statute. The journalist Jeremy Paxman also wrote a book on Englishness, and finished with the following:

> The English are simultaneously rediscovering the past that was buried when 'Britain' was created, and inventing a new future. The red-white-and-blue is no longer relevant and they are returning to the green of England. The new nationalism is less likely to be based on flags and anthems. It is modest, individualistic, ironic, solipsistic, concerned as much with cities and regions as with counties and countries. It is based on values that are so deeply embedded in the

---

[37] Kate Fox, *Watching the English: The Hidden Rules of English Behaviour* (Hodder & Stoughton, 2004), p 414.

culture as to be almost unconscious. In an age of decaying nation states it might be the nationalism of the future.[38]

The academic Stephen Wagg edited a substantial book on cricket and nationality,[39] containing much interesting discussion of how cricket has shaped nationality in each country. Then Icki Iqbal wrote a book about his experiences of growing up in England while being of Pakistani origin.[40] He called it *The Tebbit Test* and, in an inspired move, asked Lord Tebbit to supply the foreword, which he was happy to do (and to make a few concessions about his previously expressed views while he was about it). Both books show the difficulties and complexities involved in defining nationalities and consequently national loyalties.

It follows that any attempted definition of nationality based on less than tangible criteria would be unworkable. There could not, for example, be a regulation providing that a player could not be considered for inclusion in the English cricket team unless he met Paxman's definition of 'modest, individualistic, ironic and solipsistic'. Instead, there has to be a fixed and predictable set of criteria. If it were confined in the old Yorkshire fashion to those born within each state's borders, it would lead to absurd results. Among others, Lord Harris, Percy Fender, Douglas Jardine, Colin Cowdrey, Ted Dexter and Andrew Strauss could not have played for England.

Accordingly, a period of residence should also be a way of qualifying, provided that it is for a reasonable number of years. And this is precisely what the present ICC regulations prescribe. Their executive summary states:

A. CORE QUALIFICATION CRITERIA:

A Player shall be qualified to play for a National Cricket Federation where he/she satisfies at least one of the following requirements:

1. the Player was born in the relevant country;

---

[38] Jeremy Paxman, *The English: A Portrait of a People* (Penguin, 1999), pp 265–6.
[39] Stephen Wagg (ed), *Cricket and National Identity in the Post-Colonial Age: Following On* (Routledge, 2005).
[40] Icki Iqbal, *The Tebbit Test: The Memoirs of a Cricketing Fanatic* (DDKM, 2011).

2. the Player is able to demonstrate (by his/her possession of a valid passport issued by the relevant country) that he/she is a national of the relevant country; or

3. the Player is a Resident of the relevant country, in other words:

> 3.1 the Player has resided in the relevant country for a minimum of 183 days in each of the immediately preceding two years (female Players only);

> 3.2 the Player has resided in the relevant country for a minimum of 183 days in each of the immediately preceding four years (male Players only); or

> 3.3 the Player has resided in the relevant country for a minimum of 183 days in each of the immediately preceding seven years (male Players only).[41]

For those wishing to switch allegiance mid-career the following restriction is imposed:

C. REPRESENTING MORE THAN ONE NATIONAL CRICKET FEDERATION:

Nothing in the Regulations shall operate to prohibit a Player from representing more than one National Cricket Federation during his/her playing career. However, the following additional requirements shall apply:

7. where a male Player is seeking to qualify to play for a Full Member, he must not have participated in an International Match for any other Full Member during the immediately preceding four years;

8. where a male Player is seeking to qualify to play for an Associate or Affiliate Member, he must not have participated in an International Match for any other National Cricket Federation (irrespective of its membership status) during the immediately preceding four years;

---

[41] ICC Player Eligibility Regulations, effective from 18 September 2013, icc-live.s3.amazonaws.com/cms/media/about_docs/523af0cd4a1db-Player%20 Eligibility%20Rules%20-%20effective%2018%20September%202013.pdf (retrieved 23 April 2014)

9. where a female Player is seeking to qualify to play for any other National Cricket Federation (irrespective of its membership status), she must not have participated in an International Match for any other National Cricket Federation (irrespective of its membership status) during the immediately preceding two years; and

10. no Player shall be entitled to seek to qualify for a different National Cricket Federation more than once, unless the second qualification sought is for the same National Cricket Federation for whom he/she originally played prior to his/her re-qualification.

NOTE: No restrictions shall apply to any male Player seeking to qualify to play for a Full Member where he has previously participated in an International Match for an Associate or Affiliate Member.[42]

Note the disparity between male and female players. It is hard to imagine why anyone thought that was a good idea. It might be vulnerable to a challenge in English law under the Equality Act 2010. The ICC should therefore revise the rules to remove the difference. I would suggest that the longer eligibility requirement as applied to male players should be the same for all, to prevent a reprise of the nineteenth-century team-hopping and to emphasize the importance of test cricket as a game between opposing nations.

In law, a fixed test to answer a loose question is far from unusual. A fixed age for acquiring a driving licence (or voting, or drinking alcohol, or whatever) conflicts with the fact that people mature at different rates. Therefore, some people will have to wait for months or years despite being fully capable of passing their driving test, while others might become eligible and clog up the system with repeated applications when they manifestly have not developed to the requisite level. But to impose some more ill-defined criteria for assessment of a person's attributes would lead to inefficiency, uncertainty and unfairness.

Thus, in cricket, there will still be cases such as Kevin Pietersen or Darren Pattinson (see note 35) where a player technically qualifies but raises more than a few questions (and eyebrows) if selected. The answer is that the selectors retain the discretion whether to choose

---

[42] Ibid.

someone or not, and the management always retain the ability to suspend a player if he is judged not to be on message for whatever reason. Of course selectors might get it wrong, as I suspect most would agree they did in choosing Pattinson (Pietersen always divided opinion because he was such a good player, leaving more than a few patriotic Englishmen prepared to swallow their pride in order to retain him), but then selectors and managers (like everyone else) get plenty of other decisions wrong as well...

In short, while the nationality requirements might permit controversial decisions, they are about as good as we are likely to get.

THE EXEMPTION

In mid-2013, it was reported that the Australians were looking forward to being able to select the Pakistani refugee Fawad Ahmed, who had just been granted Australian citizenship.[43] Most of the initial press attention was concerned with how the selection had completed his journey of acceptance as an Australian citizen, or how he was one of very few ethnic minorities ever to represent Australia in cricket. There was an interesting debate over whether a refugee should have a shorter qualification time than other migrants, since a refugee was not changing country by choice but rather out of necessity (a view with which I would have some sympathy). Before Ahmed had even taken the field, however, a fresh set of headlines gave rise to an interesting and particularly vexing question about multiculturalism and integration, from which even the escapism that is cricket will not be spared.

A matter of principle

Ahmed's dilemma arose when he objected on religious grounds to wearing a uniform displaying the name of Australia's main sponsor, an alcoholic beverages manufacturer and distributor. In the event, the dispute was quickly resolved, with the authorities and the sponsor agreeing that Ahmed could wear a uniform with a blank space instead. But one should not expect such a swift and apparently happy resolution with every similar dispute in future. It is therefore worth

[43]   Chloe Saltau, 'Ahmed to put his spin on post-Ashes one-dayers', *The Age*, 16 August 2013.

pausing for a moment to see just how problematic it might be to allow the religious beliefs of one member of a side to alter private contractual arrangements between others, such as the national board and its sponsors. It forms part of one of the most emotive moral and political issues of modern times, namely how to accommodate different religious beliefs in public life.

A simple question

The question is a simple one to ask, but not so simple to answer. By the received interpretation of Ahmed's religion, alcohol was not permitted. He considered that not only was he forbidden to drink any, he was also precluded from promoting it by wearing the sponsor's logo. Cricket Australia, on the other hand, had signed an agreement with its sponsor requiring the promotion of alcoholic beverages by various methods including the logo placed with due prominence on the players' uniforms. The sponsor would get less value for its money if one or more players failed to display the logo for whatever reason. How does one reconcile that legitimate commercial interest with Ahmed's plea not to have to go against the grain of his religion?

There are a number of other ways in which the question might arise in a cricketing context. The question would be more acute where someone stood to gain something from advancing their religious beliefs – as opposed to Ahmed's case, where he did not ask for money or an exemption from any arduous duties, it was just that he did not want to wear a certain patch on his uniform. Suppose, for example, a player kept asking not to have to go to what all the team regarded as a tedious set of official functions, because the events were being held at a drinks manufacturer's premises. Or suppose they kept wanting breaks from training on religious days, or even asked not to play in certain matches because they coincided with religious holidays. There are precedents for this: in the 1980s, the All Black Michael Jones declined to play on Sundays for religious reasons; by and large the team accommodated his wish by allowing him to go on tour or otherwise be selected even though he would not be available for all matches. The English athlete Jonathan Edwards missed the 1991 World Championships because he refused to compete on Sundays. (He later gave up his no-Sunday policy and later still gave up religion altogether.)

The same dilemma has often arisen in the application of the criminal law or other general rules – including carrying knives, wearing crash helmets and undergoing random drug testing in prison.[44] Ahmed's case was slightly different: he was not asking the state to recognize his religion by granting exceptions to the criminal law, but seeking an exemption from a term of his *private* contract.

Some problems

All manner of problems can immediately be seen with such dilemmas. First, what is a religion? No-one would dispute that Islam such as that practised by Ahmed constitutes a religion. But there have been several legal disputes in recent years over other belief systems. In 2013, faced with the question of whether Scientology was a religion, the United Kingdom Supreme Court admitted that theological debates were not suitable questions for courts, and opted for a sort of catch-all definition:

> A spiritual or non-secular belief system, held by a group of adherents, which claims to explain mankind's place in the universe and relationship with the infinite, and to teach its adherents how they are to live their lives in conformity with the spiritual understanding associated with the belief system. By spiritual or non-secular I mean a belief system which goes beyond that which can be perceived by the senses or ascertained by the application of science[45]

Which covers more or less everything from Christianity to Jedi Knights to the Church of the Flying Spaghetti Monster.

Then there is a sub-issue of whether any purported beliefs are in fact required by any particular religion. This argument always arises in the debate over women wearing burkas in public: some argue that the burka is a cultural imposition, not required anywhere in Islam. The answer is that the courts are in no position to judge what are or are not genuine tenets of a religion. It would therefore have been no answer for someone to say to Ahmed that his religion did not really preclude alcohol; Ahmed would have to be taken at his word.

---

[44] See *Cases, Causes and Controversies*, ch 24.
[45] *R (on the application of Hodkin and another) v Registrar General of Births, Deaths and Marriages* [2013] UKSC 77 at para 57.

Even if one could define a religion and its required tenets, there would still be room for doubt over whether anyone was truly as devout as they would have others believe. Once again, this is not a suitable question for employers, courts or tribunals. Are they to follow someone around to see if they sneakily buy pork, alcohol or other taboo products? Are the employees to be required to call pastors as expert witnesses and adduce evidence about church attendance? Or should they be cross-examined in court to see how knowledgeable they are about the tenets of their professed faith?

A blunt answer

Imagine the manager of an international cricket team during a tour receiving an email on a Friday afternoon. The email explains that each member of the team has run into various street preachers during the day and each has undergone a Damascene conversion of sorts. The opening batsman does not want to attend an event the next day, because it is sponsored by an alcoholic drinks manufacturer. The opening bowler wants the training schedule rewritten to suit his prayer requirements. The wicket keeper wants to have every Sunday off, as a day of rest. So on it goes down the line, until the manager reaches the perpetual twelfth man, who is glad of a game but can't decide which of half a dozen newly vacated roles he would like to fill. Meanwhile, two secular players have started to complain that their beliefs are being wrongly subordinated to those of the others and that they are being unfairly burdened with extra duties as a result.

The most straightforward answer is that belief systems should not entitle anyone to an exemption to the general law that everyone else has to follow. This includes secular beliefs just as much as religious tenets. Accordingly, a player wanting an exception to the normal contract offered by his team should either have to negotiate the terms beforehand or put up with them. While the odd exception here and there, as with Ahmed, might not inconvenience anyone very much, it does not take much imagination to see how the situation might become unworkable, especially with a society growing more diverse by the day.

Making people stick to their contracts was the approach undertaken by the European Court of Human Rights until recently, when it decided[46] that instead of being a complete answer, a contract was only one factor to be weighed when 'balancing' whether or not a restriction on someone's religious freedom would be 'proportionate'. Applying its proportionality exercise, the court decided that it was permissible for a hospital but not an airline to have a uniform policy which banned crucifixes. The reason offered for the distinction was that the hospital was acting on health and safety grounds, which the court could not second-guess, but the airline was only applying a uniform policy as part of its public relations strategy. That seems feeble to say the least: as the court rightly recognized that it knew nothing of hygiene in hospitals, why did it think it knew something more about an airline's public relations? It is true that it is hard to see what harm the wearing of a small cross might have caused the airline, and it would be offensive to most (not just the wearers) if the airline were to refuse to allow anyone in uniform to wear a turban or a kippah to work, but these are not simple matters on which to issue legislation or court guidance.

In the messy world of commercial operations, including international cricket, not many people have time to indulge in academic exercises balancing rights to x with duties to y, still less any of the other problems identified above. The better approach, as it seems to me, would be for everyone to be given the freedom to arrange their affairs by private contract (subject to limitations to prevent exploitation or certain forms of discrimination) and then be held to them, sudden changes of mind notwithstanding. If a player could convince the cricketing authorities to grant him an exemption à la Ahmed that would be unobjectionable, but it is hard to see why there should be a legal right to enforce such a demand. I would stress that the approach I have advocated has the advantage that it would not discriminate for or against any particular religion; all would be treated the same.

Away from the vexed question of what constitutes nationality for international questions, there has always been the issue of players playing domestic cricket in other countries. The most popular

---

[46]   See *Eweida and others v United Kingdom* (Application nos 48420/10, 59842/10, 51671/10 and 36516/10). I have discussed the case in greater length in *Cases that Changed Our Lives*, vol II (LexisNexis, 2014).

destination has long been England, for two reasons: first, for a long time English county cricket was the only domestic fixture which had enough money and teams to support a professional career for overseas players; and secondly, the English summer season corresponds with most other cricketing nations' off-seasons. I turn next to one of the best-known legal controversies arising from nationality and first-class cricket.

THE KOLPAK SAGA

Introduction

In March 1997 a Slovakian handball player signed an agreement to play for a team in the second division of the German domestic league. It is probably fair to say that at the time he was thought unlikely to go down in handball history, still less that of any other sport. And yet not only did Maroš Kolpak go on to have an important effect on his own sport across Europe, he also managed to become more famous in English cricketing circles in the early twenty-first century than just about anyone who actually played the game. His impact in rugby was not much less significant. In legal terms the story is a good example of the law of unintended consequences, since it is doubtful that the drafters of the international agreements which led to the outcome in Kolpak's case had in mind how they might affect English county cricket.

The litigation

Kolpak's fame derived from legal action he felt compelled to take in the early 2000s against the German handball authority, Deutscher Handballbund eV, after it had issued him with a player's licence marked with his Slovak nationality. At the time the authority imposed limitations on clubs concerning the amount of overseas players they were entitled to hire. Kolpak challenged the decision to grant the licence in that form.

He argued that the Slovak Republic was one of the non-member countries whose nationals were entitled to participate without restriction in competitions under the same conditions as German and EU players. He relied on the prohibition of discrimination resulting from the combined provisions of the EC Treaty and the association agreement between the EU and Slovakia.[47]

The German courts referred the case to the European Court of Justice for a preliminary ruling concerning the interpretation of Article 38(1) of the association agreement. Art 38(1) provided:

> Subject to the conditions and modalities applicable in each member state:

> • treatment accorded to workers of Slovak Republic nationality legally employed in the territory of a member state shall be free from any discrimination based on nationality, as regards working conditions, remuneration or dismissal, as compared to its own nationals...

The question was whether Art 38(1) was to be construed as precluding the application to a professional sportsman, who was a Slovak national and was lawfully employed by a club established in a member state, of a rule drawn up by a sports federation in that state under which clubs were authorized, during league or cup matches, to field only a limited number of players from non-member countries that were not parties to the Agreement on the European Economic Area (EEA).

The court's decision was given in May 2003.[48] It first recognized that Art 38(1) had direct effect, with the result that Slovak nationals who invoked it were entitled to rely on it before national courts of the host member state. Hence Kolpak had been entitled to bring his case. Secondly, following earlier decisions,[49] the court held that Art 38(1) of the association agreement applied to a rule drawn up by a sports federation.[50]

---

[47] The agreement establishing an association between the European Communities and their member states and the Slovak Republic, approved on behalf of the Communities by Council and Commission Decision (ECSC, EEC, Euratom) 94/909.

[48] *Deutscher Handballbund eV v Kolpak* (Case C-438/00).

[49] *Union Royale Belge des Sociétés de Football Association ASBL v Bosman* [1996] All ER (EC) 97; *Land Nordrhein-Westfalen v Pokrzeptowicz-Meyer* [2002] ECR I-1049.

[50] It reached this part of its decisions from a comparison of the aims and context of the association agreement with those of the EC Treaty. There was no ground for giving to the first indent of Art 38(1) of the association agreement a scope different from that which was recognised as being the scope of Art 39(2) EC (formerly EC

It then held, in the laboured technical language that it customarily employs, that the first indent of Art 38(1)

> precluded any application to a worker of Slovak nationality, lawfully employed in a member state, of a rule such as that in [Kolpak's case] in so far as that rule gave rise to a situation in which the national, in his capacity as a national, although lawfully employed in a member state had, in principle, merely a limited opportunity, in comparison with players who were nationals of member states or EEA member states, to participate in certain matches which constituted the essential purpose of his activity as a professional player.

In other words, sporting clubs in EU member states were not entitled to discriminate against professional players from association countries by imposing quotas on them.

The result

Given the broad scope of the reasoning of the court, the ruling was not confined to handball. Crucially, nor was it confined to Slovakia. Other countries with materially identical association agreements included South Africa and some of the constituent nations of West Indies. And there was the bombshell for cricket. If there was no restriction on counties hiring players from those countries, then, conceivably, a single county side could turn up with present-day equivalents of Barry Richards and Desmond Haynes opening the batting and Dayle Steyn and Michael Holding opening the bowling, with George Headley and Jacques Kallis in the middle order. There would not be much room for aspirant English players in those circumstances.

Moreover, counties would be a lot less minded to put time and money into developing young English cricketers if there were ready-made South African and West Indian alternatives. Aside from star players, it would also be attractive to counties to make up their numbers with overseas players who were perhaps not contenders for the top echelon of test cricket, but who would outperform the average county journeyman and not be at risk of an international call-up.

Treaty, Art 48(2)) (on the abolition of discrimination based on nationality between workers of the member states).

It was hard enough for county cricket to resist clubs preferring overseas players as it was, since any with an EU passport would already have freedom to work in the United Kingdom, thus enabling (say) an Australian with a Portuguese grandmother to be considered the same as an English player for quota purposes. Worcestershire chief executive Mark Newton told the BBC in 2004 quite bluntly: 'Like any other business we are subject to European Union employment laws. And under those laws there is nothing we can do to stop it.' Such was proved when the ECB tried to restrict 'Kolpak players' to those who had not played international cricket for another country in the previous 12 months. They were forced to back down when Yorkshire signed the South African Jack Rudolph in 2007.

Overseas players in county cricket were nothing new. Many of the great players of the 1970s and 1980s cut their teeth there, including Viv Richards, Joel Garner, Malcolm Marshall and Gordon Greenidge from West Indies and Glenn Turner and Sir Richard Hadlee from New Zealand. In those days, however, when the EEC was more akin to a trading bloc and before it grew into the EU of today, the ECB and its predecessor (the TCCB) was able to impose a quota system on the numbers who could be hired.

By 2008 there were more than 60 Kolpak players on the county circuit. The ECB tried again by imposing a financial penalty to counties of £1,100 for every game where a side fielded a Kolpak player. Since that was classified as a way of encouraging counties to develop young players who could go on to play for England, rather than a restrictive quota system, it was considered compatible with EU rules. As anyone could have predicted, however, it was only partially effective given the potential benefits for counties of Kolpak players, which most considered were worth more than £1,100. The situation reached crisis point in the 2008 season when over half the players in one fixture were Kolpak players.

The shockwaves were not confined to cricket: many Pacific Island nations as well as South Africa had association agreements with the EU, and therefore rugby union clubs stood to benefit almost as much as county cricket sides.

The reprieve

Finally the ECB found a reprieve, when in 2008 the EU altered the effect of the association agreements so that they only applied to goods and services rather than labour. The Home Office was therefore able to restrict Kolpak players to those who had held a valid work permit for four years, which was similar to the old rules by which overseas players had to qualify for England.

Kolpak's cricketing fame and legacy therefore started to diminish. In 2005, while it had still been in its ascendancy, *Wisden* sought out the man himself for his thoughts.[51] He had heard of cricket but never seen a game. He conceded his intentions had been limited in their scope: 'I did it for myself,' he explained. Perhaps unsurprisingly, when told certain competitors in that very different sport across the North Sea were known as 'Kolpak players', his response was to roar with laughter…

[51] *Wisden* 2005, p 1706.

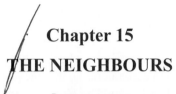

Chapter 15
THE NEIGHBOURS

INTRODUCTION

The modern law of negligence began in the early 1930s with the legendary case of *Donoghue v Stevenson*,[1] in which the House of Lords had to decide whether the manufacturer of a bottle of ginger beer owed a duty to the ultimate consumer, even though there was no contractual connection between them. Lord Atkin, drawing on the biblical parable of the Good Samaritan, famously laid down a test for whom owes a duty of care to whom:

> You must take reasonable care to avoid acts or omissions which you can reasonably foresee would be likely to injure your neighbour. Who, then, in law is my neighbour? The answer seems to be persons who are so closely and directly affected in my act that I ought reasonably to have them in contemplation as being so affected when I am directing my mind to the acts or omissions which are called into question.

This first case in this chapter, *Bolton v Stone*, was an important step in the development of negligence after *Donoghue*. The second, *Miller v Jackson*, is probably the most celebrated of all intersections of cricket and the law, thanks to the inimitable prose of Lord Denning and his unashamed celebration of village cricket. In both cases, the plaintiffs brought claims in both negligence and nuisance. The interplay between those two torts can give rise to complex legal issues, going well beyond the scope of this book. For present purposes it is sufficient to note that the same plaintiff can sue in both. Negligence in this context usually involves a particular incident or incidents of balls being hit over the fence, while nuisance involves the persistent playing of games on a ground where there are adjoining properties into which balls are regularly hit.

Away from the scenario of neighbours and passers-by being hit by balls is a more ominous prospect for sporting participants – a law suit

---

[1]   [1932] AC 562. I wrote about the case for the *New Law Journal*: see 'Love thy neighbour', 11 October 2013.

for negligence concerning something happening on the field. That possibility is considered here as well.

BOLTON V STONE

The facts

On 9 August 1947, one Miss Stone was standing on the road outside her house at 10 Beckenham Road, Manchester. The road was adjacent to Cheetham Cricket Ground, and perpendicular to the crease. The ground had existed since about 1864, whereas Beckenham Road and its houses dated from 1910.

At the time of the road's construction, the developer of the houses had come to an agreement with the club that a small strip of ground at the Beckenham Road end would be exchanged for a strip at the other end. The exchange left the distance facing the road from a batsman on strike of about 78 yards, while the road at the other end was much further away. There was a fence seven feet high along the Beckenham Road end, which with the upwards slope of the ground reached a height of about 17 feet above the pitch. Where Stone was standing was just under 100 yards from the batsman, although there were other houses closer to the ground.

In short, for a ball to land anywhere near where Stone stood would take a straight drive of extraordinary power, at least by the standards of club cricket. Unfortunately, on the day in question, a visiting batsman managed just such a remarkable shot, and Stone was hit by the ball. She brought a claim against the club, contending that they should be found liable in negligence or nuisance for her injuries.

The claim

Stone alleged: (i) the pitch was too near the road; (ii) the fence was too low to prevent balls being hit into the road; and (iii) the club had negligently 'failed to ensure that cricket balls would not be hit into the said road'. In respect of nuisance, she alleged that the matches at the ground constituted an intrinsic hazard for which the club was responsible.

One of the witnesses at trial was a Mr Brownson, who occupied the house closest to the ground. He said that five or six times during the previous few years he had known balls hit his house or come into the yard, although he was vague about exactly how many. The club members said – and the judge accepted – that it was only very rarely that a ball was hit over the fence during a match. One member, of 33 years' standing, said that he had never heard of a complaint about a ball being hit into that road. Another said that he knew of about six hits into the road in question over the course of 28 years.

The judge found for the club in respect of both negligence and nuisance, and Stone appealed. The Court of Appeal agreed with the judge that a public nuisance had not been established, but it allowed Stone's appeal in respect of negligence. The club appealed in turn to the House of Lords.

The judgment

In the House of Lords, each of the five judges gave a separate reasoned judgment, a somewhat tiresome practice that modern appellate judges still have not quite grown out of.[2] All five ruled in favour of the club and thus allowed the appeal. In essence, they considered that it was simply not reasonable to expect the club to have thought that they were posing a danger to anyone standing in the street. There had accordingly been no obligation on them to have either changed where they played or stopped the matches altogether.

The decision was a classic example of the law of negligence in action: even though their activity had been the direct cause of the plaintiff's injury, the club was not at fault because the event had been so improbable. The law – quite correctly – does not insist on perfection in human affairs. As Lord Oaksey put it:

> The standard of care in the law of negligence is the standard of an ordinarily careful man, but in my opinion an ordinarily careful man does not take precautions against every foreseeable risk. He can, of course, foresee the possibility of many risks, but life would be almost impossible if he were to attempt to take precautions against every risk which he can foresee. He takes precautions against risks which are reasonably likely to happen. Many foreseeable risks are extremely unlikely to happen and cannot be guarded against except

---

[2]   See Alexander Horne and James Wilson, 'Judgment matters', *New Law Journal*, 17 December 2010.

by almost complete isolation. The ordinarily prudent owner of a dog does not keep his dog always on a lead on a country highway for fear it may cause injury to a passing motor cyclist, nor does the ordinarily prudent pedestrian avoid the use of the highway for fear of skidding motor cars. It may very well be that after this accident the ordinarily prudent committee man of a similar cricket ground would take some further precaution, but that is not to say that he would have taken a similar precaution before the accident.

The legacy

The club might have won the case, but it does not seem to have survived to the present day.[3] The site of the ground is now occupied by another housing development, presumably to the relief of the residents of Beckenham Road, which remains relatively unchanged. What happened to Stone is not recorded.

The case itself, on the other hand, became very well known in legal circles, as part of the development of negligence in English law. I will return to that subject shortly, when considering how the law of negligence might apply to the actual playing of the game. First, however, I should record that thanks to the judgment of the House of Lords, village cricketers were left in peace until a couple of decades later when a certain Mr and Mrs Miller made an ill-judged house move.

THE DELIGHT OF EVERYONE

Unquestionably the most cherished example of cricket and the law interacting is the opening paragraph of Lord Denning's judgment in *Miller v Jackson*:

> In summertime village cricket is the delight of everyone. Nearly every village has its own cricket field where the young men play and the old men watch. In the village of Lintz in County Durham they have their own ground, where they have played these last 70 years. They tend it well. The wicket area is well rolled and mown. The outfield is kept short. It has a good club house for the players and seats for the onlookers. The village team play there on Saturdays and Sundays.

---

[3] It should not be confused, incidentally, with the nearby Cheetham Hill Club, which was founded in 1847 and is still in existence at the time of writing.

They belong to a league, competing with the neighbouring villages. On other evenings after work they practise while the light lasts. Yet now after these 70 years a judge of the High Court has ordered that they must not play there any more. He has issued an injunction to stop them. He has done it at the instance of a newcomer who is no lover of cricket. This newcomer has built, or has had built for him, a house on the edge of the cricket ground which four years ago was a field where cattle grazed. The animals did not mind the cricket. But now this adjoining field has been turned into a housing estate. The newcomer bought one of the houses on the edge of the cricket ground. No doubt the open space was a selling point. Now he complains that when a batsman hits a six the ball has been known to land in his garden or on or near his house. His wife has got so upset about it that they always go out at week-ends. They do not go into the garden when cricket is being played. They say that this is intolerable. So they asked the judge to stop the cricket being played. And the judge, much against his will, has felt that he must order the cricket to be stopped: with the consequence, I suppose, that the Lintz Cricket Club will disappear. The cricket ground will be turned to some other use. I expect for more houses or a factory. The young men will turn to other things instead of cricket. The whole village will be much the poorer. And all this because of a newcomer who has just bought a house there next to the cricket ground.

Around about this point in the judgment, the respondents to the appeal, Mr and Mrs Miller, would have started to realize things were not going their way.

The facts

The cricket ground in question was located in Burnopfield, County Durham. As Lord Denning recorded, cricket had first been played there in 1905, after the ground was leased to Lintz Cricket Club. In the early days, the ground was surrounded by agricultural fields, so few issues with neighbours would have arisen. In 1965, part of the adjacent pasture land was sold to the local council, who sold it in 1970 to property developers, and it was only then that problems began. The club objected strongly to the grant of planning permission for residential houses to be built adjoining the ground, but to no avail: permission was granted and the developers built a line of houses next to the ground. They installed a six-foot-high concrete fence around the boundary, but it was inevitable some balls were going to be hit over on a reasonably consistent basis – it certainly did not require anything like a hit of the scale of that in *Bolton v Stone* to reach the houses.

The Millers bought their particular house in 1972. They were new to the village. The rear garden had a boundary with the ground. Soon after taking possession they began to complain of incidents causing actual damage to their house, and the fear they had of personal injury whenever cricket was being played. In 1975, the club increased the height of the boundary fence to almost 15 feet to try and alleviate the situation, but some balls still continued to land in adjacent properties including the Millers'.

Claiming to be at their wits' end, the Millers brought an action against the club (the named defendant was Bob Jackson, then the club chairman) seeking damages for negligence or nuisance. They also sought an injunction to restrain the club from playing cricket on the ground without first taking 'adequate steps' to prevent balls being struck out of the ground onto their house or garden. While the club might be able to afford some damages, the injunction would in all probability have been fatal as far as playing cricket on the ground was concerned, since at the time it was thought the fence could not be raised any higher.

Financially, the litigation was quite a challenge for the club (the Millers were in receipt of legal aid). However, it received funds from the TCCB and also established a 'fighting fund', the latter being so successful in the event that it had a £3,000 surplus.[4]

The Millers gave particulars of 13 incidents of balls being hit into their property between July 1972 and July 1975. Some had caused damage to roof tiles, while others had struck window hinges or had landed in the garden. The club denied negligence. It argued that the Millers had contributed to any damage they might have suffered, because they had refused offers to fit shutters and unbreakable glass

---

[4]   The club paid the surplus to the TCCB. In recognition of the generosity, the TCCB made a coaching film with the money and put an appreciation of the club in the credits.

at the rear of their house. It also pointed out that since it had increased the height of the fence in 1975, only one ball had been hit over.

Then a bit of suburban spite began to creep into the case. The Millers testified that the cricketers often banged on the door and asked for their ball back, and were rude while they were about it. The club countered that it was Mrs Miller who was the rude one, and said that she often quite unreasonably refused to return the ball.

The trial was heard by Mr Justice Reeve, who found in favour of the Millers. He awarded them damages totalling £174.14, being £24.14 agreed special damages and £150 representing £30 per year for five years for personal inconvenience and interference with the enjoyment of their home and garden. More significantly, he granted them the injunction in the terms asked for, with the result that the cricket seemed doomed. The club appealed to the Court of Appeal.

As with the High Court, the Court of Appeal had to determine whether the club was liable in negligence and nuisance. The fact that far fewer balls had been hit into the Millers' property after the high fence was added effectively split the claims into two separate time periods. From the club's point of view, however, much the most important aspect of the case was the granting of the injunction preventing matches from continuing, rather than the damages which the Millers claimed.

The three judges each gave separate judgments, and the result was, in boxing parlance, a split decision.

Lord Denning

After his famous opening paragraph, Lord Denning pointed out that all the trouble had arisen from the fact that the developer had been allowed to build the houses too close to the ground. He then turned to the suburban sniping:

> In the first three years – 1972, 1973, and 1974 – quite a number of balls came over or under the boundary fence and went into the gardens of the houses: and the cricketers went round to get them. Mrs Miller [the second plaintiff] was very annoyed about this. To use her own words: 'When the ball comes over, they [the cricketers] either ring or come round in twos and threes and ask if they can have the ball, and they never ask properly. They just ask if they can have the

ball back, and that's it ... They have been very rude, very arrogant and very ignorant ... and very deceitful' and that to get away from any problems they made a point of going out on Wednesdays, Fridays and the weekends.

Lord Denning was in no doubt about who was telling the truth on that one. He dismissed Mrs Miller's complaint as 'most unfair': the cricketers, he was sure, had done their 'very best' to be polite. But it was still the case that some damage had been done before 1974. Lord Denning added that the householders had spotted an opportunity and managed to get their rates reduced. Then the club had built the higher fence and urged players to follow Bradman's strategy and try to hit the ball for four rather than six. Their efforts were so successful that the local authority withdrew the rates reduction.

Lord Denning also made use of the statistics compiled by the local equivalent of Bill Frindall:

Despite these measures, a few balls did get over. The club made a tally of all the sixes hit during the seasons of 1975 and 1976. In 1975 there were 2,221 overs, that is, 13,326 balls bowled. Of them there were 120 six hits on all sides of the ground. Of these only six went over the high protective fence and into this housing estate. In 1976 there were 2,616 overs, that is 15,696 balls. Of them there were 160 six hits. Of these only nine went over the high protective fence and into this housing estate.'

He turned to the law, and was in a particularly forceful mood:

In support of the case, the plaintiffs rely on the dictum of Lord Reid in *Bolton v Stone* [1951] AC 850, 867: 'If cricket cannot be played on a ground without creating a substantial risk, then it should not be played there at all.' I would agree with that saying if the houses or road was there first, and the cricket ground came there second. We would not allow the garden of Lincoln's Inn to be turned into a cricket ground. It would be too dangerous for windows and people. But I would not agree with Lord Reid's dictum when the cricket ground has been there for 70 years and the houses are newly built at the very edge of it. I recognise that the cricket club are under a duty to use all reasonable care consistently with the playing of the game of cricket, but I do not think the cricket club can be expected to give up the game of cricket altogether. After all they have their rights in their cricket ground. They have spent money, labour and love in the making of it: and they have the right to play upon it as they have done for 70 years. Is this all to be rendered useless to them by the thoughtless and selfish act of an estate developer in building right up to the edge of it? Can the developer or a purchaser of the house say to the cricket club: 'Stop playing. Clear out'? I do not think so.

For Lord Denning, everything came down to whether or not it was reasonable for cricket to be played on the ground in all the circumstances. And in his view, playing cricket was not just a reasonable option, but the right one. He added a final verdict on Mrs Miller and her claim:

> Mrs Miller is a very sensitive lady who has worked herself up into such a state that she exclaimed to the judge: 'I just want to be allowed to live in peace. Have I got to wait until someone is killed before anything can be done?' If she feels like that about it, it is quite plain that, for peace in the future, one or other has to move. Either the cricket club has to move: but goodness knows where. I do not suppose for a moment there is any field in Lintz to which they could move. Or Mrs Miller must move elsewhere. As between their conflicting interests, I am of opinion that the public interest should prevail over the private interest. The cricket club should not be driven out. In my opinion the right exercise of discretion is to refuse an injunction; and, of course, to refuse damages in lieu of an injunction. Likewise as to the claim for past damages. The club were entitled to use this ground for cricket in the accustomed way. It was not a nuisance, nor was it negligent of them so to run it. Nor was the batsman negligent when he hit the ball for six. All were doing simply what they were entitled to do.

Thus, Lord Denning would have thrown the case out altogether if it had been up to him. He noted, however, that the club had 'very fairly' agreed to pay for any past or future damage, and he fixed the amount of £400 to cover both. But the most important thing from the club's perspective was that the injunction was refused.

Lord Justice Geoffrey Lane

Lord Justice Geoffrey Lane gave the second judgment. He was slightly more diplomatic about the troubled life Mrs Miller had found herself leading, but shared the scepticism of Lord Denning about who was minding their manners when the cricketers were trying to get their balls back:

There is no doubt, however, that of all the residents in Brackenridge the plaintiffs were the people who seemed to have suffered the most. Judging from the evidence, Mrs Miller – whether justifiably or not – seems to have become almost neurotic about this trouble. Certainly the plaintiffs now take themselves off elsewhere while cricket is in progress, so that they will not be troubled by the incursions of cricket balls and of those who seek to retrieve them. It is perhaps worth remarking in passing that one of the things Mrs Miller said she objected to was the attitude of club members who came to No 20 in search of the balls. Although the judge made no specific finding on the matter, it seems that she may have been unduly sensitive on this aspect of the affair at least.

That aside, he took a more legalistic view of proceedings than Lord Denning. He considered that the club was liable in nuisance, based on a firm line of precedent[5] which held that 'coming to the nuisance' was no defence. In other words, the fact that the club had been playing cricket long before the Millers moved next door was no defence if it was proved that the cricket did constitute a nuisance.

As to negligence, he was not prepared to disturb the finding of the judge that when cricket was played on the ground, 'any reasonable person' would have to anticipate that injury would likely be caused to the Millers' property or its occupants. He concluded:

> In the present case, so far from being one incident of an unprecedented nature about which complaint is being made, this is a series of incidents, or perhaps a continuing failure to prevent incidents from happening, coupled with the certainty that they are going to happen again. The risk of injury to person and property is so great that on each occasion when a ball comes over the fence and causes damage to the plaintiffs, the defendants are guilty of negligence.

On that basis he reached the opposite conclusion to Lord Denning, and held that the appeal should be dismissed and the injunction preserved. To lessen the blow to the club, he held that the injunction should be suspended for one year to allow it time to find new premises.

---

[5] Including *Sturges v Bridgman* (1879) 11 Ch D 852.

Lord Justice Cumming-Bruce

Lord Justice Cumming-Bruce therefore had the casting vote. He agreed with Geoffrey Lane LJ's summary of the facts and his conclusions on negligence and nuisance. On the crucial question of the injunction, however, he agreed with Lord Denning. He described his task in the following terms:

> So on the facts of this case a court of equity must seek to strike a fair balance between the right of the plaintiffs to have quiet enjoyment of their house and garden without exposure to cricket balls occasionally falling like thunderbolts from the heavens, and the opportunity of the inhabitants of the village in which they live to continue to enjoy the manly sport which constitutes a summer recreation for adults and young persons, including, one would hope and expect, the plaintiffs' son.

The reason was that injunctions were a remedy of equity, which allowed for a more flexible and 'just' approach than the rigid application of the common law actions of nuisance and negligence. And in determining whether equity should allow the injunction, the court would take account of the fact that the Millers had bought the house knowing full well that there was a cricket ground next door. They had to have realized that there was a risk of balls being hit into the back yard.

Mrs Miller then received her third judicial barb:

> As it turns out, the female plaintiff has developed a somewhat obsessive attitude to the proximity of the cricket field and the cricketers who visit her to seek to recover their cricket balls. The evidence discloses a hostility which goes beyond what is reasonable, although, as the judge found, she is reasonable in her fear that if the family use the garden while a match is in progress they will run risk of serious injury if a great hit happens to drive a ball up to the skies and down into their garden. It is reasonable to decide that during matches the family must keep out of the garden. The risk of damage to the house can be dealt with in other ways, and is not such as to fortify significantly the case for an injunction stopping play on this ground.

The key point was that in determining whether or not to grant the injunction, the interests of the community as a whole had to be considered, not just those of the Millers. And the interests of the community undoubtedly favoured the retention of the cricket ground which had been there for seven decades. Those were special circumstances justifying the discharge of the injunction.

The result

Cumming-Bruce LJ therefore agreed with Lord Denning that the club's appeal against the injunction should be allowed, and the Millers left to make do with £400 damages.

Factual aftermath

Not long afterwards, and to no great surprise, the Millers moved house. There had been few issues with any other neighbours (only one had sided with the Millers), who seem to have appreciated the club's policy of sending a club officer around quickly to apologize. The fence was later raised much higher (as can be seen on the dustjacket of this book), by means of using netting between telegraph poles.

Bob Jackson eventually retired as chairman in the early twenty-first century, after 35 years' service. He recalled that the club secretary, John Cromarty, had suffered a heart attack just before the hearing in the Court of Appeal, so had been unable to attend. It was the view of most that the stress of the case, which had been ongoing for about three years by then, had contributed to Cromarty's health problems.

The club itself has continued to prosper. The case is still known among the more senior members, though its significance is perhaps not realized by the younger ones, who were born long after it was concluded.[6] Should any of them go on to study law, however, then I suspect they will find that Lord Denning's inimitable prose has retained its appeal, never more so than in the case of *Miller v Jackson*. For that reason alone the case will never be forgotten.

Legal aftermath

Several cases concerning disgruntled neighbours of village cricket grounds have since been heard in the county courts. In the 1994 case of

---

[6] I am grateful to Bob Jackson for providing his personal memories of the case. See also Fabian Muir, 'When cricket was called a tort', Cricinfo, 19 February 2012, www.espncricinfo.com/magazine/content/story/554175.html (retrieved 23 April 2014).

Lacey v Parker, the court rejected an injunction sought by neighbours of Jordans Cricket Club in Buckinghamshire that would have required the club to put up a 25-foot-high fence along the boundary. 'Thank God for the winter arriving soon,' said the claimant's wife afterwards, but the cricketers generously moved the pitch 150 yards anyway, to a site where they thought there would be 'a lot less hassle'.[7]

The case received a short mention in *Wisden* at the time, and a few years later in an article by the barrister Richard Colbey.[8] Colbey stated that the decision 'was seen by many as proof that the doctrine of *Miller v Jackson* had survived'. With due respect, a county court (as Colbey acknowledged) cannot challenge a decision of the Court of Appeal; only the Court of Appeal itself (in limited circumstances) or the House of Lords (now the Supreme Court) may do so. Since neither had considered *Miller v Jackson* at that time, it was axiomatic that the decision was still good law in 1994.

In 2010, *Wisden*[9] mentioned the case of one Mr Burgess, heard in Guildford County Court (and thus not so far from where John Derrick and his friends had played the game all those centuries earlier), which also rejected an application for a mandatory injunction requiring the installation of a barrier to stop cricket balls. Elsewhere, a resident of the Isle of Wight did not bother with legal niceties when he became concerned for the safety of his children because of the balls being hit into his garden. Instead, in a scene worthy of a 1970s sitcom, he drove his car onto the pitch and left it there.[10]

---

[7] *Wisden* 1994, p 1361; 1995, p 1373.

[8] Richard Colbey, 'Court on the Boundary', *Wisden* 1998, p 36.

[9] At p 1646.

[10] See Marc Dawson, *Outside Edge: An Eclectic Collection of Cricketing Facts, Feats & Figures* (Pitch, 2013), p 284. Dawson also mentions (pp 232–3) a Mrs Chiappini, who, embracing the spirit of Mrs Miller, became fed up with cricketers on the ground adjoining her house in Bearstead, Kent, hitting balls over her fence. She walked onto the pitch and remonstrated with the players in person. As it happened, two of the players were off-duty police officers. They arrested her, detained her in a cell and issued her with an £80 penalty notice for public disorder and offensive language.

Both the *Daily Telegraph* and the *Daily Mail* wrote articles highly critical of the police response (see for example David Hughes, 'Arresting a woman at a match in Kent just wasn't cricket', *Daily Telegraph*, 7 September 2011). Allowing for the journalistic slant, the police response does seem heavy handed, and Chiappini

Away from cricket, *Miller v Jackson* was relied upon in a High Court action in 2006, *East Dorset District Council v Eaglebeam Ltd and others*,[11] where the claimant successfully obtained an injunction preventing motocross races; the races were held to be a public nuisance because of the noise. In 2014, in another case involving motor racing,[12] the Supreme Court took some time to consider *Miller v Jackson* and in particular the issue of coming to the nuisance. Lord Neuberger held that the rule that coming to the nuisance was no defence was too well established to be overturned. Thus, where the claimant used her property for essentially the same purpose as that for which her predecessors had used it since before the alleged nuisance started, the defendant could not raise a defence of coming to the nuisance.

Lord Neuberger went on to say that there was much more room for argument that a claimant who built on, or changed the use of, her property, after the defendant had started the activity alleged to cause a nuisance by noise, or any other emission offensive to the senses, should not have the same rights to complain about that activity as she would have had if her building work or change of use had occurred before the defendant's activity had started. He concluded:

> It is unnecessary to decide this point on this appeal, but it may well be that it could and should normally be resolved by treating any pre-existing activity on the defendant's land, which was originally not a nuisance to the claimant's land, as part of the character of the neighbourhood – at least if it was otherwise lawful. After all, until the claimant built on her land or changed its use, the activity in question will, *ex hypothesi*, not have been a nuisance.

That seems to me to be a sensible approach, and if it had been applied in *Miller v Jackson*, the cricket club would certainly have won the case. Lord Neuberger also reiterated the unfettered discretion the court enjoyed in deciding whether to grant an injunction even when a nuisance had been established: it could always substitute damages instead – just as the Court of Appeal had done in *Miller v Jackson*.

---

could and should have challenged the fine and complained to the Police Complaints Authority.

[11]   [2006] All ER (D) 405 (Jul).

[12]   *Lawrence and another v Fen Tigers Ltd and others* [2014] UKSC 13.

A human right?

I will finish with some provocative speculation. I wonder if neighbours of cricket grounds owned by a local authority (and hence an emanation of the state, though that might not be a necessary pre-condition) could claim that their right to a private and family life under Article 8 of the European Convention on Human Rights was being infringed by balls being hit into their property? Or could the cricketers in such a case mount a defence by saying that playing the game formed part of *their* way of life under Art 8?

There is no doubt what answers Lord Denning would have given to both questions, and his present-day successors in the English Court of Appeal might be tempted to agree. But the ultimate arbiter of Art 8 is the European Court of Human Rights in Strasbourg, whose judges are not widely known for their appreciation of cricket. Personally, I doubt a neighbourly claim based on Art 8 would succeed if the cricketers were not found to be negligent or to constitute a nuisance, but I feel compelled to raise the possibility…

Having set that hare running, I now turn to a potentially even worse cricketing legal nightmare, which is the possibility that the tort of negligence might extend to the playing field itself.

NEGLIGENCE ON THE FIELD

The Caparo test

Bolton v Stone and *Miller v Jackson* were just two of numerous cases that developed the law of negligence as started by *Donoghue* back in the 1930s. Other cases were brought in respect of such diverse activities as auditors writing reports of company accounts, employers writing references and the Home Office supervising known juvenile troublemakers.

The most important post-*Donoghue* decision is probably *Caparo v Dickman*,[13] where the House of Lords expanded upon Lord Atkin's test for who owes a duty to whom. The House stated that there were three criteria for the imposition of a duty of care: (i) foreseeability of damage, (ii) proximity of relationship and (iii) the reasonableness

---

[13]   [1990] 2 AC 605.

or otherwise of imposing a duty. There is no doubt that, in general, organizers, players, instructors and umpires or referees owe a duty of care to participants in all sports. The question I am concerned with now is how such liability might arise on the field of play in a cricket match.

Owners and occupiers of grounds

Owners or occupiers of cricket grounds would probably owe a duty to the players[14] to remove known hazards, the more so for bespoke grounds hosting organized matches than for fields in which people occasionally play impromptu games.[15] Suppose a club's ground contained a known trip hazard on the bowler's run-up that the owners had not managed to remove before a match started, or even warn the players about, and a promising fast bowler went on to suffer an injury *à la* Glenn McGrath at Edgbaston in 2005.[16] At common law, the injury would be foreseeable; there would be a close enough relationship between the owners of the ground and the players; and in all the circumstances it would most likely be considered reasonable for the owners to be held liable to the bowler. (The same might apply with an especially dodgy pitch, I suppose, if one can imagine suitable facts.) That sort of case would be analogous to established authority from other sports such as boxing, where the organizers have been held in breach of their duty to provide adequate ringside medical care,[17] or jump racing,[18] where an action was recently brought by a jockey

[14] In England the duty is established under the Occupiers' Liability Act 1957.

[15] See for example *Slack v Glenie* [2000] All ER (D) 592, where the owner and occupier of an unsafe motorcycle racing track was found liable to an injured competitor, under the Occupiers' Liability Act 1957.

[16] On the morning the test was due to start, McGrath trod on a ball that had been left lying around and twisted his ankle. He had to withdraw from the match; the English batsmen's eyes lit up, especially when Ricky Ponting decided to bowl anyway, and the entire course of the series turned as England scored 400 in less than a day.

[17] See *Watson v British Boxing Board of Control Ltd and another* [2001] QB 1134. In February 2012, the *Australian* newspaper reported the former player Nathan Bracken suing Cricket Australia for not managing his knee injuries correctly.

[18] See for example *Hide v Jockey Club Racecourses Limited and others* [2013] EWCA Civ 545. Hide won not at common law but under a more stringent European directive. I for one found the decision controversial, but the Supreme Court refused permission for the club to appeal, so the case undoubtedly represents the present state of English law.

against those responsible for the track, concerning the adequacy of the barriers.

Players and umpires

Could an action be brought against the umpire or even the opposition bowler and captain, if there was a sustained barrage of fast bowling at a tail-ender, neither umpire took steps to warn or stop the attack, and the fielding captain kept the bowler on? Or could a tail-ender sue his own captain, if the latter failed to intervene as the Indian captain Bishan Bedi, did in Kingston in 1975/6 and declared the innings to save his players from injury?[19]

In 1985, the Court of Appeal considered *Condon v Basi*,[20] a case where a football player was said to have tackled another in a negligent fashion. The court expressed surprise that there was little authority on what would be the duty of care between players in sport, and ended up applying essentially the *Donoghue* test. It ruled that participants in competitive sport owed a duty of care to each other to take all reasonable care *having regard to the particular circumstances*. The last point was key: the expected circumstances of a game of rugby league for example, would be very different from the circumstances of a walk in the park (hard tackles by multiple individuals not being an expected feature of the latter). In the *Condon* case, the defendant was held to have tackled the plaintiff in such a way as to cause serious, foreseeable damage.

In other words, competitors in sport could sue each other if one performed an action that was tangibly beyond the expected circumstances of a normal match. In judging those circumstances, the court would consider factors including whether the sport was a contact or non-contact sport; whether the accident was in the 'heat of the moment' or during a quiet passage of play; whether the laws

---

[19]   In a match where some leading Indian batsmen had already been severely injured, Bedi refused to allow his tail-enders to risk the brutality being meted out by the West Indian fast bowlers, and hence effectively surrendered the match by declaring.

[20]   [1985] 2 All ER 453. I have not considered other jurisdictions, so the position might well be different in other countries. It certainly would be in New Zealand under the Accident Compensation scheme.

of the game were broken; what were the costs and availability of precautions; and overall what level of risk was involved.[21]

In cricket, one possibility might be if a fielder threw the ball in a deliberate and aggressive fashion at a batsman when there was no chance of a run-out and the batsman's back was turned, and thereby caused the batsman a serious injury.

What of the umpires? In two separate cases, rugby union players successfully sued the referee for failing to control the scrum collapse which led to them suffering severe injuries (both played at hooker). In both cases the Court of Appeal dismissed the referee's subsequent appeal. In the first case, *Smolden v Witworth*,[22] the Court of Appeal applied the same approach as *Condon v Basi* to establishing liability. It finished with a note of caution: '[The judge] did not intend to open the door to a plethora of claims by players against referees, and it would be deplorable if that were the result. In our view that result should not follow provided all concerned appreciate how difficult it is for any plaintiff to establish that a referee failed to exercise such care and skill as was reasonably to be expected in the circumstances of a hotly contested game of rugby football.'

In the second rugby case, *Vowles v Evans and others*,[23] the Court of Appeal again took the time to downplay fears that in future anyone would be put off refereeing an amateur match:

> Liability has been established in this case because the injury resulted from a failure to implement a law designed to minimise the risk of just the kind of accident which subsequently occurred. We believe that such a failure is itself likely to be very rare. Much rarer will be the case where there are grounds for alleging that it has caused a serious injury. Serious injuries are happily rare, but they are an inherent risk of the game. That risk is one which those who play rugby believe is worth taking, having regard to the satisfaction that they get from the game. We would not expect the much more remote risk of facing a

---

[21] See Michael Beloff QC and Rupert Beloff, 'The Field of Play' in Simon Hetherington (ed), *Halsbury's Laws of England Centenary Essays 2007* (LexisNexis, 2007), p 147 at p 155.

[22] *The Times*, 23 April 1996 (first instance); [1997] PIQR P 133 (CA).

[23] [2003] All ER (D) 134 (Mar).

claim in negligence to discourage those who take their pleasure in the game by acting as referees.

It is not easy to think of an analogous situation in cricket where an umpire might be found liable. The only common danger in cricket is from short-pitched deliveries, but they are a normal part of the game, to which everyone implicitly consents by coming out to bat. Close infielders have occasionally suffered injury too, but again they consent to field there and the risk is known and obvious. For a negligence action to succeed, it would have to be brought in respect of something clearly outside the laws of the game – a close scrutiny of the current laws regarding bouncers would be required in such a case.

The consensual aspect of facing bouncers is heightened by the fact that any batsman would have the option of retiring at any point if he felt unable to deal with a particular bowler. If a bowler produced something freakish – in the order of a trundling medium pacer suddenly developing the arm speed of Wasim Akram – any negligence claim by an injured batsman would probably fail on the basis that the damage was not foreseeable. If on the other hand the bowler bowled a series of totally illegal deliveries – in the nature of beamers delivered from half way down the pitch – it would be a different story. The batsman might sue him for negligence, and the umpire as well if it was repeated behaviour and the umpire did nothing to intervene. Possibly the opposition captain might be sued too, if he refused to take the offending bowler off. Moreover, a fast bowler acting in that rather demented (and consequently highly improbable) fashion would probably be committing a criminal assault, which I will consider in the next section.

Realistically, though, if it became clear that a bowler was insisting on some deranged behaviour and no-one was prepared to stop him, then presumably the batsman would simply walk off.[24] If he did not, he would be found contributorily negligent at least, and would have any damages awarded reduced accordingly. If the bowler performed

---

[24] Aside from malicious actions of other players, in theory negligence actions might result from things such as substandard equipment (a faulty helmet), or inadequate medical care by a doctor appointed to a match, but that is moving away from negligence resulting from the players' actions alone.

the offending delivery without warning, then he alone would be liable, since no-one else would have had a chance to respond.

The fact that few cases from any sport, let alone cricket, have followed in the wake of *Condon*, *Smolden* and *Vowles* suggests that the game does not have too much to fear from ambulance-chasing lawyers. But the possibility of actions for negligence arising out of a cricket match cannot be dismissed completely.[25]

Financial loss

Leaving aside the possibility of injury to players, the umpires in modern professional games are responsible for the fate of millions of pounds. A wrong decision at a crucial stage of a tournament might have very substantial financial consequences.

The general principle, which I have already mentioned in different contexts, has always been that the courts do not interfere with the private activity that is sport, even professional sport. To the extent they have, it has generally been confined to enforcing contracts and club rules, righting unjust post-match procedures and suchlike, but not actions on the field of play that were in the ordinary course of events. Thus, they have steadfastly refused to hear law suits trying to rewrite the result of matches said to have been distorted by incompetent refereeing. This rule is found throughout the common law world, and even in the United States, despite all the stereotypes about American litigation culture.[26]

In England, the rule was confirmed in the early 1970s in a case brought by the professional footballer Ernie Machin, who nevertheless won a victory on different grounds. Machin had been sent off, fined and suspended for allegedly kicking an opponent in a match at

---

[25] Note also that I have been considering the matter more as one of general principle; I have not tried to assemble a complete list of the cricketing claims that have been brought, let alone all sporting claims. I suspect most would be brought in a county court in the first instance (and hence would not reach the law reports) and of those many would be settled out of court anyway. Anyone wanting a more comprehensive survey of the legal position should consult a specialist sports law text such as Michael Beloff et al, *Sports Law* (Hart, 2nd edn, 2012) or one of the major torts books such as Ken Oliphant (ed), *The Law of Tort* (LexisNexis, 2nd edn, 2007).

[26] See for example *Georgia High School Association v Waddell* 285 SE 2d 7 (Georgia Supreme Court, 1981).

Newcastle. The television evidence proved that he had not committed the offence. The Football Association upheld the disciplinary sanction anyway, because it claimed he was guilty of something else. Machin sued. Although the courts reiterated that they could not interfere with the refereeing on the field of play, they quashed the sanction because Machin had been denied natural justice in the subsequent process: he had not been properly charged or given the proper opportunity to put forward a defence.[27]

The Court of Arbitration for Sport

In the early 1980s, the Court of Arbitration for Sport (CAS) was established under the auspices of the International Olympic Committee but became independent of the committee following reforms in the early 1990s.[28] The CAS hears two types of dispute: commercial cases concerning sponsorship, organization and the like; and disciplinary hearings. Most of the disciplinary cases seem to have concerned doping, but the CAS has also heard appeals against sanctions arising out of violence on the field of play and abuse of referees.

The CAS forms the apex of the private law arrangement that is sport, much in the same way that some commercial entities have chosen to create their own dispute resolution process in the form of international arbitral tribunals.[29] As with the mainstream courts, the CAS has refused to hear complaints about on-field umpiring, unless bias or corruption has been alleged. For example, a complaint was

---

[27]   *The Times*, 21 July 1973. See also *Griffith v Barbados Cricket Association*; *Byer and another v Barbados Cricket Association* (1989) 41 WIR 48, where the High Court of Barbados held that it had jurisdiction to intervene in a case where natural justice had not been observed by the defendant cricket association, concerning a hearing into a match where the result had been reached after a contrived declaration agreed between the two captains. It is important to note, though, that the case turned on the local legislation and hence would not be of much relevance elsewhere.

[28]   The CAS has an informative website, which includes a useful summary of its history: see www.tas-cas.org.

[29]   The rationale is that the tribunals comprise experts in the relevant fields and can generally reach decisions much more quickly and cheaply than equivalent court proceedings. The courts supervise and enforce awards where necessary, but (in English law at least) are very slow to interfere with the findings of arbitrators, reasoning that the parties ought to be held to their bargain, one aspect of which is the dispute resolution procedure in that bargain.

made to the CAS by the South Korean gymnast Yang Tae-Young in respect of the 2004 Summer Olympics. Yang argued that the judges had misunderstood one aspect of his routine and incorrectly marked him down. If they had not made the error, he would have won gold rather than bronze. The CAS dismissed the complaint, confirming that the decisions of the judges in the field of play could not be challenged, absent corruption. It might be added that corruption on the part of a referee would usually be a criminal offence anyway.

Neither just nor reasonable

Accordingly, despite more than 80 years of development of the modern law of negligence, no precedent has yet been set for a player – or anyone else with a legitimate financial stake in the outcome of a cricket match, such as clubs and sponsors – bringing a claim against an umpire for a blatantly wrong decision. This is despite the fact that at least the first two stages of the *Caparo* test could certainly be met in such an action, because the damage would be foreseeable and the relationship proximate (very much so in the case of a wronged player).

The reason is the third stage of the *Caparo* test: it would not be just and reasonable in all the circumstances to render an umpire's decisions reviewable. On the field there is the cast-iron rule dating back to the 1744 code: the umpire's decision is always right. Thus, even on those occasions where the batsman hits the cover off the ball and everyone barring the umpire hears the noise, the umpire's decision is deemed correct by the laws of the game. An umpire making a decision to the best of his or her ability is not being negligent, whether he or she gets it right or wrong.

I should add two related notes of caution. First, simply because no-one has yet successfully brought a case regarding an umpire's negligence does not guarantee that it will never happen; after all, few prior to 1932 would have given Mrs Donoghue much hope of succeeding against Mr Stevenson. Secondly, even if the courts preserve the general rule of not adjudicating umpires' decisions, they might find some room at the margins – say if an umpire is found to have been listening to his MP3 player instead of the game, or leaves his prescription glasses at the hotel but does not tell anyone and goes on to stand in the match without them. Clearly the umpire in those circumstances would have been negligent in the lay sense. I would still maintain, however, that the appropriate remedy would usually be for the ICC to subject the umpire to disciplinary proceedings, and *in extremis* to nullify the result of the game and order it to be replayed. It should not be for the courts to interfere by way of allowing negligence claims. Sport remains a private activity whose conduct is for the relevant sporting authorities, and if those authorities can apply a sufficient sanction there is no need for the state to interfere. The time for the courts to intervene would be if there was some evident breach of natural justice in the ICC's decision-making process similar to the *Machin* case, or, obviously, corruption.

All of that is not to say that cricketers and cricket matches are in some way above the law. If they commit actual crimes, then the fact they do so wearing flannel and with a bat or ball in their hands should not (and would not) provide an excuse, as we will now see.

Chapter 16
CRIME ON THE FIELD

INVASIONS AND INCURSIONS

Drunken invaders

The most common sort of criminal activity at cricket grounds has involved errant spectators interrupting play for some reason – almost always a bet or a dare combined with a lot of alcohol. Usually the miscreants have been removed by stewards or the police reasonably promptly. In some cases they have gone on to receive a judicial slap on the wrist in the form of a fine for a public order offence.[1] In modern times, most broadcasters and print media have also made a conscious decision to ignore the troublemakers and thereby deprive them of their presumably hoped-for fifteen seconds of fame. Then again, they may now be thwarted in that respect by smartphones and YouTube.

One of the more serious incidents occurred at Perth during the 1982/3 Ashes, when an unemployed Englishman by the name of Gary Donnison ran on the field and punched the Australian bowler Terry Alderman on the back of the head. Alderman, a former Australian Rules player, did not take the abuse lightly, and tackled Donnison to the ground. Unfortunately, Alderman dislocated his shoulder in the process and was out of competitive cricket for a year. Donnison was convicted of assault, fined A$500 and ordered to undertake 200 hours' community service. He was one of 26 people who were arrested at cricket matches around the same time in what seems to have been an outbreak of poor crowd behaviour. Most of the 26 received fines but three were actually imprisoned.

---

[1] 'The criminal law in respect of public order offences is intended to penalise the use of violence and/or intimidation by individuals or groups' ('Public Order Offences Incorporating the Charging Standard', Crown Prosecution Service website, www.cps.gov.uk/legal/p_to_r/public_order_offences (retrieved 23 April 2014)). Most public order offences are dealt with at the level of the magistrates' court, involving fines or other low-level punishments, and this is the case for most references to 'public order' offences in the book, though they also include much more serious crimes (such as those relating to rioting), involving the right to trial by jury and potential imprisonment.

By contrast, when Abdul Qadir punched a spectator during Pakistan's tour of West Indies in 1987/8, it was he who ended up paying $1,000 to settle the matter, in order to avoid facing any criminal charges. Qadir's fellow countryman Inzamam ul-Haq also once took matters into his own hands when faced with an abusive fan. In an exhibition match in Canada in the late 1990s, Inzamam picked up a bat and moved to take issue with someone who had been harassing him from the sidelines, but was stopped by the security guards before reaching his tormentor.

In January 2010, during a limited-overs match against Australia at the WACA, the Pakistani Khalid Latif was tackled by an Australian intruder, a drunken fan called David James Fraser. Fraser pleaded guilty to trespassing and assault. He was fined $9,000 and banned from the WACA for life. Twenty-four other fans were also thrown out of the ground in what seems to have been a particularly unruly occasion.

Arlott's Freakers and human rights

With a bit more levity, some of the other better-known pitch invasions have involved streakers, or 'Arlott's Freakers' as they became known in England after the commentator's famous genteelism during the 1975 Ashes.[2] The streaker on that occasion was a Merchant Navy chef with the phonetically amusing name of Michael Angelow. Angelow claimed to have done it as a bet, and to have immediately regretted the action, not least because his father had been watching on television at the time. Angelow junior received some unsolicited requests to appear in adult films (despite Arlott's slightly disparaging description of his physique). He was fined for the incident, though not by a judge without a sense of humour: the amount of the fine corresponded precisely with the amount of the bet on which Angelow had collected.

After a while, the novelty value of streaking started to wear off quicker than the participants' clothes. In the Snooker World Championship one year, Steve Davis described a streaker as 'old hat',

---

[2]   Richard H Thomas, 'You can quote me on that: John Arlott', *All Out Cricket* website, 7 December 2012, www.alloutcricket.com/blogs/sundries/john-arlott-commentates-on-lords-streaker-in-1975-ashes#Wem0umQMWkRSqGck.99 (retrieved 23 April 2014).

though he was quickly corrected by the journalist Giles Smith, who quipped that it was more a case of 'no hat'. Less humorously, in 1977 Greg Chappell caught one streaker by the hand and hit him a few times across the buttocks with his bat. It occasioned some mirth until people realized how stressed Chappell had become by the incident. Away from international matches, some sort of record was probably set in 1996 during a match between Neyland and Lawrenny in the Pembrokeshire League, when no fewer than eight male streakers interrupted play. Apparently they had been at a stag party.

Another Australian streaker, one Robert Ogilvie, was foolish enough to run towards Andrew Symonds, who shoulder-charged him in a fashion that would have done the professional rugby league players with whom he trained proud. Although Section 4.2 of the ICC code of conduct provided that players could be punished for assaulting spectators (it says rather a lot that the ICC felt it had to provide specifically for such an event), Symonds was not charged. Instead, he received the explicit support of Cricket Australia, who pointed out slightly superfluously that he had been entitled to do his job as a batsman without being rushed at by a naked spectator. Ogilvie, on the other hand, was not so fortunate and was subsequently prosecuted for charges including 'wilful obscene exposure'.[3] Bizarrely, Ogilvie's experience in being flattened by Symonds did not stop yet another spectator from attempting to take off his clothes and to the field in the same match, but the police and security removed him before he could get near any of the players.

Test matches across the Tasman have been poorly attended for many years now, but among those still making the effort have included some prepared to seek such attention as they could find by streaking. One was in the Wellington test in January 2011 between Pakistan and New Zealand. In his report of the 'plays of the match' for Cricinfo, Andrew Fernando described how events and the streaker's clothes unfolded:

> Sidestepping the guard at fine leg, the poorly covered intruder sprinted onto the field, donning nought but a cape and wielding a plastic sword. He circumvented the pitch as he ran towards the opposite end

---

[3] Ogilvie was fined A$1,500 but was allegedly paid A$7,500 by a television station to tell his story, so might not have regretted much at the end of the day.

of the ground, shaking his sword at the security personnel who were closing in. He ran into trouble at long-on though, as he was cornered by three guards who tackled him to the ground, forcibly covered his genitals and escorted him out of sight.[4]

There had been another streaker when Pakistan had played England the previous August, so their players must have started to wonder if there was a conspiracy.

Female streakers have usually caused more of a stir. One was Sheila Nicholls, who performed a cartwheel in front of the commentary box at Lord's during the 1989 Ashes. She later moved to America and forged a career as a pop singer, but took the time to record her moment of cricketing infamy on her website: 'Yeah Baby... I still crack myself up about that one,' she wrote, after explaining to her American readers that the Lord's test was the 'super bowl [*sic*] of cricket'.[5]

Nudity and the law

As with most of society's taboos, it seems likely there will always be people who think wearing clothes in public is a rule to be broken. Stephen Gough, also known as the Naked Rambler, gained some publicity in 2013 after his court appearances during an attempted walk from John O'Groats to Land's End. After being convicted of a public order offence by the magistrates, he argued on appeal[6] that his right to free expression under Article 10 of the European Convention on Human Rights had been breached by the conviction. The courts accepted that being naked was a form of 'expression', and accordingly Gough's rights under Art 10 were engaged. But they went on to find that there was a 'pressing social need' to restrain Gough's rights by means of the public order offence. In other words, society's needs outweighed Gough's, and his conviction therefore stood. So far as I am aware no cricketing streaker has raised any human-rights grounds

---

[4]   Andrew Fernando, 'Harper's howlers, and a streaker stops play', Cricinfo, 17 January 2011, www.espncricinfo.com/new-zealand-v-pakistan-2010/content/ story/497107.html (retrieved 23 April 2014).
[5]   See www.sheilanicholls.com/main.htm (retrieved 23 April 2014).
[6]   *Gough v Director of Public Prosecution* [2013] EWHC 3267.

to try and escape punishment, and if they did, then following the precedent of Gough's case they would be most unlikely to succeed.

Not all outré pitch invasions have taken place during the course of play. In 1983, one Robert Shedan, who worked as an engineer by day, was charged with causing criminal damage to the Oval wicket after he was caught urinating on it. He was fined £10 and ordered to pay compensation to Surrey County Cricket Club. In 2011, a homeless couple went one further when they were caught *in flagrante* on a cricket pitch after hours. They were convicted of a public decency offence and fined £50 plus costs.[7]

Troublemakers and rioters

In contrast with streaking, no levity whatsoever has been involved in the various riots at cricket matches over the years. At the start of the book I mentioned a fracas from 1731 involving the Duke of Richmond's team. Riots also took place from the dawn of international cricket, one of the worst occurring in 1879 during a match between an English XI and New South Wales at what became the Sydney Cricket Ground. The trouble broke out after the leading New South Wales batsman Billy Murdoch was given out. Some of the crowd – including a young Banjo Paterson – ran on the pitch and attacked the umpire, George Coulthard, and some of the English fielders. After the match it was speculated that the crowd had had it in for Coulthard, on the basis that he was a Victorian employed by the English – giving the New South Welshmen two reasons not to like him. It seems Australian inter-state rivalry could plumb serious depths of bitterness in those days.[8] The troublemakers were probably egged on by any illegal gamblers at the

---

[7]   Marc Dawson, *Outside Edge: An Eclectic Collection of Cricketing Facts, Feats & Figures* (Pitch, 2013), p 233.

[8]   The uncompromising stances of Victoria and New South Wales led to the construction of Canberra to ensure that the Australian capital was geographically midway between the two states. Cricket matches at the time reflected that rivalry, with both sides having no qualms about choosing 'chuckers'. The bad behaviour at Australian cricket grounds was not confined to inter-state competitions: at a match between Melbourne CC and South Melbourne CC in 1873, with W G Grace in attendance, the crowd invaded the pitch to protest at what they thought was a wheeze by the organisers to prolong the game and fleece them for some cash; the Melbourne side had to be escorted out of the ground by police. Again, the bookmakers may have influenced events.

ground who had bet on New South Wales, since they would have seen a chance to have the match abandoned (England were on course for victory at the time of the incident): the *Sydney Morning Herald* in particular had complained about the way in which illegal betting was being conducted with impunity at the ground.

Apparently some 2,000 people in total participated in the pitch invasion, out of about 10,000 at the ground, though only two were charged with anything afterwards. They escaped with fines, perhaps all concerned having a feeling that the case was not exactly representative of what had taken place. A war of words ensued between the two sides – not the first or last time a cricketing fixture in Australia involving a touring English side led to ill-feeling between the respective countries. The English then cancelled what would have been the fourth-ever test match, but relations were patched up soon enough and the famous 1880 Australian tour of England went ahead.

Betting at the venue was apparently stamped out not long afterwards, but the standards of crowd behaviour at Australian matches remained of variable quality – not that the angry sections were always without provocation, at least when Douglas Jardine's Englishmen tested the crowd's patience almost to breaking point during the Bodyline series. The nadir was the Adelaide test, in which Jardine by encouraging his fast bowlers in their attack committed 'the most unsportsmanlike act ever witnessed on an Australian cricket field' in the opinion of an Australian selector.[9] The presence of mounted police kept the crowd restrained, but only just. 'Not to put too fine a point on it, pandemonium reigned' reported *Wisden* in the 1934 edition. It went on to say: 'Altogether the whole atmosphere was a disgrace to cricket. One must pay a tribute to Jardine.'[10] Decades later, during the Sydney test in the 1970/71 Ashes, memories of Bodyline came flooding back after England's John Snow hit Terry Jenner with a bouncer. Objects

---

[9]   See Martin Williamson, 'A near riot at Adelaide Oval', Cricinfo, 7 December 2013, www.espncricinfo.com/australia/content/story/697733.html (retrieved 23 April 2014).

[10]   Recently a local historian mentioned to Jonathan Agnew that it could not have helped matters that almost all the crowd would have been wearing heavy tweed suits in the midday sun, evidently not heeding Noël Coward's advice about mad dogs and Englishmen. See Jonathan Agnew (ed), *Cricket: A Modern Anthology* (Blue Door, 2013).

were thrown at Snow by an agitated and less well-dressed crowd, and he was accosted by a drunken fan on the boundary. England captain Ray Illingworth's response was to take the team off the field for seven minutes. During the delay, a ground attendant was knocked unconscious by a beer can thrown from the crowd. In all 14 spectators were arrested and a further 190 removed from the ground. In fact, according to one authority,[11] the second day of the test between India and Australia as recently as 2011/12 was the first time in the history of cricket in Australia that no spectator had been ejected for unruly behaviour during a test match, although that seems a slightly improbable statistic, to my mind anyway.

Obviously, Australia has not had a monopoly on bad crowd behaviour. One incident in New Zealand found its way into the law reports, although it came from the lower end of the scale of yobbishness. It started when the defendant was nearly hit by a beer can lobbed in his direction. He attempted casually to throw it against a pile of rubbish along the fence, but inadvertently struck a woman who was working at a stall selling food. The defendant was charged with disorderly behaviour, pursuant to s 4(1)(a) of the Summary Offences Act 1981. He was convicted in the district court and the conviction was upheld by the High Court.[12] It was held that he had thrown the can with little, if any, regard to where it might land and it was a readily foreseeable consequence that the can would strike and upset a person. Having regard to the classic legal test of time, place and circumstances (found in several different contexts in this book), his action amounted to an interference with the rights of others and was serious enough to justify the intervention of the criminal law.

In England, cricket has generally been spared the mindless tribal violence which blighted football for many years, though there has still been the occasional disturbance. In 1984, for example, when Sri Lanka played its first test on English soil, the match was interrupted by Tamil protestors. One of them tried to damage the pitch with a utensil; as it was a plastic spoon, he met with something less than success. At Edgbaston in 1987, Pakistani and English supporters fought a running battle on the terraces that did bear some similarity to

---

[11]   Dawson, op cit, p 284.
[12]   *Wilde v Police* [1984] 2 NZLR 673.

football hooliganism. Fifty supporters were ejected from the ground and 16 were arrested. The trouble continued even after the match, with Ian Botham being attacked by a stump-wielding Pakistani fan after an argument during (but not over) a traffic jam. As seen elsewhere in the book, English and Pakistani players, umpires and administrators employed less violence but probably greater animosity on and off the field during the same tour, which did not improve greatly during Pakistan's next visit in 1992. At Headingley in 1997, the ground staff hired some rugby league forwards to police the ground, perhaps following the lead of the Rolling Stones, whose management once hired some of the Hell's Angels motorcycle gang to police a concert, with disastrous results. The Yorkshire experiment did not reach quite the same level of violence, but the new stewards did manage to flatten an unfortunate spectator who had been unwise enough to run on the field dressed as the back end of a pantomime cow.

Some of the worst disturbances have taken place on the subcontinent. On the services' tour just after the Second World War, the team arrived in what was then still known as Calcutta while a major riot by pro-independence supporters was in progress. The match went ahead, but thousands of protestors invaded the pitch on the first day and halted play for about an hour. No-one was hurt, though elsewhere in the city 23 people were killed. On the final day another pitch invasion occurred, but the intruders were apparently charmed into leaving by Dennis Compton and Lindsay Hassett, the latter wondering if they might spare a cigarette first.[13] A riot was quelled by police using tear gas and baton charges in Calcutta in 1967, during a match involving West Indies; an inquiry placed the blame on the Bengal Cricket Association for mismanaging ticket sales and thereby causing overcrowding. Then, in Bombay (again, using the old name still in use at the time) in 1969, the Australians had to leave the pitch for 20 minutes while the riot police plied their trade in burning stands and amid flying bottles. Initially the Australian captain, Bill Lawry, had thought that the spectators were simply trying to delay play because Australia was on top; he might have been reinforced in

---

[13]   It was on that occasion that the leader of the rioters apparently said 'Mr Compton, you very good player, but you must stop', a line with which Compton's friend Keith Miller taunted him on every subsequent occasion they met on the field.

that view by the fact that Bombay at the time had no history of crowd trouble. Many years later, the semi-final between India and Sri Lanka in the 1996 World Cup had to be abandoned after some Indian fans rioted rather than watch their team slump to what they thought would be a humiliating defeat. In retrospect, losing to that particular Sri Lankan team should not have been seen as humiliating at all, given that Sri Lanka went on to win the tournament in convincing fashion. And in 2000, at a one-day match during England's tour of Pakistan, tear gas was used once again after a crowd tried to storm the stadium at Rawalpindi.

The Caribbean has also seen its share of troubles. In 1968, after an unpopular umpiring decision during a test match against England, the crowd threw various bottles onto the pitch. The respective captains, Colin Cowdrey and Garry Sobers, appealed for calm. They seemed to succeed, only for the riot police to assault the crowd and set things off again. Afterwards, the media was divided as to how blame should be apportioned, although Clement Freud in the *Sun* newspaper also took the time to express admiration at the athleticism of some of the bottle throwers.[14] Similar trouble occurred when the World Series Cricket tournament visited West Indies in 1979. In a match in Guyana, the crowd lost patience waiting for play to restart after rain, and once again bottles started to be thrown. Spectators broke into the pavilion (one stole the till from the bar), forcing the players to take refuge in a hastily fortified dressing room. The police eventually brought the situation under control by using tear gas with what appears to have been rather more justification than in 1968. In 1999, the touring Australian team went through a similar experience during a one-day match at Sabina Park. The trouble on that occasion started after the crowd took exception to a collision in the middle which resulted in a potentially crucial run-out of a West Indian batsman. The players left the field but eventually returned and completed the game, after the police warned that their safety could not be guaranteed otherwise. After the match, the Australian captain, Steve Waugh, not a man given to cowardice or hyperbole, gave a blunt verdict: 'We were risking our

---

[14] Nigel Henderson, *The Worst of Cricket: Run-Outs to Riots – Malice and Misfortune in the World's Cruellest Game* (Pitch, 2008), p 101. Clement Freud was a popular media figure in Britain for many decades, the brother of the artist Lucian and the grandson of the psychoanalyst Sigmund.

lives again for a game of one-day cricket. If it keeps on like that, there's no point in us playing.'[15]

There have been many more incidents, major and minor, in most test match countries, but the above should suffice for some flavour of what has occurred across the cricketing world over the years.

G Davis is… the subject of numerous proceedings

In the same series as Michael Angelow's streak came probably the most infamous example of a pitch incursion, when protestors destroyed the pitch overnight at a crucial stage of the Headingley test. They were acting in support of the London minicab driver George Davis, who was serving a 20-year sentence for armed robbery. A campaign started in which graffiti would announce 'George Davis is innocent' and the Headingley incident was the apogee, or nadir depending on one's point of view. The vandals struck at night after the fourth day's play had concluded, with Australia (one up in the series) 220 for three, needing another 225 runs to win – in other words, a classic finish was in store, with England the probable favourites. The outcome was left wholly academic when the covers were removed and it was found that someone had poured oil over the wicket (evidently with a certain amount of cricketing knowledge, since they left it precisely where a good-length ball would have landed), and three-inch holes had been dug in various places. The groundsman said that the holes might be repaired in time but not the oil damage. The captains would have had to agree on another strip – and to no great surprise Australia's Ian Chappell was not in an agreeable mood, reflecting the state of the match and the series. The match was therefore abandoned, but in a properly English turn of events it rained at noon, meaning that barring an Australian collapse of severe proportions the same result would have happened anyway.

The leader of the campaign, one Peter Chappell (not of the Australian cricketing dynasty), was convicted of offences arising out of the incident and a few other antics including organizing a naked display at an East London boating lake (clearly 1975 was the year for

---

[15]   See Henry Blofeld, *'It's Just Not Cricket!': Henry Blofeld's Cricket Year* (Pocket Books, 2000), p 278. Blofeld also pointed out that on every such occasion the ICC would make a few feeble remarks and then offload responsibility to local boards.

removing clothes in public). He was sentenced to join George Davis for 18 months. Not that he would have seen Davis very much – nine months after the Headingley protest, Davis was released from prison by the Home Secretary, Roy Jenkins, despite the Court of Appeal having refused to overturn the conviction not long before. Jenkins exercised the Royal Prerogative of Mercy because of doubts over the evidence at the trial. In 1978, Davis pleaded guilty to being the getaway driver at a different armed robbery, and was sent back to jail. He was released in 1984 but jailed yet again in 1987 after he pleaded guilty to attempting to steal mailbags.

In 2007, having been free for some time and with no further convictions, Davis went to the Criminal Cases Review Commission to complain about his 1974 conviction. He was realistic enough to concede that his reputation would not be much affected either way, since he did not challenge the convictions in the two cases in which he had pleaded guilty. The case was referred to the Court of Appeal, which quashed the conviction, though it made no finding as to his innocence, only holding that the evidence had not been sufficient to convict – which is not the same thing.

A straight hit

All of the cases to this point have been straightforward from a legal point of view, in that clearly a non-participant has no business being on the playing field, and therefore there would be a general consensus that each should have been subjected to a public order offence or other sanction proportionate to the scale of their wrongdoing. Peter Chappell's offending was also well over the line of legal protests, as even a young Peter Hain might have conceded. There is therefore no cause for a discussion on matters of principle or morality.

A question might be asked, however, about how effective the ICC has been in responding to the various issues with crowds over the years. It forbade spectators to bring alcohol into grounds, which was a farcical measure in two respects. First, the ban applied to all grounds, when several had not had any crowd trouble for years (or, in some depressing cases, any crowds at all), rendering a blanket ban inappropriate. Second, there was no ban on buying alcohol inside the grounds, inevitably priced to reflect the sellers' new-found monopoly.

Any determined and well-resourced drunkard could therefore carry on as before. If it was not acceptable for crowds to drink alcohol to excess, it should not become acceptable because the sellers and organizers make a large profit at the same time.

Instead, the proper response from the ICC and national boards to any poor crowd behaviour should have been a simple economic one: withdraw the right of any offending venue to host international matches. The ground would therefore have every incentive to take appropriate measures, as would the local law enforcement, given the loss of revenue to the community. But that would involve the ICC in making a swift, decisive and punitive decision; not something for which it is renowned.

Next, however, is a slightly trickier question: potential criminal acts between players, including the act of playing the game itself.

CRIME BETWEEN PLAYERS

On-field fights

How might a crime occur between players? The most obvious would be if one player assaulted another, as some have come close to doing at various points over the years. One well-known incident was the Lillee–Javed contretemps of the early 1980s. It produced the dramatic photograph of Javed, bat raised in the manner of the Royal High Executioner of years past, squaring up to a pugilistic-looking Lillee, with the umpire bravely stepping between them. Nevertheless, the incident shown in full (easily found on YouTube at the time of writing) reveals less drama and more a childish display from Lillee – something unworthy of a player otherwise rightly considered one of the greatest fast bowlers in history.

Not long before, an even better photograph had been taken of Michael Holding kicking the stumps in over a manner almost as stylish as his bowling action. The picture is usually likened to a rugby union fly-half kicking a conversion, though the Moulin Rouge might be an equally apt comparison. Holding's petulant place kick or can-can audition took place during a thoroughly forgettable tour of New Zealand by West Indies in 1979/80. The tourists more or less gave up when things did not go their way both on and off the pitch. There is no question they had some provocation in the form of amateur (in both senses) umpiring on the field and poor organization away from it, but, as they eventually conceded, their response was disproportionate. The low point was not even Holding's tantrum, but rather Colin Croft losing his temper and barging into the umpire (Croft claimed it was unintentional; once again YouTube enables modern readers to make up their own minds), closely followed by Clive Lloyd's studied indifference, when he forced the umpire to walk to him in a most demeaning fashion.[16]

As objectionable as his conduct was, any technical assault committed by Croft was rightly not deemed worthy of troubling the public prosecutors. Only a severe offence would warrant police attention, because a milder form of pushing or shoving would – and should – be dealt with satisfactorily by captains and their team management in the first instance, and if not then the ICC, who could fine or suspend those responsible.

More recently, in the IPL a famous piece of petulance occurred when Harbhajan Singh slapped his India team-mate Shanthakumaran Sreesanth during the course of a match. The incident was a good example of prosecutorial authorities not needing to be involved (not that the hit was serious enough anyway), since, following a hearing, Harbhajan was banned by the IPL from the rest of the tournament and was deprived of his salary. The BCCI also banned Harbhajan for five international limited-overs matches, on the ground that he had broken the code of conduct in his national contract. The affair was about the least of Sreesanth's worries in the long run, since in 2013 he pleaded guilty to match-fixing.

It would take something like a player being seriously injured by a punch, or assaulted with a bat,[17] before the police would be justified

---

[16] For a short account of the tour see Simon Lister, 'Ding-dong in Dunedin', Cricinfo, April 2006, www.espncricinfo.com/magazine/content/story/241985.html (retrieved 23 April 2014). I should note that to their credit both sides were anxious to rebuild bridges in their subsequent meetings in the 1980s; interestingly, West Indies still struggled in New Zealand with the local conditions. For much the same reason in reverse New Zealand has rarely been competitive in the Caribbean at any point in history.

[17] Dawson, op cit (p 233) has a dramatic example from an unspecified match in Bangladesh in 2012, when a teenage fan apparently ran onto the pitch to complain to

in intervening. As a general principle, there should be no reason for an assault to be treated differently just because it takes place in the course of a cricket match as opposed to a darts match at the local pub. That said, it is important to recall that with all criminal offences the prosecution has a discretion whether or not to charge anyone, even if an offence has technically been committed. It would therefore be in order for the police not to intervene even in a clear case of assault if, as would have been the case with the Harbhajan–Sreesanth incident, they were satisfied that a fine and suspension imposed by the cricketing authorities on the players involved had been punishment enough.

In recent times, in certain Western countries the new crime of 'hate speech' has been introduced, thus rendering sledging a potential criminal offence. The sometime England football captain John Terry was charged with just such an offence following a verbal exchange on the field with Anton Ferdinand. He admitted using racist words, but claimed that he had done so when questioning what he thought had been an allegation of racism from Ferdinand. Expert lip readers affirmed that he had used the words but could not come to a conclusive view on Terry's claim about the context. The judge held that it could not be proved beyond reasonable doubt that Terry had used the offending words as an insult rather than 'a challenge to what he believed had been said to him' (although the acquittal did not prevent the Football Association from subjecting Terry to separate disciplinary proceedings).

Hate speech offences are well intentioned: no-one in their right minds would believe that racial abuse should be acceptable. Yet there remains a legitimate question to be asked as to whether it should be a separate crime from general harassment or assault. Terry admitted – he could hardly do otherwise – that he was in the midst of a highly abusive exchange with Ferdinand. The police would never have gone near the incident had there not been the suspicion that Terry had referred to Ferdinand's race. One can think of ways in which Terry might have been equally offensive without such a reference, and therefore it is not clear why the police would get involved for

---

an umpire about a dismissal. The umpire allegedly grabbed a bat and hit the fan over the head with it, causing fatal injuries.

one type of abuse as opposed to another. It is not an answer to keep adding different categories of abuse (gender, disability, ethnicity, culture, religion, whatever) in the hope that the legislators can think in advance of every category they might like to ban. Instead, as I have said elsewhere,[18] there should be a general definition of unacceptable behaviour. To the extent that one kind of abuse (aimed at the victim's race, disability or whatever) is thought worse than another, that would be an aggravating factor in sentencing – or perhaps for considering whether to bring a prosecution in the first place – but not for the creation of wholly separate offences.

Assault by cricket

I well remember a batsman's advice on how to deal with close infielders: hit the ball towards them as hard as possible, and let go of the bat. Depending on the circumstances, that action might stretch to a criminal act, but it would have to be rather extreme, in the nature of a blatant and intentional attempt to hit someone.

What of intentional injury from short-pitched deliveries? In the mid-1970s, following the Lillee and Thomson assault on England in 1974/5 and the near-death of Ewen Chatfield,[19] and then the West Indian assault on Brian Close and John Edrich, there were whispers in the government that cricket might be made subject to health and safety regulations, though nothing came of it. It is true that for the inaugural World Cup in 1975, at the behest of the Pakistan Board of Control, a special sitting of the ICC came up with a special regulation that any ball over the batsman's head (judged by his normal stance) would be called wide. That regulation might be added to the reasonably long list of bad laws (cricket and otherwise) that could be compiled from over the years, since a ball above head height would necessarily be harmless, whereas many of the worst injuries over the years have been from balls that would not even have risen to shoulder height.

Nowadays, with bouncer restrictions and protective gear, short-pitched bowling is less of an issue than in the 1970s. If there ever was a chance of someone finding a criminal act in anything resembling a

---

[18] See *Cases, Causes and Controversies*, ch 39.
[19] Not, as it happens, from a bouncer as such, but a shortish delivery that Chatfield unfortunately deflected onto his temple, a point often lost in accounts of the incident.

conventional cricket delivery, it must be vanishingly small by now. Perhaps if a fast bowler ran half way down the pitch and intentionally bowled beamers at the batsman's head, that might cross the line and warrant a criminal prosecution. The West Indian fast bowler Roy Gilchrist bowled several such deliveries on the Indian subcontinent in the 1960s, and was sent home from the tour as a result. (Gilchrist was a volatile character: at one stage he was sentenced to three months' probation for assaulting his wife.) It would be akin to a boxer stamping on the head of an unconscious opponent – an action where obviously no consent had been given.

Short of that type of occurrence, however, which would not be cricket in any sense, it is hard to imagine the prosecutorial authorities finding cause for intervening in the normal course of a cricket match, even if someone was being hit repeatedly by a particularly venomous fast bowler. As with possible civil actions for negligence, the reason is straightforwardly one of consent: anyone going out to bat is taken to have consented to the possibility of being hit by the ball as a result of a legitimate delivery.

The fact is that cricket, like rugby, boxing, free diving, or countless other sports, is not free from danger. The criminal law does not exist to remove all risk of injury from society, any more than the law of negligence does. Cricket is for umpires in white coats on the field of play, not judges in robes inside cloistered halls. That does not mean that cricketers are above the law, only that the criminal law, as the ultimate weapon of the state against its citizens, must remain a weapon of last resort.

Chapter 17

THE LAWS OF THE GAME:
THE SPIRIT AND THE LETTER

Introduction

Cricket is a game full of forlorn hopes and sudden dramatic changes of fortune and its rules are so ill-defined that their interpretation is partly an ethical business.

— George Orwell

Up to this point I have looked at various ways in which cricket has interacted with the law of the land. In the course of doing so I have touched on a few of the more intractable theoretical issues, including the spirit of the law versus the letter. I have also mentioned disputes about legal decision-making processes, including the pros and cons of the jury trial. In this final section I will seek to apply some of the lessons learned to the laws and legal conundrums of the game of cricket itself.

I shall consider first the spirit of cricket and how it affects the laws and their enforcement, beginning with a few thoughts on the spirit of cricket in the abstract, and then turning to some real-world examples where it has been said to have been breached or upheld. I shall then turn to the ultimate symbol of cricket's law and spirit: umpiring and umpires.

The spirit of the law

'The spirit of the law' is a concept usually invoked where a person is able to do something which might be permitted by the letter of the law, but which was clearly intended by the drafters of the law to be forbidden. In philosophical terms this is known as an 'idiomatic antithesis'. A neutral example, well away from the cricketing world, is the ban on smoking in public places introduced in Minnesota in the mid-2000s. An exemption was granted in the case of theatrical performances, because it was thought necessary for actors to be able on occasion to depict smoking literally (showing a distinct lack of imagination: they should have remembered the prologue, spoken by

Chorus, to *Henry V*[1]). One person who did have some imagination was the proprietor of a bar who declared each evening a 'performance' by the customers. He encouraged them to come in costume (as it was a heavy metal-themed bar, it might have been hard to tell if they were or not) and put playbills on the walls, and explained to everyone that the customers were taking part in a production called *Before the Ban*. The idea was that the customers were playing themselves before the date on which the smoking ban came into force. The ruse might not have worked in English law,[2] but assuming it did, it would be the clearest example of the spirit or intention of the law being thwarted by the inadequacy of the letter.

Law and justice

Loopholes are one thing, but injustice is another. It is something of a jurisprudential truism that not everything legal is moral.[3] An obvious example is the apartheid system to which Basil D'Oliveira was subjected; it might have been the law of the land at the time, but moral it was not. Then again, nor should everything immoral be illegal: the days of criminalizing adulterers have thankfully passed even though the act is still morally taboo.

There are accordingly two points to bear in mind from the general law: first, the spirit or intent of the law might be confounded by loopholes; and secondly, it is possible for an action or omission to be legal but at the same time not moral or just, and vice versa. Or, as Dickens's Mr Bumble would have put it, it is possible for the law

---

[1]   Chorus implores the audience to use their imagination: 'For 'tis your thoughts that now must deck our kings, Carry them here and there; jumping o'er times, Turning the accomplishment of many years into an hour-glass…'

[2]   It would be vulnerable to the action known as fraud on a statute: see *R v J* [2005] 1 All ER 1 at [64].

[3]   For some, known in jurisprudential circles as 'legal formalists', the law says what it says, and justice and morality never enter the equation. What is moral and right is what is legal. I had always assumed that concept never gained much favour outside law school tutorials, but a few years ago it found an unlikely defender in a member of the clergy. See Peter Mullen, 'If tax avoidance is immoral, then our laws and our morals have parted ways', *Daily Telegraph*, 22 June 2012, and my reply, 'Jimmy Carr and the morality of tax avoidance', Halsbury's Law Exchange, 26 June 2012, www.halsburyslawexchange.co.uk/jimmy-carr-and-the-morality-of-tax-avoidance (retrieved 25 April 2014).

to be an ass. Both points are all well and good in the abstract, but in both cases the problem comes in the detail. Not every example is as clear as those given above. The question of what is and what is not a loophole gives rise to hundreds of pages in the law books every year, while the question of what constitutes justice and fairness provides ample fodder for philosophical treatises the world over.

What, then, of the spirit of cricket?

The spirit of cricket

Just as it is not enough to say that morality is whatever is contained within the general law, it is also not enough to say that the spirit of cricket is simply playing within the laws of the game. Instead, the spirit of cricket has to mean some form of moral code, sitting above what one can merely get away with under a technical interpretation of the laws, which is precisely why the saying 'not cricket' has been part of the vernacular for well over a century.

In 2000, an attempt was made to incorporate the spirit of cricket expressly into the laws themselves. A preamble was inserted, which begins with the declaration 'The captains are responsible at all times for ensuring that play is conducted within the Spirit of the Game as well as within the Laws'.[4] The preamble then gives some examples of the spirit in play:

2. Fair and unfair play

> According to the Laws the umpires are the sole judges of fair and unfair play.

> The umpires may intervene at any time and it is the responsibility of the captain to take action where required.

3. The umpires are authorised to intervene in cases of:

Time wasting

Damaging the pitch

Dangerous or unfair bowling

---

[4] This is reiterated in the laws themselves, by law 1(4) and 42(1).

Tampering with the ball

Any other action that they consider to be unfair

4. The Spirit of the Game involves RESPECT for:

Your opponents

Your own captain and team

The role of the umpires

The game and its traditional values

5. It is against the Spirit of the Game:

To dispute an umpire's decision by word, action or gesture

To direct abusive language towards an opponent or an umpire

To indulge in cheating or any sharp practice, for instance:

(a) to appeal knowing that the batsman is not out

(b) to advance towards an umpire in an aggressive manner when appealing

(c) to seek to distract an opponent either verbally or by harassment with persistent clapping or unnecessary noise under the guise of enthusiasm and motivation of one's own side

6. Violence

There is no place for any act of violence on the field of play.

7. Players

Captains and umpires together set the tone for the conduct of a cricket match. Every player is expected to make an important contribution to this.

Some of the provisions are plainly redundant. Paragraph 3 lists a number of actions which are breaches of the laws anyway. As for paragraph 6, there never has been any place for violence on the field of play (disputes about the classification of short-pitched bowling notwithstanding) and a law to that effect seems otiose. Some of the concepts are purely abstract, such as 'sharp practices', 'dangerous', 'unfair' or 'traditional', and do not belong in a set of laws without some clear definition or at least a body of jurisprudence establishing what they mean. Then there are provisions which seem more like wishful thinking or cheerleading than anything that properly belongs in a set of laws: how can one judge the importance of each player's expected contribution in paragraph 7?

It is questionable how much improvement can be expected from players just by putting into the laws exhortations about behaving nicely. It is reminiscent of the signs one sees on public transport identifying priority seats for the elderly or disabled, or the signs in hospitals asking patients not to abuse or assault staff: none of those instructions were thought necessary in the past and the people who would indulge in that sort of conduct would probably not be put off by a sign telling them otherwise.

It was therefore not altogether surprising that Mike Atherton dismissed the inclusion of the spirit in the laws as 'nothing more than a remarkably successful marketing strategy' and called the preamble 'a lot of well-meaning guff'.[5]

A note of caution is required, though: it might be thought that puffery in laws is harmless, but a few have been caught short over the years making that assumption. Courts will usually try to give effect to the words in front of them, even if the drafters had only intended the provision to be meaningless waffle. Notably, the Carbolic Smoke Ball Company made a wildly optimistic claim in its advertising, which it was called upon to honour.[6]

---

[5] See Sahil Dutta, 'A fresh voice to an ancient debate', Cricinfo, 13 June 2010, www.espncricinfo.com/magazine/content/story/462728.html (retrieved 23 April 2014).

[6] The company advertised its product as an influenza remedy. In an 1891 advertisement it said that it would pay £100 to anyone who caught influenza after using the product according to the instructions; see *Carlill v Carbolic Smoke Ball*

Assuming the preamble is meant to be given substantive effect, two points stand out. First, there is a clear reiteration throughout that the umpires are the sole judge of what constitutes unfairness, and that it is the responsibility of captains to act if the umpires draw it to their attention. Secondly, as with the provisions on ball-tampering considered earlier in the book, there are some wide-ranging catch-all sections, such as the prohibition on 'sharp practice' – doubtless because the drafters were keenly aware how unwise it would be to try and come up with a comprehensive definition of the spirit of the game and every possible manifestation. The author Rob Smyth did not attempt an exhaustive definition even after writing an entire book on the subject.[7] Exercising similar caution, I shall not attempt to do so either. Instead, I will consider a few of the better-known instances over the years where the spirit of cricket has been questioned and offer a few comments from a legal and philosophical perspective.

Hoodwinking the batsman

When discussing W G Grace, I noted how the Ashes were born after the 1882 one-off test at the Oval in England. The match remains one of the closest test matches of all time. *Wisden* 1883 reported: 'Jones was run out in a way which gave great dissatisfaction to Murdoch and other Australians. Murdoch played a ball to leg, for which Lyttelton ran. The ball was returned, and Jones having completed the first run, and thinking wrongly, but very naturally, that the ball was dead, went out of his ground. Grace put his wicket down, and the umpire gave him out.'

Grace's feat has been repeated numerous times since. For example, on his first-class debut, Sid Barnes, the troubled genius discussed earlier in the book, ran out a batsman after over had been called. The square leg umpire had not heard the call and so gave the batsman out. The batsman happened to be the opposition captain, Victor Richardson (grandfather of the Chappell brothers), who made his feelings clear. Barnes's captain, another great player, Stan McCabe, withdrew the appeal, though he was not obliged by the laws to do so.

Company [1893] 1 QB 256.
[7]   Rob Smyth, *The Spirit of Cricket: What Makes Cricket the Greatest Game on Earth* (Elliott & Thompson, 2010).

Many years later, the New Zealand wicket keeper Brendon McCullum managed no fewer than three similar dismissals. On the last of them,[8] in 2009, he ran out an absent-minded Paul Collingwood, who had left his crease under the mistaken impression that over had been called. The New Zealanders withdrew the appeal, though Collingwood conceded that he would only have had himself to blame if the dismissal had stood.

England were again the beneficiaries of opposition generosity in 2011, when Ian Bell was dismissed by India in similar circumstances to those of Collingwood. Bell thought a ball had gone for four and tea had been called. Neither was true, and he was run out by the short-leg fielder. The stakes were particularly high, since Bell had played brilliantly for 137 at the time of the incident. Yet the Indian captain, M S Dhoni, agreed to withdraw the appeal over the tea break. Dhoni was lauded for upholding the spirit of the game, although two recently retired England captains, Nasser Hussain and Michael Vaughan, both said they would certainly have appealed under the same circumstances.[9]

In each of those cases, the spirit of cricket was said to be called into question because the spirit centres on the contest between bat, ball and fielders, in the course of ordinary play. That is the ultimate test which players undertake and others pay to watch. No aspiring player dreams of winning a vital match through sneakily dismissing an absent-minded batsman; instead every bowler dreams of uprooting a middle stump and every fielder wants to take a brilliant one-handed catch, just as every batsman dreams of hitting a good ball to the boundary rather than one the bowler accidentally drops during his delivery stride.

To start with, therefore, a definition of the spirit of cricket involves scoring runs and taking wickets in the ordinary course of play, not taking advantage of an opposing player's misfortune or misapprehension. Equally, however, test cricket is supposed to

---

[8]   On the two earlier occasions (in 2005 against Zimbabwe and 2006 against Sri Lanka) he ran out batsmen who had left their crease to congratulate their partners on reaching a milestone.

[9]   Paul Weaver, 'Ian Bell's run-out: sportsmanship prevails thanks to M S Dhoni', *The Guardian*, 31 July 2011.

be a tough game, batsmen should keep their wits about them, and they should not expect too many indulgences if they do not bother to satisfy themselves that over has been called before leaving their crease. There is no novelty in that stance; *Wisden* 1883 continued with its description of Jones's dismissal: 'Several of the team spoke angrily of Grace's action, but the compiler was informed that, after the excitement had cooled down, a prominent member of the Australian eleven admitted that he should have done the same thing had he been in Grace's place. There was a good deal of truth in what a gentleman in the pavilion remarked, amid some laughter, that "Jones ought to thank the champion for teaching him something".'

Those points apply even more strongly with the sharp bowling practice known as 'Mankading'.

Mankading

'Mankading' is the act of a bowler running out the non-striker for backing up too far. It is named after the Indian test cricketer Vinoo Mankad, who performed the action twice against Bill Brown during India's 1947 tour of Australia. A few other players have performed the action since, though the most famous example is probably Courtney Walsh's refusal to Mankad Saleem Jaffar of Pakistan in a group match in the 1987 World Cup. Pakistan went on to win the match, which cost West Indies a place in the semi-final.

Mankading differs from running out absent minded batsmen in at least two respects: (i) none of the absent-minded batsmen in the examples considered earlier were engaged in ordinary play, having instead left their crease under a misapprehension; and (ii) none of them were seeking or in a position to gain any advantage by leaving their crease, they just thought the ball was no longer in play. By contrast, a Mankaded non-striker is leaving his crease in the run of play and, especially in the age of short singles, stands to gain a tangible advantage by doing so. Indeed, it is a breach of Law 42(16) to try to steal a run during a bowler's run-up.

Instead, Mankading can only be said to be a breach of the spirit because a convention has grown up over time that the bowler should give a warning – as Mankad himself did back in 1947. In much the same way, in the general law sufficiently strong common understandings or representations can give rise to legally binding obligations, even against contrary written agreements.[10] I have to say I never thought Mankading fell very far outside the spirit of the game. It might be opportunistic on the part of the bowler, but it is equally opportunistic on the part of the offending non-striker to be backing up too far.

A second principle can therefore be added to the spirit of cricket: identifiable conventions should be respected, even if they might be breached within the law.

In recent times the laws have been amended so that a bowler may only Mankad a batsman before entering his delivery stride.[11] That being the case, I would argue that Mankading no longer falls outside the spirit of the law at all, since any non-striker who has started backing up even before a bowler has reached his delivery stride is clearly taking liberties. But the general principle of respecting conventions still applies.

Substitutes

A team playing in the spirit of the game should wish to defeat the strongest possible opposition. For that reason, many a captain over the years has allowed a last-minute substitution before a match even if they might legitimately have objected. During the 1986 tour of England, New Zealand's captain, Jeremy Coney, allowed England to play two substitute wicket-keepers, partly out of general sportsmanship, but also because he did not want it said that New Zealand had only won thanks to England's misfortunes. Far better, he reasoned, to beat England's best side and leave them devoid of excuses (for the record, New Zealand drew the match but won the series).

All of that is laudable enough, but the practice of substitution can also be abused by fielding sides wishing to give their fast bowlers a break, rather than where there has been a genuine injury. Ricky Ponting formed the view that that was what England were up to during the 2005 Ashes with their four-pronged pace attack. Ironically, when he finally lost his temper in public, it was after he was run out

---

[10] Usually by the doctrine of estoppel in contract law or that of legitimate expectation in administrative law.

[11] See Law 42(15).

by a legitimate substitute (Gary Pratt was on the field after Simon Jones had suffered the injury that would end his test career, though Ponting did not know that at the time). Not that anything new was going on: in the 1911/12 tour S F Barnes apparently went off the field for a cigar and a massage.

The manipulative use of substitutes was something which became particularly tempting for fielding sides after the introduction of minimum over rates. Previously, sides with a lot of fast bowlers were able to slow over rates down to a level which tried the patience of even their most loyal supporters. At times the four-pronged West Indian attack managed little more than ten overs per hour, about half that of Larwood and Voce half a century earlier.[12] Dilatory over rates amounted to another breach of the spirit of the game, as well as being commercially detrimental since they put off anyone watching.

Respect for the game

As seen above, paragraph 4 of the laws provides that the spirit of the game involves respect for the game and its traditional values. A nice illustration comes from Jeremy Coney again, during New Zealand's 1983 tour to England. He had hit the winning runs to secure his country's first ever test victory on English soil. When asked what his thoughts were just before the final delivery, he explained: 'The main feeling was thinking of all the New Zealand players who have been coming here for 52 years, better players than myself, and making sure that their sweat and effort had not been in vain.' Coney thus recognized that the game has a long and continuous history, and that no player is bigger than the team – or other teams past and present.

For perhaps a more concrete example in the other direction, Dennis Lillee's infamous attempt to use an aluminium bat in 1979 might have been within the rules, but it was still an action which showed no regard to cricket's history, tradition or spirit. Equally, the petulance he displayed when objections were made showed little respect to his opponents, the umpires or the spectators – and even his own captain, who had asked him to change it.[13] One does not need to

---

[12]   David Frith, *Bodyline Autopsy: The Full Story of the Most Sensational Cricket Series –Australia v England 1932–33* (Aurum, 2002), Kindle location 113.
[13]   That said, Lillee's captain, Greg Chappell, may have been engineering things

fashion a Betjemanesque description of cricket's past to understand the significance of willow to the game (or even to bother with poetry at all: Lillee's bat apparently damaged the ball and for that reason alone should have been stopped).[14]

The ICC too is occasionally apt to forget or ignore cricket's history and traditions. I mentioned earlier how it decided to award full test status to the 2005 Rest of the World series in clear breach of its own pre-existing rules. Even if the decision had been within those rules, it struck at the very essence of test cricket as it had existed for nearly 140 years. Then there was the even worse decision to experiment with substitutes (lamely called the 'supersub') in a flawed effort to spice up the flagging 50-over one-day international format.[15] International cricket had always involved eleven-a-side matches[16] and the spirit required respect for that convention. The supersub rule was an abysmal idea even on its own terms, since it blatantly favoured the team which won the toss.

Another bad rule from years past was the use of net run rate to determine the winner of rain-affected limited-overs matches. The nadir was the famous World Cup semi-final in 1992, when South Africa were left having to score 21 off a single ball[17] to win a match after a rain interruption, prior to which they had needed 22 off 13 balls. That farce led to the development of the Duckworth–Lewis

rather cynically; it has been said that he allowed Lillee to go out with the bat, knowing that it would be banned, because he also knew Lillee would be incensed and would take out his frustration on the English batsmen shortly thereafter – which he did and Australia won the match by 138 runs.

[14] Incidentally, *Wisden* 1997 pointed out a good example of the law of unforeseen consequences – an exemption had to be granted to bat manufacturers from a regulation which would have required trees to be cut down only with 28 days' notice. See p 1379.

[15] The experiment was carried out in the early 2000s, and did not last. Before it was finally put down in early 2006, several captains had come to gentlemen's agreements not to use it; they would name a supersub as required and treat him as a normal twelfth man.

[16] The Victorian odds matches mentioned in Chapter 2 were the exceptions that proved the rule, since the reason the 1877 MCG match was retrospectively deemed the first ever test match was that it was the first time representatives of England and Australia faced each other on equal terms.

[17] The scoreboard erroneously showed 22 still needed off the final ball, as if it mattered.

method (D–L) which, for all its flaws (chiefly its complexity, but that seems unavoidable, and to some of cricket's quirkier followers even a virtue), seems to have been a significant improvement.[18] Most importantly, it has resulted in many fewer matches where the losing side has been able to blame the system. With a touch of pathos, the next time South Africa were ousted in a rain-affected World Cup knockout match, it was because they had not done their sums correctly rather than because the sums rendered the task impossible. The D–L method can thus be said to be much more in keeping with the spirit of the game than its predecessor.

Respect for opponents

The great South African all-rounder Jacques Kallis once said:

> To me, the spirit of cricket is reflected in the way I've always tried to play the game: that's to play hard on the field, but at the end of the day or at the end of your career to be able to pick up the phone and call the guy you've played against. That is a good judge of whether you've played in the right way or not. It is [a] tough, tough game, but it's important to keep control of your emotions and not cross the line. As much as anything, it's born of a respect for your opponents and teammates. You want to treat someone the way you want to be treated. That's not to say you can't have a harsh word occasionally, but it's vital that you don't cross the line.[19]

An archetypal example of Kallis's sentiment is the image of Andrew Flintoff consoling Brett Lee at the end of the Edgbaston test in 2005, when both teams had spent the preceding five days in cricket's equivalent of what the army would call close-quarter battle.

As ever, there is ample scope for arguing over the margins of Kallis's ideal. Allan Border gained the sobriquet 'Captain Grumpy' on the 1989 Ashes tour when he demanded an end to the previous fraternization between players off the field, yet no-one seriously accused him of breaching the spirit of the game.[20]

---

[18]   Had D–L been in force in 1992, incidentally, South Africa would have had to score five off the last ball, a much fairer result which correctly reflected England's stronger position without writing off the game altogether.

[19]   Quoted in Smyth, op cit.

[20]   'I was prepared to be as ruthless as it took to stuff you,' he explained to his

Sledging and time-wasting

One of Captain Grumpy's most notable protégés, Steve Waugh, perfected (if that is the right word) the 'art' of the sledge, which he liked to call 'mental disintegration'. When he was batting, Waugh also enjoyed needling the fielders into verbally harassing him, as he found it spurred him on as a player.

One wonders whether Waugh's approach would now fall foul of paragraph 5 of the preamble, which precludes 'abusive language towards an opponent'. It would be easy to imagine some kind of excessive abuse going well beyond anything players or spectators could be expected to tolerate. At times abuse looks pathetic anyway, particularly from a losing side: in Sydney in 2014, for example, Ben Stokes, otherwise the only English player to advance his reputation on one of the worst tours in English history, did himself no favours by delivering some verbal nonsense to Mitchell Johnson, who had been far and away the player of the series. Just before this book went to press *Wisden* 2014 was published, which includes an article by Martin Crowe denouncing sledging as a mask to conceal fears.

On the other hand, no-one expects a sterile game devoid of emotion and passion. Merv Hughes, one of Australia's most aggressive sledgers, could not help delivering barrages of obscenity at the opposition at regular intervals. It is a moot point how often he crossed the line between hardened competition and breaking the spirit of the game. The umpire Dickie Bird did once chide him for his continuous abuse of the English batsman Graeme Hick. Hick's teammate Mike Atherton was less intimidated, mainly because he could never understand what Hughes was saying beyond one creative obscenity that concluded every sentence. Other players worked out that Hughes only sledged batsmen he considered a threat, and started taking his tirades as a compliment.

---

opposite number, David Gower, after the series (see Gideon Haigh, *Sphere of Influence: Writings on Cricket and Its Discontents* (Simon & Schuster, 2010), p 263). There was nothing especially new about Border's policy either: captains in Fred Trueman's day often became annoyed at Trueman's visits to the opposition's dressing room.

Hughes's clashes often made for an engaging spectacle, because not a few batsmen were quite prepared to stand up to him: since retiring, Hughes has entertained many with his tale of how not sledging Javed Miandad was no guarantee that Javed was not going to sledge him. Robin Smith also tells an amusing anecdote in which he replied to a series of 'can't bat' taunts from the burly Australian by smashing a ball to the fence and then telling Hughes they made a good pair, since he couldn't bat and evidently Hughes couldn't bowl.

Hughes was hardly the first pace bowler to employ verbal abuse: Fred Trueman was also well known for his one-liners, once telling the Warwickshire batsman Kasim 'Billy' Ibadulla during a frustrating innings: 'You've got more edges than a broken pisspot.' When a Cambridge batsman patronizingly intoned 'That was a very good ball, Mr Trueman' after being dismissed, Trueman, a former bricklaying apprentice from Yorkshire mining stock, retorted: 'Aye, wasted on thee.' After dismissing another Oxbridge player who had come to the crease in a Harlequin's cap and matching cravat, Trueman, unimpressed by that sort of finery, observed: 'Hardly worth dressing up for, was it?'

Another grey area is the prohibition in paragraph 5 against wasting time, especially when done to pressure an opponent. It is also a sound principle in the abstract, and there have been many examples of flagrant breaches over the years – such as Zimbabwe against England in 1996 (prompting England coach David Lloyd to make an ill-judged comment about murdering them to a draw), or Pakistan against England in the third test in 2000 (when England managed a famous victory in near-darkness, showing the benefit of all those gloomy late-season county fixtures). Equally, however, one thinks of Mark Taylor's masterful captaincy against Mike Gatting in the 1994/5 Ashes, as the veteran Gatting inched painfully slowly towards what would be his final test century. Taylor expertly changed bowlers and field settings as Gatting became becalmed in the nineties. No-one complained – least of all Gatting himself – and instead the consensus was that Taylor had presided over quintessential test cricket.

For cases on the borderline between hard cricket and breaking the spirit, one could recall any number of time-wasting exercises taken by batsmen during rearguard actions. In the first Ashes test of

2009, England's last pair in the fourth innings held out against all expectations to save the match, during which time they used a few old tricks such as frequently 'gardening' the pitch and having the twelfth man bring things out to the middle more than was strictly necessary. There were some protestations afterwards, though it was generally agreed that most other teams – including the Australians themselves – would have done the same in England's position.

With both sledging and time-wasting, what is acceptable depends once again on time, place and circumstances. On the field of play the question of judging those factors is a matter for the umpires and nowadays the match referee as well.

Walking

When Adam Gilchrist walked off the field during the 2007 Cricket World Cup final against Sri Lanka without waiting for the umpire's decision, he was universally praised for a fine display of sportsmanship. By contrast, when Stuart Broad refused to walk against Australia in the opening match of the 2013 Ashes series in England, even though by his own admission he knew he had hit the ball (he could hardly have claimed otherwise), he was denounced by all and sundry for poor sportsmanship. Although it was generally conceded that very few others ever walked (Gilchrist having retired by then), the fact that Broad had actively sought to deceive the umpire by a bit of gamesmanship marked him out for condemnation. Darren Lehmann, the Australian coach, called him a 'blatant cheat', though he later resiled from the comment.

The controversy led to commentators dusting off their history books and recalling some great walks and non-walks in years past. W G Grace, needless to say, never walked, and Don Bradman was not known for the practice either. A few players were thought to walk when it did not matter and stand their ground when it did, in the hope that the umpires might give them the benefit of the doubt in important cases thanks to their reputation. The experienced and well-regarded umpire Steve Bucknor once remarked that some players practically demanded it.[21]

---

[21]   Andy Bull, 'A good walk spoiled', *Guardian* website, 22 March 2011, www.theguardian.com/sport/2011/mar/22/cricket-world-cup-the-spin-andy-bull (retrieved

It seems to me that someone who never walked would actually be acting in a more moral fashion than a walker-of-convenience cynically trading on his reputation. And it has to be said that walking has always been rare in test cricket, which renders the BBC's guide to fair play in cricket[22] slightly inaccurate when it states that 'sadly this is a tradition that has gone out of the game at the highest level' – it would be more accurate to say that walking never was a tradition at the highest level in the first place.[23]

During the Broad controversy, some commentators went one further and argued that *walking* was not within the spirit of the game, since it constituted dissent from the umpire's decision. There is a superficial symmetry with this argument – if it is wrong for a batsman to stand his ground when given out, then maybe it is also wrong for him to walk when given not out; in both cases the batsman is defying the umpire. But it does not quite hold up, since a batsman who walks is sacrificing his own advantage, whereas a batsman who dissents is demanding something to which he is not entitled. I wonder, though, whether a batsman who walks should be recorded by the scorer as 'retired' rather than 'out'?

It is worth considering next whether there is a difference between a batsman not walking when standing his ground and a fielder who claims a catch he knows to be false. No less a cricketer than Ricky Ponting called for players to take the fielder's word for it regarding catches, while at the same time standing on his rights by refusing to walk when batting. It is true that claiming catches depends on the fielder's word while a batsman not walking depends on the umpire's word, but it is hard to see a moral distinction. There is no reason why the umpire should have less respect than the fielder – if anything, it should be the opposite.

It is also true that the batsman is always entitled to the benefit of the doubt, and thus it might be argued that he should be entitled to the

24 April 2014).

[22] 'Fair and Unfair Play', BBC Sport, news.bbc.co.uk/sport1/hi/cricket/rules_and_equipment/4183306.stm (retrieved 24 April 2014).

[23] Simon Rae, *It's Not Cricket: Skullduggery, Sharp Practice and Downright Cheating in the Noble Game* (Faber & Faber, 2001) has a whole chapter to this effect, and is the best place to start for readers wanting more history on walkers.

benefit of mistakes too, which the fielder should not, but I do not think that holds water. If there is doubt over a dismissal then there has to be a mechanism to resolve that doubt one way or another, and having a convention that it always falls in one direction seems sensible. It should make for more consistent decision-making and ensure that one batsman is not favoured over another.

If on the other hand a batsman or fielder knows for certain that the umpire is in error, then there is obviously a moral case for admitting it, or, if there are good reasons for one to keep quiet then they should apply to the other as well. That is, unless the underlying reason for the batsman being favoured in marginal calls is that it is thought more entertaining or otherwise more in tune with cricket for the batsman always to be favoured, in the same way as the prosecution always has to bear the burden of proof in a criminal trial. I for one do not find that convincing.

There is accordingly no principled difference between a batsman not walking and a fielder trying his luck with a catch. The two situations have been treated differently over the years because of custom or convention. That convention is now codified in the preamble to the laws, since paragraph 5 states that it is an offence to appeal knowing the batsman is not out, but nowhere is it stated that it is an offence for a batsman to stand his ground knowing that he is out.

It is hardly the only illogical distinction one can find in cricket,[24] or law for that matter. 'The life of the law has not been logic,' said the great American judge and jurist Oliver Wendell Holmes Jr; 'it has been experience.' But while I can accept the distinction between refusing to walk and wrongly claiming a catch because of convention, I believe the ICC went too far in 2013 when it ignored Stuart Broad's gamesmanship yet saw fit to fine Dinesh Ramdin for claiming a catch he had not taken.[25] Instead, Ramdin's moral transgression should

---

[24] For a random example, one might ask why the fielding side has always been supposed to applaud a hundred, but the batting side has never been expected to applaud a five-wicket haul or a hat-trick ball.

[25] For those who savour such things, it should be noted that the match referee who censured Ramdin was Stuart Broad's father, Chris – a former test cricketer who once famously lost his cool when given out during an Ashes test.

have been ignored as well, and punishment left to the court of public opinion.

In international cricket, at least, it may be that the distinction is now academic, given that the umpires can refer borderline catches to the third umpire, meaning that unscrupulous fielders will likely be caught out themselves. But the distinction remains valid for cricket below the highest level.

Bodyline and the rise of bouncers

I have already dealt with the legality of bouncers, and suggested that (within limits) they ought to be regarded as part of the game and not something for officious lawyers to try and expunge. It remains to add a few words about bouncers and the spirit of cricket.

In 1931, Lord Harris, by then the elder statesman of English cricket, said of the game: 'You do well to love it, for it is more free from anything sordid, anything dishonourable, than any game in the world. To play it keenly, honourably, generously, self-sacrificingly is a moral lesson in itself, and the class is God's air and sunshine. Foster it, my brothers, so that it may attract all who can find the time to play it; protect it from anything that would sully it, so that it may be in favour with all men.'[26] The very next year, Douglas Jardine's English side set out for Australia with one of the most notorious plans in sporting history.

As has long formed part of cricket legend, Jardine's plan was conceived to try and shift an immovable object in the form of Don Bradman.[27] In 1930, Bradman had destroyed the English bowlers (his series aggregate was still a world record at the time of writing) and left them with the fear that he would do even better on his home soil, in which case the series would effectively be over before it started.[28]

---

[26]   Quoted in Colin Cowdrey, *MCC: The Autobiography of a Cricketer* (Hodder & Stoughton, 1976), p 9.

[27]   In his book on the series Jardine denied that his plan had been formulated as a response to Bradman. He received a stinging rebuttal from Bradman in the latter's *Farewell to Cricket* (Hodder & Stoughton, 1950), the relevant part of which is reproduced in Jonathan Agnew (ed), *Cricket: A Modern Anthology* (Blue Door, 2013), ch 1.

[28]   There is a fascinating interview with Bradman filmed on the tour just before the

After the Oval test it was suggested to Jardine by a former England captain, Percy Fender, that Bradman's technique might be vulnerable to short-pitched bowling. Since Bradman had scored a double hundred in the match, it cannot have seemed much of a weakness, but it was about all Jardine had to go on.

Jardine's plan was for his fast bowlers to aim down 'the line of the body', and thereby force the batsman either to play the ball into a predictable zone on the leg side or face a potentially serious injury. He had the weapons to execute the strategy too, chiefly in the form of the fastest bowler of the day, Harold Larwood. The trouble did not start properly until the third test, when the Australian captain, Bill Woodfull, was hit on his chest – by a ball which was not bowled to a Bodyline field, though Jardine's icy remark, 'Well bowled, Harold', as the players surrounded the stricken Woodfull did not help matters (Jardine had been trying to intimidate Bradman, who was the non-striker). In the same match the Australian wicket keeper, Bert Oldfield, had his skull fractured. As seen earlier, the crowd was sufficiently riled by the spectacle that a pitch invasion seemed imminent, and some of the English players genuinely feared for their safety.

Bradman did struggle in the series, but only by his own incomparable standards – he still averaged 56 – and he was not always dismissed by a Bodyline field either. But there was enough deliberately intimidatory bowling for the Australian players, crowds and administrators to form the view that, as Woodfull famously remarked to England's manager Plum Warner during the Adelaide test, two teams were on the field but only one was playing cricket. Whatever technical, legal right Jardine had to pursue his strategy, the Australians were in no doubt that it was wholly contrary to the spirit. Towards the end of the tour, barrackers started advising Jardine not to brush the flies away, since they were the only friends he had left.

On the other side of the world, decades before live television broadcasts, the MCC haughtily dismissed the burgeoning controversy during a terse exchange of telegrams with their Australian counterparts,

---

fifth test, which can be found on YouTube. Bradman looks slightly nervous, but shows remarkable dexterity and wrist movement when demonstrating his shots. In response to the interviewer's fairly tame questions he gives rehearsed and rather clichéd answers that come across much like a press conference today. *Plus ça change…*

which had begun after the latter complained that relations between the two countries were being imperilled by Jardine's tactics. *Wisden* 1933 took a similar stance to the MCC, also unencumbered by evidence since its authors would not have seen the matches either. In his notes, the editor, Stewart Caine, said rather sniffily:

> It may at once be said that, if the intention is to hit the batsman and so demoralise him, the practice is altogether wrong – calculated, as it must be, to introduce an element of pronounced danger and altogether against the spirit of the game of cricket. Upon this point practically everybody will agree. No one wants such an element introduced. That English bowlers, to dispose of their opponents, would of themselves pursue such methods or that Jardine would acquiesce in such a course is inconceivable.

Meanwhile *The Spectator* recorded:

> There has rarely been a Test team more uniformly sound than the eleven led by Mr Jardine. To his captaincy, and particularly his judicious handling of his bowling, much of the success achieved has been due, and among his colleagues, though it is almost invidious to single out individuals for special mention, Larwood by his bowling (quite apart from any leg-trap success), and Ames by the batting with which he supplemented his brilliant wicket-keeping, stand out conspicuous.[29]

That said, a debate did ensue elsewhere in the English press, with at least some correspondents taking the view that the Australians would not be making the fuss they were without some justification.[30]

After the tour the MCC displayed all the arrogance of ignorance when demanding Larwood play the scapegoat and offer an apology, which he angrily (and correctly) refused to do, not just on the ground that he (the professional) had been following the orders of his captain (the amateur) at all times, but also on the basis that he had done nothing contrary to the spirit of cricket anyway. By that stage, both the MCC and *Wisden* had changed their tune about the use of Bodyline

[29] 'Recovering the Ashes', *The Spectator*, 17 February 1933. *The Times* maintained the same tone as *Wisden*, dismissing any thought of Jardine's wrongdoing as 'inconceivable'.

[30] See Martin Smith (ed), *Not in My Day, Sir: Cricket Letters to the* Daily Telegraph (Aurum, 2011).

somewhat. *Wisden* admitted in the 1934 edition: 'When something of the real truth was ultimately known in this country, [it] caused people at home – many of them famous in the game – to wonder if the winning of the rubber was, after all, worth the strife.' The MCC conceded in a communique that 'there is evidence that cases of the bowler making a direct attack upon the batsman have on occasions taken place during the last cricket season'. It went on to rule that bowling that was 'regarded as a direct attack by the bowler upon the batsman, and therefore unfair' should be unlawful, and instructed umpires to stop it.[31]

Larwood never played for England again. Jardine nevertheless retained the support not only of most of his English colleagues (notable exceptions including Plum Warner, Wally Hammond, Gubby Allen and the Nawab of Pataudi, the last of whom was described by Jardine during the tour as a conscientious objector for refusing to take up a position in a bodyline field) but some Australians as well, perhaps most notably Jack Fingleton. Jardine's defenders argued that leg theory was not new, nor was short-pitched bowling, and the problem in reality was that the Australians lacked the weapons to retaliate.

Fingleton observed years later that Bradman was happy to preside over some concentrated short-pitched bowling from Lindwall and Miller after the war (when asked about the effect on the batsmen, Bradman was said to have replied: 'They've got a bat in their hands'). There needs to be some caution with Fingleton's account, given the well-known animosity between him and Bradman. Either way, the reality of Bodyline as opposed to the legend was soon eclipsed by other fast bowlers over the following years, if not by Hall and Griffith in the 1960s or John Snow in 1970/71, then at least by Lillee and Thomson with their famous destruction of England in 1974/5.

Lillee and Thomson might not have bowled to a Bodyline field, but the blows which the English (including a 42-year-old Colin

[31] Quoted in Bradman, op cit, where he unleashed stinging criticisms of Jardine, Larwood and Fingleton. He also derived evident satisfaction at the reaction of Hammond to being on the wrong end of Bodyline bowling from the West Indians Martindale and Constantine in 1933. What Bradman did not add was that Jardine in that series never flinched when on the receiving end himself.

Cowdrey[32]) endured must have at least equalled, and in all probability surpassed, anything inflicted by Jardine's henchmen more than 40 years earlier. Lillee and Thomson each made public comments at the time exulting in hitting the batsman's body.[33] Both were at least as unsporting as any utterance or action of Jardine, even if they might have expressed themselves in a rather different manner from the pompous Wykehamist.[34] And when watching both teams trade bouncers during the Centenary test in 1977, Larwood reportedly remarked: 'These fellers have bowled more bouncers in this match than I ever bowled in a season.'[35]

More significant for world cricket than the Australians' vanquishing of England in 1974/5 was their equally emphatic 5–1 defeat of West Indies the following season. Rather than complain about Australian tactics, the West Indies captain, Clive Lloyd, sought to emulate them. Shortly afterwards, he put together the most feared fast bowling combinations in history (it helped that he had the resources to hand) and developed the formula that would keep West Indies at the top of world cricket for nearly two decades. The laws of cricket by then precluded the use of Bodyline fields (footage of Close and Edrich on the receiving end in 1976 suggests Lloyd and his bowlers might not have been averse to trying them otherwise). Then again, from the 1980s onwards the new protective gear such as shin guards and helmets enabled fielders to stand closer in orthodox positions such as

[32]   Cowdrey, the model English gentleman of his day, took the time to introduce himself to Thomson when he walked out to the middle. Thomson replied with some choice Anglo-Saxon phrases, explaining that Cowdrey's manners were not going to spare him from the impending barrage. It has to be said, though, that Cowdrey, despite his great reputation, was not above the odd bit of gamesmanship himself. In 1957, he and Peter May used their pads to cut short the dominance of Ramadhin and Valentine and render them ineffective. Neither bowler was the same again; intimidation, it seems, can cut both ways. See Amol Rajan, *Twirlymen: The Unlikely History of Cricket's Greatest Spin Bowlers* (Yellow Jersey, 2011) p 208.
[33]   See Frith, op cit, location 125. A forthright defence of Bodyline can be found in Michael Arnold, *The Bodyline Hypocrisy: Conversations with Harold Larwood* (Pitch, 2nd edn, 2013).
[34]   In fairness, I should add that in the years since, Thomson has become a popular commentator, always restrained and balanced in his analysis, if I may offer the compliment.
[35]   Duncan Hamilton, *Harold Larwood* (Quercus, 2009), p 201.

silly mid-on. Of course, the batsmen had the use of better equipment as well and on balance would have benefited the most.

Another change which took place during the West Indian reign was the end of the fast bowlers' union. In 1976 there was an agreement of sorts not to bounce tail-enders, though it was largely ignored. In 1978 England's Bob Willis unleashed an unpleasant assault on Pakistan's nightwatchman and batting ferret Iqbal Qasim (not even a fast bowler himself), culminating in Qasim leaving the field with a deep gash on his face. 'He had batted for 40 minutes,' explained the unapologetic England captain, Mike Brearley, afterwards, before adding the slightly redundant observation that if the ball hadn't smashed Qasim in the face there wouldn't have been a problem.

In the same year, the prospect of facing several batteries of 90mph bowlers on Australian pitches during World Series Cricket led Dennis Amiss to use the first proper protective headgear in international competition (though Graham Yallop was the first to wear something in an official test). Amiss wore a modified motorcycle helmet, and later explained: 'People did laugh. They were calling out: "Hey Amiss – where's yer skateboard?" The point is, though, that bowlers were becoming more aggressive. It wasn't "Bodyline", it was "headline". I chatted to a few of the boys and they agreed, especially when David Hookes got his jaw broken by Andy Roberts and was eating through a straw for five weeks.'[36]

Helmets were commonplace at first-class level and above within a year or so.[37] Some argued that they were against the spirit of the game, in making batsmen soft or at least nullifying one of the bowling side's legitimate weapons. *Wisden* 1979 also thought they were ugly. The Pakistani test cricketer Asif Iqbal had the best riposte when he wondered what it said about someone who wanted to protect his shins but not his head (he might have mentioned the groin as well had he been less polite). One Bodyline veteran, the Australian Leo O'Brien, a man of conspicuous courage in his playing days (and a

---

[36] Quoted in *Flying Stumps and Metal Bats: Cricket's Greatest Moments by the People Who Were There* (Aurum, 2008), p 245.
[37] Amiss's motorcycle helmet was soon replaced by the now-familiar design based on an equestrian helmet, which among other things allows the batsman to hear more easily than a motorcycle helmet.

former amateur boxer), suggested that Ned Kelly's armour would be appropriate against Lloyd's West Indians.[38]

It seems to me that although there had unquestionably been short-pitched bowling before Bodyline,[39] the manner and degree to which it was deployed in that series did exceed what was accepted at the time, even allowing for exaggeration on the part of Jardine's opponents and the extent to which the tale has grown in the telling. Bodyline can thus be said to have breached the spirit of the game, even if it fell within the letter of the law of the day. What constituted the spirit of cricket in respect of short-pitch bowling was remoulded, if not removed entirely, by the gladiatorial contests of the 1970s. That does not retrospectively redeem Jardine, but it does put his tactics in context and render the hate mail which Larwood received on the fiftieth anniversary of Bodyline in 1982 as absurd as it was anti-social. By then, Bodyline had been well and truly surpassed by the 1970s' 'headline' as Amiss called it.

Nowadays (in 2014), the protective gear available to batsmen has reached the point where both the number and severity of injuries have been greatly reduced and accordingly the spirit has perhaps relaxed a bit more in respect of short-pitch bowling. A good illustration is the fact that Australia's bowling coach, Craig McDermott, attracted no surprise or protest in late 2013 when he bluntly declared that his attack was intentionally using short-pitched bowling to dispose of England's tail-enders:

> That's been our team plan and I don't think we're going to go away from that … There's not too many tailenders around the place who bat below seven that enjoy playing a lot of balls around their helmet,

[38]   Frith, op cit, location 150. Frith also goes on to wonder (location 176) whether the Packer revolution made things worse because aggressive bowling provided better television. There seem to be few things that Packer did not get blamed for.

[39]   See Rae, op cit, and his chapter 'Flesh Will Blacken'. I have always found the story of Lionel Tennyson interesting. The grandson of the poet, he was renowned for great physical courage facing Gregory and McDonald in 1921. Yet, given that he served in the trenches during the Great War, being twice mentioned in dispatches and three times wounded, I suspect he would have ridiculed any praise he might have received for bravery in the face of a cricket ball. During the Bodyline series any cricket followers aged in their late twenties or older would likely have well remembered the 1921 series.

so, so be it. Speaking from my personal experience it never really affected my bowling but it certainly affects your batting.

The way we want to play our cricket we will continue to do, and what you want to describe that as is up to you.[40]

Some commentators[41] maintain that things have gone too far, and that because of helmets and the assorted body guards something important has been lost (even if a few recent injuries have shown that even modern helmets do not remove all risk).[42] Reflecting the arguments I made against bouncers being found negligent or in

---

[40]   Daniel Brettig, 'McDermott says bouncer barrage will continue', Cricinfo, 10 December 2013, www.espncricinfo.com/the-ashes-2013-14/content/story/698941. html (retrieved 24 April 2014).

[41]   David Gower, in his autobiography *An Endangered Species* (Simon & Schuster, 2013), wondered if Ricky Ponting would have had the same career had he played in the 1980s with superior fast bowlers and inferior helmets – not because there was ever any question mark over Ponting's courage, but because his pull shot would have left him too vulnerable. Gower, incidentally, faced Lloyd's team with such skill and fortitude that Lloyd said he was the only Englishman he would want in his side. Martin Crowe, who also distinguished himself in the same era against West Indies, was quoted recently as saying: 'Today's equipment? Unbelievable. I dread to think of the damage that Ian Botham and Viv Richards would have done with them.' (Linus Fernandes, 'Martin Crowe scratches his 14-year itch', Bleacher Report, 9 November 2011, bleacherreport.com/articles/933579-cricket-quotebook-greg-chappell-martin-crowe-waqar-younis-et-al/page/4 (retrieved 24 April 2014)).

I am not sure that there are as many express bowlers around in the twenty-first century as there were in the 1970s and 1980s. On the one hand, sport science and general living conditions have undoubtedly improved, which would suggest bowling speeds might have increased, just as athletic records continued to be broken regularly (until recently anyway; Olympic records in many sports now seem to be levelling off). On the other hand, the combination of minimum over rates and a much-increased international schedule means that pacemen have to bowl within themselves more than their predecessors.

[42]   Shane Watson, for example, was dealt an unpleasant blow by Stuart Broad in the 2013 Oval test, and a few years earlier the New Zealand batsman Daniel Flynn lost a tooth when hit flush on the grill by James Anderson. The ball which hit Watson missed his helmet, while it is sobering to imagine what Flynn's injury would have been had he not been wearing one. Away from test cricket, in 1998, the former India test player Raman Lamba died after being struck on the head while fielding at short leg during a domestic match in Bangladesh, while in 2013 a first-class cricketer, Darryn Randall, died when he was hit on the side of the head while attempting a pull shot. See also Geoff Tibballs, *No-Balls and Googlies: A Cricket Companion* (Michael O'Mara, new edn, 2013), pp 67–8.

breach of the criminal law, I would simply reiterate that the use of short-pitched deliveries within reasonable limits has always been considered not so much in breach of the spirit of cricket as one of its most important manifestations.

Therein lies a question with which lawyers grapple on a regular basis – what is reasonable? It is the sort of knotty question on which it is hard to legislate. The current version of the laws arguably goes too far with its restrictions, but it does not seem unreasonable to give umpires the power to intervene if someone does get carried away on the pitch. As to when they should intervene, to use the legal equivalent once more, the question is one of time, place and circumstances. Relevant factors would include the condition of the ball, the condition of the pitch, the ability of the batsman, the protective gear available to him, and whether anyone has been warned in the match to that point. It would be unwise to try to be much more prescriptive than that.

Underarmed, underhanded and Down Under

The ultimate clash between the spirit and the letter of the laws of cricket happened on 1 February 1981, towards the end of a limited-overs international between Australia and New Zealand. After the eighth New Zealand wicket fell, Greg Chappell, the Australian captain, was sitting on the boundary feeling, as he later related, absolutely shattered by the punishing new international programme. He had already made one controversial move earlier in the match, when refusing to accept Martin Snedden's word concerning a spectacular catch Snedden had taken in the outfield. The two umpires declined to adjudicate on the matter because they had been watching for a run-out. Chappell was therefore able to continue his innings, which everyone knew at the time was potentially critical to the match as he was Australia's leading batsman. Eventually he was caught by Bruce Edgar, whereupon he walked without hesitation. But it was as fielding captain that Chappell was about to make one of the most controversial decisions in cricket history.

One ball was left in the match, to be bowled by Chappell's younger brother Trevor. Taking guard was the New Zealand tail-ender Brian

McKechnie,[43] a dual international who had once kicked a last-minute penalty for the All Blacks, enabling them to win the Grand Slam.[44] That aroused some faint hope among New Zealand supporters that he could pull off a similar feat with the bat.

Realistically, however, McKechnie's cricketing record suggested he was not much of a candidate to hit his first ball for six on the longest boundary in world cricket. Yet there remained the slimmest of chances, and so Greg Chappell invoked his last-ditch plan. Like a diligent drink-driving lawyer or taxation accountant, he had spotted a loophole: there was nothing in the laws in black and white prohibiting the ball being bowled underarm. He instructed Trevor accordingly, and the rest is history: Rod Marsh openly showed dissent; Trevor dutifully bowled the ball; McKechnie blocked it and threw his bat away in disgust; and New Zealand's captain, Geoff Howarth, ran onto the field and protested to the umpires without success.

The reaction was near unanimous. In the television studio Richie Benaud denounced the delivery as 'one of the worst things I have ever seen done on a cricket field'.[45] Elsewhere the Australian Prime Minister, Malcolm Fraser, said in a bland political tone that Chappell had not performed in the manner expected of the Australian captain.[46]

---

[43] It is often erroneously stated that McKechnie was the number 11; in fact he was number 10. Funnily enough, the actual number 11, Snedden, did hit a massive six at the same ground a couple of years later, in the match in which Lance Cairns achieved folk hero status by hitting six of them in his innings.

[44] The penalty was in the dying moments of a match against Wales on the 1978 tour. It followed a piece of unsporting conduct to rival Chappell's: Andy Haden, the All Black lock, dived in the manner of a professional footballer to make it look as though he had been pushed in the lineout. A penalty was awarded immediately afterwards, which McKechnie duly kicked. The referee later explained that the penalty was actually awarded for a different, genuine infringement by the Welsh against Frank Oliver – but even so, that did not make Haden's conduct any better.

[45] Benaud thought that the situation had come about through Greg 'getting his sums wrong': the final over of the match should have been the responsibility of Australia's best bowler, Dennis Lillee, but Lillee had already used up his allotted 10 overs. See also Clayton Murzello, 'How Chappell's underarm clean bowled cricket', Mid-Day, 1 February 2011, www.mid-day.com/sports/2011/feb/010211-Greg-Chappell-under-arm-bowl.htm (retrieved 24 April 2014).

[46] Interestingly, Fraser himself was the beneficiary of a legal loophole of sorts a few years earlier, when the Governor-General, Sir John Kerr, arguably ignored the spirit of the Australian constitution when he employed his power under the letter to dismiss

Fraser's counterpart across the Tasman, Robert Muldoon, sneered that it was appropriate that the Australian uniform was yellow. An enterprising New Zealander quickly printed T-shirts with the slogan 'Aussies have an underarm problem'. Back in Australia the greatest cricketer of all time growled: 'The less said about that the better. I didn't enjoy it at all.'[47] The eldest of the Chappell brothers, Ian, was less than charitable in public. He is reputed to have said: 'One Chappell ordered it, the other Chappell bowled it and if the third Chappell agreed with it, they'll think we are all mad.'

Despite the furore, the Australian authorities took the *Yes, Minister* approach and told Greg Chappell off without actually disciplining him in any meaningful fashion. They changed the laws so as to ban underarm bowling, but decided (appropriately deferring to the rule of law) that since the delivery had been legal at the time, the result of the match would stand. Chappell decided not to tour England later that year, allowing counter-factual historians to wonder whether Australia might have found another 19 runs in the Headingley test had he done so.[48] He returned at the end of the year for a tour to New Zealand. In his first international innings, he was greeted with a lawn bowl being rolled onto the pitch by a spectator with a wry sense of humour. But he conducted himself throughout the tour with such courtesy and generosity both on and off the pitch that he was given a formal award at the end as 'sportsman of the series'.

Chappell went on to explain that the underarm delivery had never been about winning one match, but rather sending a message to the board that he had had enough of the relentless schedule. If so, there

the Prime Minister, Gough Whitlam. He then parachuted in Fraser, who had been the leader of the opposition, as Prime Minister. Despite all the resultant outrage at Kerr's undemocratic act, the Australian electorate showed they actually agreed with his choice by returning Fraser at the next general election.

[47]   Quoted in 'The Don on...', Outlook India, 26 February 2001, www.outlookindia.com/article.aspx?210924 (retrieved 24 April 2014).

[48]   That was of course the famous match which England won by 18 runs after following on. Chappell's replacement as captain was Kim Hughes, who endured a torrid time trying to lead senior players such as Dennis Lillee and Rod Marsh. See Christian Ryan, *Golden Boy: Kim Hughes and the Bad Old Days of Australian Cricket* (Allen & Unwin, 2010), who points out that it was not just Hughes being given the captaincy that annoyed the veterans; Lillee in particular never seemed to get along with him anyway.

was some hefty irony: as seen earlier in the book, the schedule was driven by Kerry Packer, following his successful revolt against the authorities. Packer had won because enough of the senior world players had followed him rather than the traditional authorities. And the most senior player he had managed to recruit was the Australian captain – one Greg Chappell, thereby proving the old adage about being careful what you wish for.

Years after the event, the Chappell matriarch, Jeanne, moved to defend her youngest: 'Ian criticised Greg then, but Greg said he did it because he was so tired and did not want to play another game. I can see both points of view. But I got mad because Trev was blamed. It was not his fault. My husband (Martin) said to him "Did you think that up" and Trev said "No. My captain told me to do it and I had to do it."'[49]

No-one has seriously disputed the legality of Chappell's delivery. The umpires had no choice other than to allow what the law did not expressly disallow and the Australian board had no choice other than to let the result stand and change the laws prospectively.

Was Chappell's action wholly against the spirit? There has been the odd murmur in the other direction over the years, pointing out that underarm was the traditional form of delivery for the first few centuries of the game's existence; that everyone else should have been alive to the possibility as Chappell was;[50] and that McKechnie

[49] As recorded by Murzello, op cit. It might be added that both Trevor Chappell and Brian McKechnie have freely admitted in the years since that the incident gave them much greater fame than they might otherwise have enjoyed from their cricket careers, both of which were fairly modest, or at least certainly not approaching those of Trevor's elder brothers.

[50] David Frith claimed without any pleasure that he might have been inadvertently responsible for the whole affair, having said as a throwaway line a couple of years earlier that someone might resort to an underarm ball to win a match when the opposition needed six off the last ball. Frith was writing in the aftermath of Brian Rose's declaration during a domestic limited-overs match in England, which preserved the calculations his team needed to progress in the competition. It was a piece of rule manipulation certainly on a par with the underarm, though because it did not take place in an international match it did not gain the same infamy. See David Frith, *Caught England, Bowled Australia: A Cricket Slave's Complex Story* (Eva Press, 1997), p 242. It might be added that before declarations were introduced to cricket, some nineteenth-century matches were reduced to a farce as one side

had robbed himself of the moral high ground by not even trying to hit the ball for six. The last point can be discounted – even if McKechnie was somehow wrong in not still trying to hit the ball further, it would not render Chappell's actions right, any more than a careless householder leaving the keys in the door makes a burglary morally or legally acceptable.

It is true that in those early years of limited-overs cricket, various forms of experimentation had been taking place, including Mike Brearley's controversial decision to place all his fielders including the keeper on the boundary. Fielding restrictions were later introduced to prevent a repeat of Brearley's gamesmanship, and also to encourage batsmen to hit over the top and thus produce a more popular spectacle.[51] But at the time it took place Brearley's tactic was better characterized as more desperate than dubious. Perhaps his inclusion of the wicket keeper was going too far, given the obvious settled convention about where the keeper might stand, but not otherwise. Not for nothing did John Arlott say of Brearley that 'his clarity of mind enabled him to pierce the woolly romanticism and anachronistic feudalism which so long obscured the truth of cricket'.[52]

On the other hand, Brearley probably did go too far when he cannily put a helmet on the ground in front of the wicket, to try and tempt the batsman into playing a rash shot for the five runs that would be awarded if he hit it. Again, the laws were swiftly changed afterwards to require helmets to be behind the keeper when not in use. There seems little doubt Brearley's action on that occasion was in breach of the spirit of the game, since the idea of the game is to score runs by hitting boundaries or otherwise hitting the ball into the outfield and running until the fielders retrieve it. It does not lie in hitting objects left lying around by manipulative fielding sides.

---

desperately tried to commit batting suicide and the other side tried not to dismiss them, in circumstances where a modern team would declare.

[51] Those restrictions were in place by the time of the underarm match, and it was noticed after the match that Australia were actually in breach of them when the ball was bowled, which meant it should have been called no-ball. But, just as with the Snedden catch, the umpires' attention was elsewhere.

[52] Quoted in Agnew, op cit.

That was essentially the reason later given by Dennis Lillee as to why he would have refused to bowl the underarm if he had been bowling at the time.[53] And it is the reason why it can be concluded without hesitation that Chappell was in breach of the spirit of the game when making his infamous order.

I know it when I see it

Drawing together all of the separate examples, I would still not attempt to try and offer a comprehensive definition of the spirit of cricket. At one point I started to wonder if I would be reduced to paraphrasing what an American judge once said about pornography: 'I cannot define it, but I know it when I see it', since virtually all examples of the spirit of cricket in theory and in practice have a second sentence beginning 'However...'. But that is not to say that there is nothing that could be agreed upon as counting as the spirit of cricket, any more than the existence of problems in the theory and practice of criminal law proves that there is no such thing as ethics in general society.

I would make three observations. First, most of the examples of the spirit in action, and the more useful examples provided by the laws' preamble, can be distilled down to one overarching principle: the spirit of cricket involves playing the game by the traditional methods with bat and ball, not by antics such as tampering with the ball, hoodwinking a player, wasting time or verbally (let alone physically) abusing anyone. One should neither stand on the letter of the law to take advantage of every misfortune suffered by the opposition, nor should one seek to milk the rules oneself: if there is a convention that a particular law is never enforced, then that should be respected.

Secondly, there will inevitably remain substantial grey areas in both the spirit and the letter. One no more expects an anodyne game played in silence than one expects players to engage in bullying or straining the interpretation of the laws to their limits. And the captain who is shrewd enough to spot something in the laws no-one else has thought of may not necessarily be offending the spirit but simply using his brain.

---

[53]   Dennis Lillee, *Menace: The Autobiography* (Headline, 2003).

Thirdly, the question arises 'Who decides?' In the general law, there are often tricky questions about who should have the final say in resolving some dispute, such as the scope of a court's power to review the decision of an arbitrator in a contractual case. In cricket, by contrast, at least on the field of play, there is happily no difficulty in providing an answer: the man in white is always right. Every manifestation of cricket's legislation from 1744 to the present day has restated the principle that it is the umpires who are to resolve any conflict, be it concerning the spirit or the letter, and the players have to accept it.

There are two underlying assumptions in that point: first, that the umpires always deserve respect, and second, that cricket will always have umpires in the traditional sense. In the final section of the book, I will look at the past, present and future of umpiring, which remains not simply the cornerstone of cricket's laws and its spirit but also the ultimate confluence of cricket and law.

Chapter 18

THE UMPIRE IS ALWAYS RIGHT

Some history

It is worth starting with a reminder of what the 1744 laws of the game said about umpires:

> They are sole judges of all Outs and Ins, of all fair and unfair play, of frivolous delays, of all hurts, whether real or pretended, and are discretionally to allow what time they think proper before ye Game goes on again ...

> They are sole judges of all hindrances, crossing ye Players in running, and standing unfair to strike, and in case of hindrance may order a [run] to be scored ...

> Each Umpire is sole judge of all Nips and Catches, Ins and Outs, good or bad Runs, at his own Wicket, and his determination shall be absolute, and he shall not be changed for another Umpire without ye consent of both Sides.

The meaning of those laws has not been lost in time. There is no point arguing with the umpire, the laws have always made clear, because there is no argument to be had.

Despite that resounding founding principle, every cricket fan has a store of anecdotes and memories about bad umpires and bad decisions.[1] I mentioned much earlier in the book some of the bad decisions that were forced upon the umpires by W G Grace and his bullying gamesmanship. In 1946, a few decades after Grace's career, his successor as the greatest cricketer in the world, Don Bradman, gained some notoriety when he was given not out after hitting the ball to second slip early in the first test of the first post-war Ashes. The result was arguably career-saving for Bradman, career-ending for his opposite number, Walter Hammond, and series-ending for England.[2]

---

[1] For a host more umpiring stories, see Teresa McLean, *The Men in White Coats: Cricket Umpires Past and Present* (Hutchinson, 1987).

[2] I have always thought that both Bradman and Hammond's conduct must have been informed by the war, in that neither saw front-line combat and both would therefore have felt some discomfort after the war leading men who had. Certainly, it was one

'A fine fucking way to start a series' was Hammond's reputed verdict at the end of the over (the second adjective changes from account to account of the incident).

Leaving aside the ethics of whether Bradman should have walked (he himself maintained that he had thought he hit the ball into the ground first, and therefore waited for the umpire's decision), the seemingly atrocious umpiring error was most probably due to reluctance on the part of the umpires to give Australia's icon out at a critical juncture in the series. Many great batsmen since have been thought impossible to dismiss by lbw on their home grounds – or to have the opposite problem away from home. At least, that much has often been assumed by piqued opponents.

Of course, even the best umpires can have a bad moment or a bad day, just as the best players can. Some umpires, though – like some judges, it has to be said – have carried on stubbornly into old age, despite fading abilities, until finally being silenced by death or non-selection. The once much-respected English umpire Frank Chester, for example, suffered ill health towards the end of his career. He seems to have lost the plot after the Second World War, showing overt animosity towards the Australian players on the field. In 1953 he was quietly stood down after complaints from players. On England's subsequent winter tour to West Indies, some of the less experienced umpires made decisions so bad that they had to be given police protection, such was the animosity provoked in the crowd.

Other such incidents can be found throughout cricketing history, but by the 1980s, not a few umpires must have wanted police to protect them from the players rather than the crowd.

The 1980s onwards: the case for change becomes irresistible

The decade got off to the worst possible start with West Indies' embarrassingly bad response to embarrassingly bad umpiring in New Zealand during their 1979/80 tour, which I mentioned earlier in the

reason for the tension between Bradman and Keith Miller. It would also have meant both Bradman and Hammond feeling a sense of urgency, even desperation, at re-establishing themselves on the cricket field. See further Malcolm Knox, *Bradman's War: How the 1948 Invincibles Turned the Cricket Pitch into a Battlefield* (Robson Press, 2013).

book, when considering crime on the field. The following year, when India toured Australia, Sunil Gavaskar stormed off the pitch after being given out in a test and took his batting partner, Chetan Chauhan, with him. They were met on the boundary by the team manager, who persuaded Chauhan to return and thus enabled the match to continue.

In 1982, the English umpire David Constant gave out the Pakistani batsman Sikander Bakht. Replays showed that Bakht had not edged the ball. The Pakistanis were rankled enough to demand that Constant not be appointed when they returned to England in 1987, but the English authorities ignored the request. Constant went on to make further contentious calls, as a result of which the English landed in Pakistan for the return series later the same year to the sound of numerous axes being ground. What followed with a grim inevitability was probably the most acrimonious on-field umpiring spat in test cricket history, when the English captain, Mike Gatting, squared off against the umpire, Shakoor Rana.

The trouble began when Rana misinterpreted Gatting's signal to one of his fielders. Angry words were spoken by both, and index fingers jabbed like Bren guns on full automatic as the two men stood toe to toe without, as *Wisden* later put it, a square inch of dignity between them. After the day's play, when it seemed both were ready to back off, the arch-Machiavellian Pakistani captain, Javed Miandad, goaded Rana into prolonging the dispute by insisting that Gatting provide a written apology (England had been in a strong position in the match, and thus any delay suited Javed's ends). As a result, an entire day's play was lost, injecting salt into what must have been a reasonably gaping wound in Gatting's ego at the time.[3] Under some duress from management and even the British diplomats in Pakistan, Gatting finally produced a handwritten scrawl offering an apology for 'bad language' – which he had to pass to the man who had started the exchange by calling him a 'fucking cheating cunt'. The irony was not lost on Gatting, either at the time or since.

---

[3] A few years later, the *Guardian* obtained documents from the British embassy about the affair: see Paul Kelso and Rob Evans, 'Gatting's bust-up with umpire just wasn't cricket, said British envoy', *The Guardian*, 19 December 2005, www. theguardian.com/uk/2005/dec/19/cricket.freedomofinformation (retrieved 24 April 2014).

It has to be said that Rana had some form, having prompted the generally genial Jeremy Coney to threaten to lead New Zealand from the field two years earlier in protest at a series of questionable decisions (the team gathered on the boundary, but, as with Gavaskar and Chauhan, were persuaded by their manager to continue). Nevertheless, Gatting should have taken heed of the time and the place, and exercised some restraint. That might have saved him the moral high ground and with it the England captaincy (which he lost some months later under a different pretext but with most suspecting that it was a belated punishment for the Rana rant). It is a shame that few captains of the day were inclined to follow the lead of India's Gundappa Vishwanath, who withdrew an appeal during the Golden Jubilee test in February 1980 after a protest by the batsman, Bob Taylor. Then again, there was no obligation to do so and most captains probably assumed with some justification that good and bad decisions constituted swings and roundabouts.

The 1990s began with an incident that added considerably to the case for neutral umpires, as well as bringing together several themes already seen in the book. It took place during the fourth test on England's 1989/90 tour of West Indies. The home side mounted a highly aggressive appeal against the journeyman English player Rob Bailey. It seemed to persuade the umpire, Lloyd Barker, to change his mind and Bailey was given out.[4] Bailey was so disgusted he kicked the fridge door upon his return to the dressing room and broke his toe. Similar feelings were evidently present among the opposing fans, who began a fight that had to be broken up by police. Meanwhile, in the commentary box, Christopher Martin-Jenkins muttered that if that was gamesmanship, he wondered what cheating might involve. His comments were immediately denounced as redolent of colonialism, and led to a libel action from Barker. The action was settled out of court with payment of an undisclosed sum and a statement by Martin-Jenkins that no allegation of cheating had been intended.

I find that course of events slightly hard to understand, because it seems to me that Martin-Jenkins was criticizing the West Indian

---

[4]   See Martin Williamson, 'Demented and orgasmic gesticulations', Cricinfo, 1 March 2014, www.espncricinfo.com/magazine/content/story/723865.html (retrieved 24 April 2014).

players, not the umpire. Either way, the whole affair did not seem to put Bailey off umpires, since he later became one himself.

It was therefore to no particular surprise that the calls for neutral umpires became irresistible soon after. They had first been tried in a series between Pakistan and India in 1989, but it was not until the early 1990s that they became the norm. To begin with, one neutral and one home umpire would stand in each match, but eventually the ICC went all the way and opted for two neutrals, drawn from an elite panel of supposedly the best international umpires.

Neutral umpires

Employing neutral umpires only partially mollified complaints, because disaffected players and supporters still formed the view that certain umpires were biased against them. That view persists in the present day: one only has to look at online cricketing message boards, which since their invention have been full of intemperate and often outrageous accusations about umpiring bias – and not just from a few trolls either.

For controversies on the field, one need go no further than those involving the Australian umpires Ross Emerson and Darrell Hair. In 1999, Emerson officiated in one of the most unsavoury one-day international matches in history, when Sri Lanka's captain, Arjuna Ranatunga, threw all respect for the umpire out the window in response to Emerson repeatedly calling Sri Lanka's star spin bowler Muttiah Muralitharan for a no-ball. The call was not because Murali overstepped, but because of his action, which Emerson believed unlawful and for which he (and Hair, as it happened[5]) had called Murali in the past.[6] Far from accepting the umpire's decision, Ranatunga held up play repeatedly and took his team to the boundary in protest, then

---

[5] On that occasion, in Melbourne in 1995, Ranatunga was also captaining and also took the side off for a while, before arriving at a crude compromise where Murali bowled from the other end so that Hair did not have the chance to call him. The other umpire, Steve Dunne, considered Murali's action legitimate.

[6] As I pointed out in the introduction, I have not considered throwing as a separate subject, although it is a good example of a concept easily understood but not so easily defined in a legal sense. See for example Richie Benaud, *My Spin on Cricket* (Hodder & Stoughton, 2005), ch 5.

after the match made a mockery of the ICC's disciplinary process by threatening to challenge any sanction in court.

It was a forgettable episode on all sides.[7] There were two main points from a legal perspective. First, Emerson had clearly operated to a pre-conceived agenda in calling Murali, something unworthy of a quasi-judicial officer in any circumstances. Worse, he had done so despite Murali's action having earlier been cleared by other umpires and the ICC itself. Emerson should have followed the ICC's decision that Murali's action was permissible, and if he could not manage that, then he should have declined to stand in the match. Having failed to take either of those steps, he must have been tempted to follow the English umpire Arthur Fagg's example from Edgbaston in 1973: Fagg left the field in protest against the ungentlemanly way one of his decisions was received by the West Indian captain, Rohan Kanhai. The difference was that Emerson's problems were all of his own making, at least to begin with.

Secondly, whatever Emerson's failings, Ranatunga seemed determined to outdo him for outrage, with a total disregard for any authority except his own – not just on the day, but throughout the disciplinary process afterwards. He too should have followed established precedent and accepted that the umpire's decision is always right on the field of play, then complained via the usual channels after the game.

Similar points apply to the Darrell Hair affair, which took place during Pakistan's 2006 tour of England. The trouble began with Hair's assessment during the Oval test that the ball had been tampered with and his consequent deduction of five runs from Pakistan. I trust that enough was said in the section on the ball-tampering libel actions to explain why the Pakistani team did not take kindly to that ruling. But, instead of waiting until the conclusion of the match (which, like Gatting's England nearly two decades before, they had been on course to win), they refused to take the field after a break. When the allotted time had expired, the match was quite properly declared forfeit.

---

[7]   It has been dissected in much more detail elsewhere, the best account being Henry Blofeld, *'It's Just Not Cricket!': Henry Blofeld's Cricket Year* (Pocket Books, 2000), pp 257–66.

In the ensuing controversy, the Pakistanis made the forceful point that there was no footage from any of more than 20 cameras at the ground which showed any of their players tampering with the ball. They also threw in the allegation that Hair was biased against teams from the subcontinent, thereby opening a political can of worms that has never really been closed.

From a legal point of view, three points emerge. First, obviously enough, Hair was not the only umpire on the field at the time, though no-one seemed to notice in the controversy that followed (save for a few slanderous accusations that the other umpire, Billy Doctrove, was incapable of making his own judgement and standing up to Hair). Secondly, the appropriate course of action for Pakistan, just as it had been for Sri Lanka, was to complain about the umpiring to the ICC after the match, not to throw their toys out of the pram during the match itself. If they believed Hair was biased against them because of his past conduct, then they should have objected to his appointment in the first place. Thirdly, once Pakistan had failed to take the field within the allotted time, then the *only* course of action available to the umpires was to declare the match forfeit; it was not a matter of discretion.

None of those points seemed uppermost in the ICC's collective mind, however, as it more or less disowned Hair in the days following the match. He incurred much scorn when a leaked email showed that he had offered to walk away in return for a pay-off. Yet not only is that a normal course of action in most forms of legal dispute, it is hard to rebut the suspicion that the email was leaked deliberately in order to embarrass Hair into surrendering his claim. Either way, the ICC's conduct was so unbecoming that a leading barrister offered to represent Hair for nothing when Hair subsequently brought a case before the employment tribunal.[8] And the demolition of the ICC witnesses when the case was heard mirrored the destruction of the Australian board by Sid Barnes's barrister all those years before.[9] Hair was subsequently

---

[8] See Robert Griffiths QC and Stephen Whale, 'The Ball-Tampering Affair', [2007] *New Zealand Law Journal* 89; 'Robert Griffiths QC and Stephen Whale separate fact from fiction in their report on the great ball-tampering affair and its wider implications', [2006] 156 (7253) *New Law Journal* 1897.

[9] See Mike Atherton, 'Hair tribunal highlights ICC flaws', *Sunday Telegraph*, 7 October 2007, who recorded among other things: 'One by one these well-meaning,

restored to the elite panel of umpires but retired shortly thereafter, while the ICC quite rightly attracted derision for later overturning Hair's rulings about the match, including the result.[10] The rule of law required the original decision to stand (especially since as mentioned the laws provided that the *only* possible result was a forfeit once Pakistan had failed to take the field in time); so too did the previously discussed principle that umpiring decisions on the field of play should remain sacrosanct.

The guiding legal principle

There is no point in having neutral umpires if they are not going to behave in a neutral fashion, and there is no point in having processes for complaints and discipline if the players are able to drive a coach and horses through both. The guiding legal principle is the famous one laid down by Lord Hewart: 'It is not merely of some importance but is of fundamental importance, that justice should not only be done, but should manifestly and undoubtedly be seen to be done.'[11] That principle applies to cricket just as much as to the law.

That said, there has to be a presumption in each match that the umpires are indeed neutral.[12] Thus, save for all but the most extreme circumstances, the players have to accept whatever decisions are forthcoming on the field, and rely on the established complaints process after the match. After the Hair affair, a well-publicized debate among pundits took place over whether on-field dissent was a positive part of the game, or whether the old adage of the umpire being right rendered dissent beyond the pale.[13] It should be clear by now that I favour the latter view.

certainly not racist but undoubtedly bumbling and, on this evidence, incompetent administrators shuffled to the front of the room, raised their right hands and promised to tell the whole truth and nothing but the truth. One by one they were sent packing, lacerated from head to foot by [Hair's QC's] ordered mind and razor tongue.'

[10]   See for example Ian Chappell, 'ICC out of control', Cricinfo, 6 July 2008.

[11]   *R v Sussex Justices; ex parte McCarthy* [1924] 1 KB 256 at 259.

[12]   One good example of failing to give the appearance of impartiality was the actions of the Australian umpire Peter McConnell in Melbourne in 1990. The English bowler Phil Tufnell asked an unremarkable question about how many balls were left in the over, to which McConnell replied: 'Count 'em yourself, you Pommy bastard.'

[13]   See Ed Smith, *What Sport Tells Us about Life* (Penguin, 2009), ch 11.

There are examples from other sports which show what happens when respect for the referee or umpire disappears: the unedifying sight of teenage Premiership footballers delivering strings of expletives to the referee, for example. In tennis, John McEnroe's legendary tantrums nowadays seem to be viewed with a bit of nostalgia, helped no doubt by McEnroe's superlative abilities as a commentator. At the time, however, they were rightly seen as a tiresome display of immaturity and a needless interruption to the game.

One sport which has managed to preserve the authority of the on-field official is rugby union, where the referee has the power to march the offending side back ten metres in response to any backchat. That sanction, combined with the sending-off powers for more serious transgressions, usually keeps even the most intemperate sides under control. An equivalent for cricket would be an immediate run penalty for the dissident team, though hopefully it would never be necessary: no-one would wish to see a close match decided by such a penalty. Writing in *Wisden*, following the Rana–Gatting incident, Graeme Wright hit the right tone, which I would respectfully endorse: 'In all sporting games there have been and there always will be injustices. Life is full of them, and one of the virtues of sport is that it can set an example to society in how to accept setbacks with some dignity. Umpires, on the other hand, should remember that, while being both judge and jury, they are not above the Laws.'[14]

Technological creep

In the same *Wisden* piece, Wright suggested the use of television replays to double-check umpiring decisions. There were many reasons in favour of doing so apart from the occasional on-field controversies: television replays had been around long enough for every cricket fan to have a store of indisputable umpiring howlers, especially since the introduction of multiple camera angles by Channel 9 in Australia during the Packer revolution. Moreover, American football had introduced a limited form of video replaying for refereeing decisions, so there was a sporting precedent, albeit one probably unnoticed by most cricket supporters. Most weighty of all, Sir Donald Bradman had suggested in *Wisden* 1986 the use of replays for run-outs, though

[14] *Wisden* 1988, p 46.

in those days before Hawk-Eye he had baulked at the idea of using them for lbws.

Starting from the Indian tour of South Africa in 1992/3, a limited use of technology was allowed, with the third umpire being allowed to adjudicate on run-outs and stumpings if asked by those in the middle. While the on-field umpires had no obligation to use the replays, predictably enough most took the safe option of referring all but the most obvious cases as a matter of course. By and large the system has worked: the number of run-out or stumping appeals in all forms of cricket is usually low enough not to interrupt the flow of the game greatly, and using the third umpire has saved the painful embarrassment of having millions on television seeing a poor decision replayed over and over again, along with the tedious exchanges of allegations about umpiring competence and bias. On occasion, however, the cardinal principle of giving the batsman the benefit of the doubt has been overlooked by umpires and commentators alike – a marginal call not clearly visible from any angle is not a 'difficult decision', it is a straightforward one where the normal principle of declining the appeal should be applied.

On that last point, I have to register a mild semantic disagreement with one of cricket's foremost authorities, Richie Benaud, who once wrote: 'It always astonishes me when people talk about benefit of the doubt. There is no such thing as benefit of the doubt. The batsman is never given out unless the umpire is absolutely certain he is out.'[15] The phrase 'benefit of the doubt' means that if a player looks like he might be out, but there is room for doubt, then the appeal should be declined. In other words, it is just another way of saying 'not out unless absolutely certain', analogous to 'beyond reasonable doubt' in criminal law, and hence distinct from the weaker standard of 'balance of probabilities' required in civil law claims. It is not a meaningless concept.

Returning to the advance of technology, three more recent devices have proved more controversial than television replays. The devices are the Snickometer, which employs directional microphones to measure sounds as the ball passes the bat; Hotspot, which uses infra-

---

[15]   Benaud, op cit.

red cameras to record any touch of ball on bat; and, probably the most significant, Hawk-Eye, which uses radar to predict whether a ball which has struck the pads would have gone on to hit the stumps. The use of each necessarily involves delays and, rather worse than that, threatens to destroy the role of the on-field umpires.

At this point analysis from the general legal system ceases to provide compelling guidance. In the general law, arriving at the right answer is the ultimate goal, and as new technology becomes available, the only objections to using it to the fullest are (i) how reliable it has proven and (ii) the danger of misuse of data by authorities, or the related concern of invasion of privacy by data collection. Hence, CCTV footage and DNA technology have made a substantial contribution towards crime-fighting, though there is always the concern that the authorities will abuse both to expose people's private affairs. Also, while DNA may provide compelling evidence in some cases, it is still dependent on variable factors such as the quality of the samples used.

In cricket, on the other hand, reaching the right answer is superficially the goal, but one can also say that umpires and their fallibility are part of the game, with the sort of sentimentality that would have no place in a courtroom for obvious reasons. I suspect most cricket followers would agree that something would be lost if the on-field umpires were to be reduced to holding jerseys and counting deliveries, let alone if they were done away with altogether.

DRS and ORS

In 2009, recognizing the need to balance the technology against the retention of umpiring dignity, and taking account of the fact that the new devices could not be said to be foolproof anyway, the ICC introduced the Decision Review System (DRS). The system allowed each team two unsuccessful review requests per innings during a test match, after which no more reviews could be made. As well as the teams being able to ask for a review, the on-field umpires at their own discretion could seek assistance from the third umpire for certain types of dismissal and other issues such as boundary calls.

The system was complicated by the fact that the third umpire could not substitute his own view for that of the on-field umpires; instead, if the decision was within established margins of error or was otherwise inconclusive, the 'umpire's call' would stand. That restriction was reminiscent of the traditional limitations in English law in judicial review of executive action. In both cases the reason for the limitation is to preserve the primacy of the original decision maker, and thus confirm the third umpire in cricket and the court in the general law as merely the guardians of the process rather than the ultimate decision makers.

DRS was controversial from the start, both in theory and in practice. Among its most prominent theoretical opponents was India's cricket authority, the BCCI. DRS came under particular scrutiny during the Ashes in England in 2013 (in the return series, none of the matches were close enough to generate any similar controversy). For example, at Old Trafford the Australian batsman Usman Khawaja was given out by the on-field umpire. He reviewed the decision, but to the surprise of most viewers, the decision was upheld by the third umpire. At the very least the manifest doubt should have resulted in a not-out call. If the on-field umpire had erred, that would properly have been written off as just part of the game. The third umpire, on the other hand, under less time pressure and with all the technology at his disposal, had much less excuse and much less chance of indulgence on the part of those playing and watching the game. The incident showed that human errors were not the preserve of those on the field.

The responses in the cricketing press fell into three broad categories: those who would do away with all uses of technology; those who would use it to its fullest; and those who would tinker with the DRS system for some sort of compromise. The problem with the first option is that the genie is out of the bottle. If television broadcasters still use the same technology then, absent DRS or some equivalent, umpires will consistently be humiliated in the way they were with run-outs before the third-umpire system was introduced. Theoretically, the ICC could insist on all the different forms of technology being banned from any contracted broadcaster, but I suspect they would encounter resistance on that front, both from the broadcasters and from viewers who have grown accustomed to its use.

The problem with the second option is that the technology remains imperfect, both in its ability to reach the right answer and in its application. Jacques Kallis provided an interesting quote: 'How accurate it is, I don't know … We are getting that right to a degree but I am not convinced how accurate it really is. I don't think there are any guys that are 100% sure that the thing is as accurate as they want to make it out to be. They keep saying it, but I'm not so sure and I think 99% of cricketers will say that.'[16] The flow of the game may be interrupted intolerably if every decision takes in the region of five minutes for all forms of technology to be employed. And the Khawaja decision was just one example of how the technology might fail.

It has always seemed to me that the problems associated with DRS in principle (leaving aside the technical flaws with the equipment) have been exaggerated. The real issue during the 2013 Ashes series in England (aside from the third umpire failing, as with the Khawaja dismissal) was the bad referrals which the Australians habitually made, not the system itself. After all, the system applied equally to England, who happened to use it more wisely, even though their captain, Alastair Cook, admitted they were 'confused' by it all. A better way of looking at it would be to say that a new element had been introduced to the art of captaincy, and it would take a while for captains to master it.

Various refinements to DRS might be found here and there (at the time of writing, the ICC was experimenting with an alternative called ORS – Officiating Review System – which promised to work much more quickly, because the third umpire would have access to replays immediately, rather than when provided by the broadcaster as was the case for DRS), but pending either the perfection of technology or its total abolition, some kind of compromise in the form of DRS seems the only viable option. I would argue that the current form is not far wrong. Allowing more reviews than at present will slow the game down too much, and the limitations apply equally to both sides, so there is no unfairness involved.

One change I would advocate is to remove the 'umpire's call' limitation. It does not advance the cause of umpiring dignity for the umpire to be shown to be wrong but to have his decision upheld anyway. On the contrary, it borders on the patronizing. Since the

---

[16] Firdose Moonda, 'Benefactor, friend, family-man', Cricinfo, 30 December 2013, www.espncricinfo.com/southafrica/content/story/705451.html (retrieved 24 April 2014).

evidence is there for all to see (and, if not, the benefit of the doubt should be ordered each time in favour of the batsman, irrespective of the umpire's original call) there seems nothing to be gained from the viewers seeing one result but the players being given another.

A final delivery

It has to be acknowledged that future generations may see the above discussion as a load of Luddite nonsense. Anyone born in the twenty-first century could quite possibly end up spending every day of their life from school age onwards connected to the internet via tablets and smartphones (and future equipment not yet thought of) as a basic everyday activity, even more than they do already. It is easy to imagine, for example, umpires wearing 'smart' glasses that automatically provide comprehensive and apparently foolproof information about every form of dismissal, with umpiring pay and prestige reduced accordingly. It is equally easy to imagine cricketers of the same generation seeing such technology as no more radical or unsporting than the use of a mechanized roller for the groundskeeper or a calculator for the scorer. Of course, they might also find playing the game outside with real bats and balls pointless when a 3D virtual reality simulator affords more convenience, but I should probably wait to comment on that day until it arrives.

Chapter 19

DRAWING STUMPS

'Cricket? It civilises people and creates good gentlemen. I want everyone to play cricket in Zimbabwe. I want ours to be a nation of gentlemen,' said Robert Mugabe, who went on to break every word of that pledge, and thus prove that cricket is not going to save the world. In fact, none other than Sir Neville Cardus once wrote that 'cricket more than any other game is inclined towards sentimentalism and cant', and not a few critics have said the same about law compared with other professions. 'Suffer any wrong that can be done you rather than come here!' the former court reporter Charles Dickens advised in *Bleak House* when referring to the Chancery Division.

But there is no need to end on a cynical note. The majesty of the law and much of the appeal of cricket have often been said to derive from the arcane and impenetrable rules of both, as well as the theatre and etiquette which one finds in both court cases and test matches. Rather more substantively, the best response to critics of both law and cricket is to refer to the market. The common law legal system is one of the most respected in the world, as reflected in the substantial number of international commercial transactions that choose English law as the governing law of the contract, and the number of international businesspeople who choose to come to London to settle their disputes by arbitration or litigation.

As for cricket, pundits can always be found to predict the decline of test matches, yet the twenty-first century has already produced some of the finest ever played. The 2005 series was the best Ashes ever – and the greatest test series full stop according to *Wisden*, not exactly a publication given to wild overstatement. If one disagrees, then other leading candidates can be found in some of the memorable recent clashes involving Australia, India, Pakistan and South Africa, with the only regret being that those countries no longer play five-test series against each other. Where the spirit of cricket is concerned, if the foregoing pages have covered a few of the well-known breaches, then it should be remembered that there have been a lot more matches not covered in this book precisely because they were played in an admirable spirit.

In 1997, looking back to the start of the 1980s, David Frith wrote: 'A period was unfolding in which the spirit of cricket was to be traduced time and again, forcing caring writers and broadcasters to sound quite pompous at times. But they – we – meant well. It was a beautiful and honourable game, and still is, on the whole, but there is a fragility about its natural code of conduct that has compelled legislation to be brought in here and there as a kind of splint.'[1] Writing nearly twenty years after Frith, I would say that the splints brought in by way of changes to the laws of cricket have been a mixed bag. As I have argued, the laws concerning such things as ball-tampering or nationality requirements are in a reasonable state even if their implementation is not always (and probably never will be) trouble free. The use of bouncers at the highest level has ceased to be the controversy it once was, thanks to playing restrictions and better protective gear, though things have arguably gone too far. Bad behaviour on the pitch (ball-tampering, abusive behaviour and so forth) is usually dealt with more severely nowadays, though the ICC has taken its time in this respect and has not always been able to stand up to self-interested national boards. I am also inclined to agree with Mike Atherton's assessment that the introduction of the 'spirit of cricket' in the laws was just wishful thinking.

As to the general law, I have identified two primary threats to cricket. The first is if the law becomes too intrusive; that is, if any 'activist' judge takes it upon him or herself to find someone liable in negligence for something which happens in the ordinary course of a match or, even worse, guilty of a criminal act for what has hitherto been considered an acceptable risk forming part of the game. If that were to happen then cricket as we know it would start to fade away as players would be forced to take far too many precautions against future law suits – or, more likely, choose a different sport. The second threat is that the law might fail to be *intrusive enough*, by not stopping illegal bookmakers from making a farce of international competitions.

The possibility of either is depressing enough. Then again, I can say one thing: both dangers have been around for some time now, but they haven't happened yet. Since cricket has survived Grace's

[1]   David Frith, *Caught England, Bowled Australia: A Cricket Slave's Complex Story* (Eva Press, 1997), p 242.

gamesmanship, Bodyline's brutality, Packer's plot, the underhanded underarm, and all the other crises mentioned in this book, I suspect it might just survive for a while to come.

INDEX